American Gothic

American Gothic
New Interventions in a
National Narrative

Edited by Robert K. Martin *&* Eric Savoy

University of Iowa Press Ψ Iowa City

University of Iowa Press,
Iowa City 52242
Copyright © 1998
by the University of Iowa Press
All rights reserved
Printed in the United States of America
Design by Richard Hendel
www.uiowapress.org

Printed on acid-free paper
Library of Congress
Cataloging-in-Publication Data
American gothic: new interventions in a national narrative /edited by
Robert K. Martin and Eric Savoy.
p.   cm.
Includes bibliographical references and index.
ISBN-13: 978-0-87745-622-3, ISBN-10: 0-87745-622-4 (cloth)
1. American fiction — History and criticism.   2. Gothic revival
(Literature)— United States.   3. Horror tales, American — History
and criticism.   4. National characteristics, American, in literature.
5. Psychological fiction, American — History and criticism.   6. Women
and literature — United States.   7. Race relations in literature.
8. Narration (Rhetoric).   I. Martin, Robert K., 1941– .
II. Savoy, Eric.
PS374.G68A83   1998
813'.0872909 — dc21   97-32722

ISBN-13: 978-1-58729-349-8, ISBN-10: 1-58729-349-8 (pbk)

CONTENTS

ROBERT K. MARTIN & ERIC SAVOY

Introduction

If gothic cultural production in the United States has yielded
neither a "genre" nor a cohesive "mode" but rather a discursive
field in which a metonymic national "self" is undone by the return of its repressed Otherness, then a critical account that attempts to reduce the gothic to an overarching historical consistency—a matter of "essentials" and "accidentals"—will be of
limited use. For the gothic coheres, if it can be said to cohere,
around poetics (turns and tendencies in the dismantling of the
national subject), around narrative structuration, and in its situation of the reader at the border of symbolic dissolution. The
multivalent tendencies of the gothic have not been particularly
illuminated by recent attempts at generic categorization: Donald
A. Ringe's *American Gothic* and Louis S. Gross's *Redefining the
American Gothic* provide insightful readings of texts, of moments,
but their gestures toward comprehensivity, toward "tradition,"
by way of rather uniform synecdochic examples fail to convince.
This book approaches the persistence of the gothic in American
culture not by seeking historical comprehensivity or even critical consensus but, committed to pluralism in a field that is in-
choate, by providing a composite of "interventions" that explore
specific issues—in the histories of gender and race, in the cultures of cities and scandals and sensations, in the psychodynamics of representation—in order to advance particular and distinct
theoretical paradigms.

It is our hope, however, that this book's commitment to particularity does not preclude a genuine conceptual resonance
both among its various interventions and with a fairly broad

spectrum of theories of Otherness that have been influential in
the current academy. While this project is post-Fiedlerian in its
movement beyond archetypal criticism, it is indebted and in
many ways supplementary to Leslie Fiedler's pioneering conjunction of historicism and psychoanalysis. His insistence on the
dialogic relation between the American national symbolic and
the tendencies of the gothic—"How could one tell where the
American dream ended and the Faustian nightmare began?"
(143)—and his understanding of this dialogism as fundamentally
ironic—an "essentially gothic" culture produced by a civilization
driven "to be done with ghosts and shadows" (144)—have lost
none of their freshness and indeed provide the cultural frame
for subsequent inquiry. Such a frame is enriched by the incipient or tacit "gothic" preoccupations of a variety of poststruc-
turalist theories: deconstruction, in its twin obsessions with
the Otherness of figurative language and the dismantling of signification's coherence by the eruption of Otherness; psychoanalysis, committed to the temporality of the subject as organized around repression and return; the new historicism of racial
inquiry, which dismantles sanctioned national narrative by exposing its silencing predications; and gender studies (the continuum from feminism to queer theory), which illuminates the
definitional centrality of genders and sexualities that have been
culturally marginalized, abjected, othered.

   American Gothic: New Interventions in a National Narrative,
then, emerges at the intersections or interstices among these
assorted critical trajectories and attempts to orient the gothic
toward "theory" even as it understands "theory" as emerging
from, and predicated upon, the gothic tendencies in Western
culture. The entire history of the gothic lies behind—to cite one
influential example—Julia Kristeva's understanding of the abject, that which is "radically excluded" from individual and national self-definition yet which "draws [the subject] toward the
place where meaning collapses," for "from its place of banish-
ment, the abject does not cease challenging its master" (2). Like
psychoanalysis, like revisionist historiography, the project of the
gothic turn in narrative has been to take the ego, or the story
generated by the national ego, "back to its source on the abom-

inable limits from which, in order to be, the ego has broken away," and Kristeva's metaphor for this uncanny cultural encounter might well illuminate the gothic tendency itself: "[i]t is an alchemy that transforms death drive into a start of life, of new significance" (15).

Such convergence of theory's illuminations with the recurring impulses in various representational venues surely constitutes the matrix of "work" on the gothic in the postmodern moment: literature, cinema, painting, news broadcasts, journalism are not merely "diagnosed" or "analyzed" by theory, despite its privileged status of knowingness in our late culture; rather, these diverse sites are organized around a common tropics, a shared set of metaphors that, in the most general sense, are "performative" in the sense that their very limitations are the basis of their productivity. This convergence is to be seen everywhere, and if the gothic may be said to be everywhere, then it will cohere *nowhere in particular*. This is precisely why an appreciation of the possibilities of "resonance" is preferable to a totalizing or comprehensive critical enterprise. There are sites, there are moments. There is no All. It is this matrix, arguably, that has enabled a critical discourse about the gothic that moves fluidly between disciplines, between specialized discourses. Thus Michelle A. Massé can negotiate between feminism and Freudian psychology to argue that "'normal' feminine development [is] a form of culturally induced trauma and the Gothic novel its repetition" (7). Thus it is no accident that Eve Kosofsky Sedgwick's entire project of mapping the epistemological regulations of the heteronormative subject in the social field—its predication on the terrible potentiality of otherness that is inflected through "homosexual panic"—originated in her work on the homoerotics of the "paranoid Gothic" (89). And thus Anne Williams can pose the question "What noun would 'Gothic' appropriately modify, then? I would suggest the term 'complex'" (23). Finally, the role of the gothic as the site of discursive convergence between an academic, theoretical project and the regulatory imperatives of culture is exemplified best in the figure, and the figures, of Stephen King, who "likes" to see the horror film "as lifting a trap door in the civilized forebrain and throwing a basket of raw meat to the hungry alligators swimming around in that subterranean river beneath" (460).

—*Eric Savoy*

The "new" in our title—*New Interventions*—indicates more than the fact that the essays in this volume were written recently. For the gothic, even if it has been seen as definitional of American writing since Leslie Fiedler's work in 1960, has undergone a paradigm shift remarkable in its extent. These essays are *new* in that they ask *new questions* based on *new assumptions*.

One of the most important aspects of the shift is linked to a radically different conception of psychology and psychological criticism. Not that many years ago, Donald Ringe warned against psychological readings, which "always distort the works they treat . . . they blind us to what the authors themselves were trying to do" (11). Such a view of intentionality betrays a critical blindness and an apparent innocence of the most fundamental lessons of psychoanalysis—that the subject is unaware of his or her own intentions. No one after the death of the author could make such a case for a fixed and unified consciousness seriously.

The most important recent study of the gothic argues in very different terms that "Freudian theory and Gothic sensations are 'homologous realms' of discourse" (Williams 94). The underground and the unconscious offer similar closets and similar catastrophes, occupied as they are by demons not readily kept in their place. The breakdown of the law (as well as of the Law) is a condition of being. As Anne Williams puts it, reading Freud as one would read Balzac or Proust, his "collected works . . . tacitly constitute a generic theory; let's call it *The Mysteries of Enlightenment*" (290).

For earlier critics the alternative to studies of the author's "intention" was recourse to the universal. Hawthorne, in this view, offers a study of the "dark view of human fate" (Ringe 173) rather than a historically grounded understanding of the representation of "darkness", that is, an acknowledgment of the cultural embeddedness of the emergence and definition of a genre. As Elizabeth Kerr suggestively put it in her study of Faulkner, "[t]he revival of the Gothic in the twentieth century, the age of technology, is parallel to its birth in the eighteenth century, the age of reason" (8). In cultural texts high and low, postmoderns inscribe their mixed fascination and horror at the effects (one wants almost to say, as they do in Hollywood, the *special effects*) of the technological somehow installed in the bedrooms of the suburbs and no longer simply in Transylvania.

In place of a symbolic or allegorical reading, we propose a set of concretized readings. The tradition of reading American literature in a symbolic mode has led to distortion and repression, as Nina Baym has shown through the examples of women's writing. It has similarly been easier to read blackness in terms of demonology than of race. The crucial gothic trope of darkness has been transformed in the critical tradition to a moral or psychological flaw in a manner that effaces the "real," that is, the ways in which a concept of "light" has provided no space for accounts of black experience except through Othering, providing, as Ralph Ellison's great gothic text puts it, the ten drops of black that define whiteness (175).

If the texts we have brought together here are, we hope, new in their concerns, they are also interventions; that is, they seek to do more than record. A political engagement is necessary if the various darknesses and secrets are to be more than tropes. The gothic our authors explore in different ways is national, or part of a collective self. Like the famous Grant Wood painting that gives its name to this collection, the sense of prim propriety may conceal a haunted heritage, with a pitchfork that can do more than toss hay.

The Wood painting, like Truman Capote's *In Cold Blood* (1965), may also serve to remind us of what lies beneath the landscape, of the flatness that conceals the secrets of the prairie. If most of our contributors locate the horror neither in a Conradian colonial Other nor in a vacant stare of the land, they prefer the horrors of the urban landscape and, perhaps even particularly, the suburb, that territory that David Lynch has mined for its once again repeated story of American innocence and the violence that disturbs/constitutes it.

—*Robert K. Martin*

WORKS CITED

Ellison, Ralph. *Invisible Man.* New York: Signet, 1952.

Fiedler, Leslie. *Love and Death in the American Novel.* 2nd ed. New York: Doubleday, 1966.

Gross, Louis S. *Redefining the American Gothic: From Wieland to Day of the Dead.* Ann Arbor, MI: UMI Research P, 1989.

Kerr, Elizabeth. *William Faulkner's Gothic Domain.* Port Washington, NY: Kennikat P, 1979.

King, Stephen. "Why We Crave Horror Movies." *Reader's Choice.* Ed. Kim Flachman et al. 2nd Canadian ed. Toronto: Prentice-Hall, 1996, 458–460.

Kristeva, Julia. *Powers of Horror: An Essay on Abjection.* Trans. Leon S. Roudiez. New York: Columbia UP, 1982.

Massé, Michelle A. *In the Name of Love: Women, Masochism and the Gothic.* Ithaca: Cornell UP, 1992.

Ringe, Donald A. *American Gothic: Imagination and Reason in Nineteenth-Century Fiction.* Lexington: UP of Kentucky, 1982.

Sedgwick, Eve Kosofsky. *Between Men: English Literature and Male Homosocial Desire.* New York: Columbia UP, 1985.

Williams, Anne. *Art of Darkness: A Poetics of Gothic.* Chicago: U of Chicago P, 1995.

This collection of essays grew out of a joint research project supported by the Social Sciences and Humanities Research Council of Canada, to whom we express our gratitude. Further support from SSHRCC and from the Université de Montréal made the first American gothic conference possible. We wish to thank all participants for their stimulating responses to our collective questions. As one of our speakers put it, "Let's have a reunion . . . I loved that conference—it was incredibly invigorating, and I adored Montreal." Such enthusiasm makes it all worthwhile. Particular thanks go as well to Michelle Braun, indefatigable, professional, and generous, and to George Piggford, who organized the conference with superb tact, skill, and grace.

PART I

Framing the Gothic
Theories and Histories

ERIC SAVOY

The Face of the Tenant
A Theory of American Gothic

"Think of him," she said, placing a finger against the
front-view portrait of the blond young man. "Think of those eyes.
Coming toward you." Then she pushed the pictures back
into their envelope. "I wish you hadn't shown me."
TRUMAN CAPOTE, *In Cold Blood*

A "theory" of gothic cultural production in the United States is
necessarily invested in a poetics of terror—a tropics, a recurring
turn of language. If such generally structuring turns are most
strikingly conceptualized in particular moments, then this brief
excerpt from Capote's work suggests the multiple, inevitable,
and even casual ways in which narrative might take a decidedly
gothic turn. These chilling words are spoken by Marie Dewey—
the wife of Alvin Dewey, an agent of the Kansas Bureau of Investigation—late in 1959 as she studies the photographs of two
men who, without apparent motive, murdered a farm family "on
the high wheat plains of western Kansas, a lonesome area that
other Kansans call 'out there'" (3). While the photographs give
a face, a human agency, to a crime whose horror lies in its absence of meaning and its distance from the rationally explicable,
her discourse betrays the desire to situate the static image of the
face in a narrative, a desire from which she immediately recoils.
What is most striking in Marie Dewey's language—what is most
suggestive of the gothic turn—is her syntax of reiterated imperative. "Think of . . ." insists upon both the imaginative reconstruction of a historical event—a moment just prior to violent

3

annihilation—and what might be called "being out there," an intuitive, visceral knowledge of terrible affect that approaches the experiential. In the queerly hybrid "nonfiction novel" that Capote attempted in the writing of *In Cold Blood*, Marie Dewey's brief appearance signifies both the act of reading "America" and the writerly turn toward the fascination of the fearful, a fascination that, she implies, ought not to be indulged but inexorably is.

Her fleeting comments suggest that the gothic tendency in American culture is organized around the imperative to repetition, the return of what is unsuccessfully repressed, and, moreover, that this return is realized in a syntax, a grammar, a tropic field. Once instigated, Marie Dewey's impulse to narrate the body that violates and the violated body can only escalate in the structure of haunting textual return: the photograph of Richard Hickock's face, especially his eyes, gives her what might be colloquially called a "turn," which is turned into a narrative obligation, which subsequently recurs in the rumor that Hickock bequeathed his eyes "'to an eye doctor. Soon as they cut him down, this doctor's gonna yank out his eyes and stick them in somebody else's head'" (338). This final gothic turn provides a compositional vanishing point in which there is no vanishing; horrific history acquires a body, a face, a figure that recedes into futurity. The failure of repression and forgetting—a failure upon which the entire tradition of the gothic in America is predicated—will be complete in those conscious eyes. Such a return is not merely monstrous and unthinkable, it is uncanny. And the writing of the uncanny is the field—or, more precisely, the multivalent tendency—of American gothic, an imaginative requirement by which, as Leslie Fiedler pointed out, "the past, even dead, *especially* dead, could continue to work harm" (131).

In the thirty years since the publication of *Love and Death in the American Novel*, Fiedler's genealogy of American gothic has remained vitally suggestive; indeed, his broad connections between historiography and psychoanalysis have shaped the parameters of subsequent conceptualization. He insists on the absolute centrality of the gothic in American literature, for "until the gothic had been discovered, the serious American novel could not begin; and as long as that novel lasts, the gothic cannot die" (143), while gesturing toward its essentially paradoxical status in "America," that eighteenth-century construction "pledged to be done with ghosts and shadows, committed to live a life of yea-saying in a sunlit, neoclassical world" (144). Influenced by his argument that "the whole tradition of the gothic is a pathological symptom rather than a proper literary movement" (135), much post-Fiedlerian analysis has been preoccupied with accounting for the role of the gothic as a negation of the Enlightenment's national narratives. Maggie Kilgour and Anne Williams, whose work in British contexts is often applicable to American ones, understand both the binary logics that have required a darkness as the Enlightenment's Other and the interlinearity of gothic cultural production and the rise of psychoanalysis. Williams argues, via Foucault, that "Enlightenment thought characteristically ordered and organized by creating institutions to enforce distinctions between society and its other. . . . Like the haunted Gothic castle, the Freudian discourse of self creates the haunted, dark, mysterious space even as it attempts to organize and control it" (248). Kilgour's declaration that "psychoanalysis is a late gothic story" (221) surveys the cultural matrix that enabled the narrativization of irrepressible Otherness.

In the American scene, it may be that broad generalizations about the gothic—overshadowed as they are by the genealogical tracing of British and continental influences—have reached a limit of conceptual or explanatory usefulness, and further particularization is urgently required. Louis S. Gross is surely right to read the gothic as a "demonic history text" (2) in *Redefining the American Gothic* and to grasp its "common thread" as "the singularity and monstrosity of the Other: what the dominant culture cannot incorporate within itself, it must project outward onto this hated/desired figure" (90). However, this observation raises the question of *how* the project of narrating "Otherness"—which indeed is a "dominant" cultural mode—embodies a "figure" that it "cannot incorporate within itself." I suggest that the difficult task of such incorporation—of gesturing toward that which resists an explicit lexicon—has situated American gothic continuously in a tropic field that approaches allegory: the gothic is most powerful, and most distinctly American, when it strains toward allegorical translucency. Given the thinness, the blankness of the American historical past and much of the American landscape, allegory—which is not, properly speaking, a "figure" but which is supremely conducive to the ghostly figures that we commonly associate with gothic, particularly prosopopoeia—provided a tropic of shadow, a kind of Hawthornian "neutral territory" in which the actual is imbued with the darkly hypothetical, a discursive field of return and reiteration. It is, of course, the lesson of Melville that nothing is so terrible as nothingness itself, the absence of a coherently meaningful symbolic: it is precisely the semantic impoverishment of allegory, the haunting consequences of its refusal of transparency, that impelled American gothic's narrativization of Otherness toward its insubstantial shadows, and vice versa.

Like allegory, the gothic is a fluid tendency rather than a discrete literary "mode," an impulse rather than a literary artifact. Such thinking seems to prompt Anne Williams's refusal to consider the gothic—"a 'something' that goes beyond the merely literary"—as simply a genre, a tradition, or a set of conventions; rather, in asking "what noun would 'Gothic' appropriately modify," she suggests the term "complex," which denotes "an intersection of grammar, architecture and psychoanalysis" (23–24). A model of gothic "complexity" that tends toward allegory—and I shall have more to say about the particular figures that are generated by allegory—is a useful corollary to theories of the historiographical orientation of gothic narrative.

"American gothic" does not exist apart from its specific regional manifestations; the burden of a scarifying past is more typical of New England and southern gothic than, for example, that of the prairies, yet common to all is a narrative site that tends to be an epistemological frontier in which the spatial division between the known and the unknown, the self and the Other, assumes temporal dimensions. The gothic cannot function without a proximity of Otherness imagined as its imminent return; consequently, allegory's rhetoric of temporality—its gesturing toward what cannot be explicitly recovered—aspires to a narrative of the return of the Other's plenitude on a frontier in which "geography" supplements the impossibilities of language, of both national and personal historiography.

According to David Mogen, Scott P. Sanders, and Joanne B. Karpinski, "gothicism must abide on a frontier—whether physical or psychical"; despite the specific locatability of frontiers in various cultural moments, American gothic historiography generally "derives from [a] conflict between the inscripted history of civilization and the history of the other, *somehow immanent* in the landscape of the frontier" (17, my emphasis). A symbolic Otherness that is "somehow immanent," that must be figured forth in narrative, suggests the resonance between gothic historiography and the haunting insubstantialities of allegorical trope. Also conducive to the allegorical corollary—a mode of narrative that is organized around semiotic gaps or "rifts"—is their model of the historical matrix that is inhabited by the gothic. "Gothicism results," they argue,

> when the epic moment passes, and *a particular rift* in history develops and widens into a *dark chasm* that separates now from what has been. The history that suffers this rift is the inscripted past, the literal re-presentation to ourselves of a [hi]story that integrates people, events, and places, and makes of the world and its landscape a locale ... whose experience is comfortable, confident, coherent and known. This inscripted history is privileged; it functions as the logocentric past. . . . When we become aware of breaks in the logocentric history, of gaps in the authorized text of the past, the inscriptions of another history break through into meaning. (16)

This model suggests that logocentric historiography is an essentially nostalgic mode, if nostalgia is understood as a will to sustained cultural coherence, a desire for the seamless authenticity of national narrative; the fracturing of this mode by the irruption of "another history" is explained by Mogen, Sanders, and Karpinski as an ever-widening "dark chasm," a spatial or structural metaphor that, once again, evokes an allegorical temporality. This chasm is opened by the strategies of gothic signification, for it is not simply the case that a horrific "alternate" history emerges as a cohesive or fully explanatory corrective that is superimposed upon nostalgic history. Rather, it irrupts by fits and starts in a semiotic that is fragmentary, one that is more suggestive than conclusive. As such, the gothic "turn" toward compelling but unthematizable narrative might be conceptualized as the emergence of the Lacanian Real, which, according to Judith Butler, "is that which resists and compels symbolization" (70). The congruent and compatible strangenesses of gothic and allegorical image manifest what Anne Williams describes as "a pattern of anxiety about the Symbolic" and reveal "the fragility of our usual systems of making sense of the world," for "an extraordinary number of Gothic conventions . . . imply disorder in the relations of signifiers and signifieds" (70–71).

While gothic narrative emphatically refuses nostalgia, it seems to be the case that nostalgic representations of "America" veer toward the gothic with remarkable frequency; invariably associated with self-consciously "late" cultural production, this turn problematizes nostalgia's simplicity by invoking a darker register that, ironically, emerges as the very consequence of nostalgic modes of knowing. A prototype might be Henry James's return to America at the turn of the century: his late writing explores the contrast between sunny myths of return and the pull toward a tropics of devastation and the attractive threat of a hypothetical, unlived American life. Such contrasts recur but in very different terrains: in the spring of 1996, the highly popular film *Twister* locates the terrible in the vertical that descends from the sky upon the horizontal stretch of America from Iowa to Oklahoma, geographically contiguous with the mythic "West" that, according to Jonathan Raban, is a "bleak and haunted landscape" that "looks like a landscape in an allegory" (81). While its primary nostalgic referent is *The Wizard of Oz*, the narrative turns and twists in its uneven course toward gothic historicity.

In one spectacular sequence, a tornado spirals through the face of a cinematic screen at the Galaxy Drive-In, upon which is projected the most memorable scene from Stanley Kubrick's 1980 film of Steven King's novel *The Shining*. In a perfect moment of ironic congruence, the tornado destroys the image of Jack Nicholson axing through a door, behind which Shelley Duvall cowers in terror. The point of this intertextual strategy is thoroughly allegorical; while it is in keeping with a long tradition in American gothic of attributing terrible violence to the muteness of landscape, it "explains" this terror by juxtaposing nature—literally—against cinematic culture, against what it is *not*, in an escalating spiral of signification that laminates the Symbolic into a coherent order even as it blows it apart. *Twister's* framing of the cinematic screen—the cultural face fleetingly inhabited by Nicholson and then imploded—mediates an exchange of attribute between human and natural agency in an aesthetics of the gothic sublime; the tornado itself veers toward allegory, a personification of the qualities of Nicholson's performance which David Thomson describes as "the wicked naughty boy, the thwarted genius, the monster of his own loneliness. No one else could have been so daring and yet so delicate" (546). Yet, such a maneuver is not entirely new; it represents a further development of what Fiedler called "the grafting of Jamesian sensibility onto the Southern gothic stem" (476). Such are the strange, defamiliarizing uses of the gothic in a late culture that wants nostalgia simultaneously to have a playful edge and to approach the unthinkable.

If allegory is the strangest house of fiction, haunted by a referentiality that struggles to return in a narrative mode that is committed to repress what it is compelled to shadow forth (for allegory's suspension between avowal and disavowal must somehow fail to repress if it is going to "work"), then it is not surprising that the house is the most persistent site, object, structural analogue, and trope of American gothic's allegorical turn. Consider a partial catalog of American gothic houses: Poe's House of Usher, Hawthorne's Custom House, James's house on the "jolly corner," Sutpen's Hundred, Stephen King's Castle Rock, and Capote's Kansan farmhouse are structures whose solid actuality dissolves as they accommodate (and bring to spectacular figure) a psychic imperative—the impossibility of forgetting. In accounting for this imperative, Freud reveals the gothic origins of his conceptual lexicon by bringing forward the gothic's major architectural metaphor; to illustrate his theory of the uncanny (*das Unheimliche*) as "something repressed which *recurs*"—resonant with "Shelling's definition of the uncanny as something which ought to have remained hidden but has come to light"—he points out that some languages "can only render the German expression "an '*unheimlich* house' by 'a *haunted* house'" and suggests that "this example [is] perhaps the most striking of all, of something uncanny" ("The Uncanny" 241).

Freud's illustration seems to confirm the participation of psychoanalysis in gothic epistemology and narrative structures; he asserts that "psychoanalysis, which is concerned with laying bare these hidden forces, has itself become uncanny to many people" ("The Uncanny" 243). What is the status, the discursive materialization, of such "hidden forces" in narrative? Can language ever "lay bare" the Other? The entire tradition of the gothic suggests that a "haunting" return requires a poetics of the ephemeral and the indistinct. Crucially important for this project of conceptualizing the gothic as a tropic field is the narrowing focus of Freud's translation across languages and cultures, the figurative turn toward a spatialized, "architectural" psyche in the slide of signifiers from *unheimlich* to "uncanny" and its gothic equivalent, "haunted." If the Freudian text, and its translation, might be understood as *allegorizing the uncanny* in its figurative turns, then it does so under the auspices of the gothic's tendency to generate an allegorical sign—a human agency, a prosopopoeia—that returns the repressed Other to the vitally performative.

The psychic "house" turns toward the gothic only when it is "haunted" by the return of the repressed, a return that impels spectacular figures. More specifically, prosopopoeia may be conceptualized as the master trope of gothic's allegorical turn, because prosopopoeia—the act of personifying, of *giving face* to an abstract, disembodied Other in order to return it to narrative—disturbs logocentric order, the common reality of things. Paul de Man observes not only that "prosopopoeia is hallucinatory," because "to make the invisible visible is uncanny" (49), but also that such uncanny trope generates epistemological incoherence: "it is impossible to say whether prosopopoeia is plausible because of the empirical existence of dreams and hallucinations or whether one believes that such a thing as dreams and hallucinations exists because language permits the figure of prosopopoeia.

The question 'Was it a vision or a waking dream?' is destined to remain unanswered. Prosopopoeia undoes the distinction between reference and signification upon which all semiotic systems . . . depend" (49–50). This theory can be broadly extended to the gothic's allegorical turn, which, in complicating the "distinction between reference and signification," veers away from the clarity of denotation toward the ghostly realm of connotation: accordingly, the gothic registers a trauma in the strategies of representation as it brings forward a traumatic history toward which it gestures but can never finally refer.

Paradoxically, the various kinds of trauma represented by the gothic—the proximity of Otherness which occasions allegorical approximation—constitute both a return and a loss, and the gothic might be broadly conceptualized as a cultural ritual of inscribing the loss of coherent ego formation, the negation of national imaginary, and the fragmentation of linguistic accountability. For the uncanniness of the gothic is simultaneously terrible and melancholy, and the conjunction of fear and sorrow is powerfully annihilating of the ego's investment in things as they comfortably "are." This conjoined gothic affect is to be located not exclusively in the irruption of the id or in Lacan's revision of the death drive that posits the id's overwhelming of the ego but perhaps more immediately in the agency of the superego. This is suggested by a striking repetition in Freud's diverse writings that move toward the conceptualization of the superego. In his 1919 essay on "The Uncanny," he takes up the gothic figure of the double, which he seems to understand as an allegorization of the splitting of the ego: while the double originates in primary narcissism, its Otherness becomes "the uncanny harbinger of death" in later stages. "A special agency is slowly formed there, which is able to stand over against the rest of the ego, which has the function of observing and criticising the self." This "special agency" is arguably the site of the uncanny return of the repressed both in psychosis and in the paranoid gothic, for "in the pathological cases of being watched, this mental agency becomes isolated, dissociated from the ego . . . able to treat the rest of the ego like an object" ("The Uncanny" 235). The superegotistical double emerges into discourse, into narra-

tive, through allegorical personification, a turn that entails both
the loss of a coherent self and the fracturing of a transparent,
clearly referential lexicon of the self, a turn that marks loss as terrible. Previously, in his 1917 essay on "Mourning and Melancholia," Freud explained that melancholia arises from the traumatic loss not of an object but in regard to the ego, and he did
so in virtually the same language. The "melancholic's disorder,"
he argues, manifests when "one part of the ego sets itself over
against the other, judges it critically, and, as it were, takes it as its
object" ("Mourning" 256). If gothic trauma can be understood
as the imminence of the ego's violation, as something to be
scared of, then such possibility is signifiable only through the
tropic turn toward the hypothetical face of the Other, a face that
haunts the house of the psyche and its allegorical narrativization.

The doubleness of American gothic's allegorical impulse—
which represents "trauma" in a traumatized discourse that splits
the sign from the referent—appears early in the tradition, most
remarkably in Poe's architecture of remembering and return,
"The Fall of the House of Usher." Poe's "house" might be called
a master text for the subsequent history of American gothic,
both in its sense of what might accrue as "story" and its indirect
strategies of narration, the complex that Eve Kosofsky Sedgwick
describes as "the difficulty the story has in getting itself told"
(14). The content of Gothic story remains radically inaccessible:
the occasion of the Ushers' melancholia inheres in the strange
relation between Roderick Usher and his sister, Madeline, a
historical dimension that lies in the realm of the proscribed and
the unspeakable and as such is not subject to recovery. Consequently, the narrative must gesture toward the absent explanatory core of the story by organizing a tension between two allegorical currents. The first represents what might be called the
volition toward repression: Madeline must die, and her body
must be interred in the deepest recess of the house. The second
represents the return of the repressed secret, the rise of the Real,
the irruption of history in Madeline's ascent as revenant, uncannily anticipated by, or predicated upon, the act of reading an old
romance.

In the work of conceptualizing a poetics of American gothic, the narrative trajectory of Poe's "House" is less important than the allegorical signs it generates, the most striking of which occurs in the final moment of Madeline's interment, when the narrator allows himself to gaze upon her face:

> we partially turned aside the yet unscrewed lid of the coffin, and looked upon *the face of the tenant.* A striking similitude between the brother and sister now first arrested my attention; and Usher, divining, perhaps, my thoughts, murmured out some few words from which I learned that the deceased and himself had been twins, and that *sympathies of a scarcely intelligible nature* had always existed between them. Our glances, however, rested not long upon the dead—for we could not regard her unawed. (329, my emphasis)

This passage sustains and is organized around a complex resistance between its literal level—the gaze upon the face of the dead—and its allegorization of this gaze as an act of intuitive, incomplete historical reconstruction. As a sign, the countenance of Madeline Usher remains stubbornly mute in its somatic materiality, yet Poe's "gothic" emerges precisely as such only when this sign turns faintly toward prosopopoeia and generates the narrator's allegory of reading, a moment in which Poe's writing performatively gestures toward the reading *of* the gothic text by hermeneutic energy *in* the text. I regard this passage as typical of how American gothic requires a discursive matrix of preterition: an unspeakable, irrecoverable historical preterite is marked, and its consequences brought forward to the present, only in a species of circumlocution. Thus, Madeline's face becomes the text of the double, the twin, the Other, inscribed with the faint traces of an illegible history of "sympathies of a scarcely intelligible nature." Poe anticipates the fullness of prosopopoeia, Madeline's return as revenant, in the metaphor of tenancy, of a house within the House of Usher: Madeline is not completely consigned to the realm of the dead, nor is her historical significance; a mere "tenant" of the coffin, she will return to consciousness. Perhaps it is a critical inevitability to read an allegorical sign allegorically, that is, to situate it as a suggestive trope in an explanatory narrative of one's own; I argue that the entire tradition of American gothic can be conceptualized as the attempt to invoke "the face of the tenant"—the specter of Otherness that haunts the house of national narrative—in a tropics that locates the traumatic return of the historical preterite in an allegorically preterited mode, a double talk that gazes in terror at what it is compelled to bring forward but cannot explain, that writes what it cannot read. Such a model might go far in expanding the American grain of the gothic that Donald A. Ringe sees as fully realized in Poe's refusal to "vacillate . . . between the rationally explained and the frankly supernatural" and his assumption of "a position that can best be called noncommittal" (151). If American gothic flourished in the noncommittal strategies of the allegorical, then the overarching tendency of the gothic has been toward a suspension between the immediacy of terrible affect and its linguistic and epistemological unaccountability.

The prevailing tendency of critical discourse to explain gothic's allegorical strategies by a reversion to allegory itself suggests the tenacious power that gothic tropologies and epistemologies continue to exercise. In particular, the architectural metaphor of the haunted house is frequently transferred from its gothic origin—where, as I have suggested, it functions simultaneously as site and structure of narrative, as the vehicle for representing the return of the repressed Other and the prosopopoeial mode of its signification—to deconstructive and queer theoretical projects. Here, the "house" denotes both the text that is inhabited by the specters of referentiality and the subject who is haunted by the repudiated Other. It is not surprising that Eve Kosofsky Sedgwick's model of homosexuality's closet and its epistemological rigors emerged from her work in *The Coherence of Gothic Conventions* (1980), where she locates the gothic convention's requirement that the "self is spatialized": at issue within this architectural model is self-knowledge, which is urgently compelled even as it is preterited. In the turn toward personification allegory, "it is the position of the self to be massively blocked off from something to which it ought normally to have access. . . . The inside life and the outside life have to continue separately, becoming counterparts rather than partners [which creates] a doubleness where singleness should be" (12–13). She compares the occluded knowledges of gothic narrative to "the Watergate transcripts. The story does get through, but in a muffled form, with a distorted time sense, and accompanied by a kind of despair about any direct use of language" (15).

Sedgwick's model of the psychically spatialized self is predicated upon the social construction of "normative" and "Other," and the function of the gothic is to trouble "the stable crystalline relation . . . that enforces boundaries with a proscriptive energy" (38). The gothic disrupts the regulatory relations of proscription by returning the "blocked off" Other from the temporal field of the preterite to signification: in this sense, the gothic might seem to arise when the will to preterition *fails*. Yet, while preterition resembles a discursive tactic of repression, the two are not identical; more accurately, the "muffled form" of the gothic is constituted by the double impulses of preterition, which, as a particular manifestation of allegory, articulates indirectly what it cannot obliterate. Suspended between a knowledge that is blocked and a knowledge that is repudiated, preterition tracks and mobilizes, marks the course while it serves as a discursive *recourse*, of "return" across violated boundary. As both "form" and "content" of narrative, it figures the uncanny while it uncannily figures, which might explain why the gothic houses the Freudian "uncanny" in the several senses connoted by the adjective "queer," an adjective that strains toward prosopopoeial nomination.

Predictably, the recent queer theoretical project conceptualizes the interplay between repression and preterition by redeploying the allegorical tropes of the gothic, in particular by personifying the haunting "Other." Diana Fuss broadly surveys the domain of queer critique through a revisionist cartography of the unstable borders between heterosexuality and homosexuality: "[e]ach is haunted by the other, but . . . it is the other who comes to stand in metonymically for the very occurrence of haunting and ghostly visitations." Current work in the field of gender and sexuality, she observes, reveals "a certain preoccupation with the figure of the homosexual as specter and phantom, as spirit and revenant, as abject and undead." Thus, she concludes in a statement that marks the convergence of the queer and the tropic field of the gothic, "homosexual production emerges . . . as a kind of ghost-writing, a writing which is at once a recognition and a refusal" (3–4). It is ironic, perhaps, that the current academy—driven by the imperative to illuminate the margins of America's national narratives, to bring the occluded and excluded others of sexual, gendered, and racialized difference to presence—performs its revisionist work in the conventional house of the gothic's allegorical structuration, epistemology, and tropic discourse. However, these cultural and discursive returns indicate not a failure of the critical imagination but rather the revolutionary potential of American gothic, its long history of accommodating new interventions.

This introductory overview of the representational strategies of the gothic—and their persistence in American cultural work of various kinds—concludes in Iowa, where this collection of essays originates. Much of the preceding argument about the gothic's straining toward allegory, its historiographical matrix of prosopopoeial return that attempts to invoke "the face of the tenant," is suggested by Grant Wood's 1930 painting, *American Gothic*, the national icon under which this text is produced. In keeping with the general refusal to interrogate the national symbolic, Grant Wood's art was dismissed as simplistic, as merely regional, as naively realistic, until a major retrospective of his work in 1983–84 shifted the current of reception. A subsequent flurry of commentary responded to Wood's implication that the Midwest, in the words of Donald B. Kuspit, "is fertile with more than neat rows of wheat and corn" (139): Thomas Lawson detects "an edge of unsettledness" in Wood's career that bespeaks "a claustrophobia of the spirit among the rolling fields" (77), while Kuspit sees Wood as a painter of "an inward strangeness" whose enduring subject is "a powerful psychological undertow . . . under the veneer of Social Realism" and whose mode is a "temptation by allegory" (141). The doubleness of allegory is suggested, too, by Karal Ann Marling's opinion that *American Gothic* inflects nostalgia through irony to frame a "tension between modernism and tradition, between corrosive self-knowledge and delusional retrospection" (97). Representational "tensions," like an inconclusive or incomplete turn *toward* allegory that fails fully to achieve its semiotic, are critical models that are solicited by the liminal, the indirect, the shadow of signification that is cast by *American Gothic*. As James M. Dennis observes, the figures in Grant's painting "are permanently armed against any conclusive speculation as to what they stand for.... The spectator therefore confronts interminably the quiescent couple that haunts the national imagination" (85).

American Gothic achieves, among other things, an allegorization of American gothic: like all allegories, its silence inheres in the gap between signification and reference, but, more particularly, this allegory sustains a paradoxically illuminating silence in the space between the planes of composition, between foreground and background, between the couple's performance of preterition and the historical preterite that resides in the "Carpenter Gothic" house. Wood's subject is less the stubborn hardness of a mythic prairie character than what Fiedler calls "the *pastness* of the past" (137), the inexplicable, melancholy continuity between historical suffering and the visible textures of the present. According to Wanda M. Corn, Grant Wood intended *American Gothic* to be primarily a study in vertical composition: the architecture of Carpenter Gothic "appealed to Wood because of its . . . emphatic design—particularly the verticals . . . and the Gothic window, prominently placed in the gable. With his fondness for repeating geometries, Wood immediately envisioned a long-faced and lean couple, 'American Gothic people,' he called them, to complement the house and echo its predominantly vertical lines" (129).

I would argue, however, that the energy of the painting is divided between its upward reach—the vanishing point above the gothic arch and the gable peak—and its inward reach that laminates the silent couple to the supplementary resonance of the house across a supremely suggestive narrative gap. If this painting strains toward allegory, then it does so by invoking the historical preterite that resides in that house and haunts the national couple, a preterite that, typically, is preterited. As such, the house allegorizes historical consciousness itself, subject to the imminent irruption, the proximate quality, of the not-forgotten. Grant Wood's *American Gothic* suggests the regional precision, the very specificity, of the gothic's recurring manifestations: it belongs to what Jonathan Raban calls "that sad and unlamented West where bitterness and fury were the natural offspring of impossibly great expectations" (62); like all gothic, it haltingly brings forward the underside, the Otherness, of the narratives of national self-construction. The sign of the house yearns not for reconciliation with the past but for inhabitation by the past, the ghosts of return, as it strains toward prosopopoeia. It leaves us more or less in Capote's "out there," attending to the "whisper of wind voices in the wind-bent wheat" (343).

WORKS CITED

Butler, Judith. *Bodies that Matter: On the Discursive Limits of "Sex."* New York: Routledge, 1993.

Capote, Truman. *In Cold Blood: A True Account of a Multiple Murder and Its Consequences.* New York: Random House, 1965.

Corn, Wanda M. *Grant Wood: The Regionalist Vision.* New Haven: Yale UP, 1983.

de Man, Paul. *The Resistance to Theory.* Minneapolis: U of Minnesota P, 1986.

Dennis, James M. *Grant Wood: A Study of American Art and Culture.* 2nd ed. Columbia: U of Missouri P, 1986.

Fiedler, Leslie. *Love and Death in the American Novel.* New York: Doubleday, 1960, rpt. 1992.

Freud, Sigmund. "Mourning and Melancholia." *On Metapsychology: The Theory of Psychoanalysis,* vol. 11 of *The Penguin Freud Library.* Trans. James Strachey et al. New York: Penguin, 1984, 245–268.

———. "The Uncanny." *The Standard Edition of the Complete Psychological Works of Sigmund Freud,* vol. 17. Trans. James Strachey et al. London: Hogarth Press, 1955, rpt. 1991, 219–252.

Fuss, Diana. "Introduction: Inside/Out." *Inside/Out: Lesbian Theories, Gay Theories.* Ed. Diana Fuss. New York: Routledge, 1991.

Gross, Louis S. *Redefining the American Gothic.* Ann Arbor: UMI Research P, 1989.

Kilgour, Maggie. *The Rise of the Gothic Novel.* London: Routledge, 1995.

Kuspit, Donald B. "Grant Wood: Pathos of the Plain." *Art in America* 72.3 (March 1984): 138–143.

Lawson, Thomas. "Grant Wood: Whitney Museum of American Art." *Artforum* 22.3 (November 1983): 77.

Marling, Karal Ann. "Don't Knock Wood." *Art News* 82.7 (September 1983): 94–99.

Mogen, David, Scott P. Sanders, and Joanne B. Karpinski, eds. *Frontier Gothic: Terror and Wonder at the Frontier in American Literature*. Rutherford: Fairleigh Dickinson UP, 1993.

Poe, Edgar Allan. *Poetry and Tales*. Ed. Patrick F. Quinn. New York: Library of America, 1984.

Raban, Jonathan. "The Unlamented West." *New Yorker*, May 20, 1996, 60–81.

Ringe, Donald A. *American Gothic: Imagination and Reason in Nineteenth-Century Fiction*. Lexington: UP of Kentucky, 1982.

Sedgwick, Eve Kosofsky. *The Coherence of Gothic Conventions*. New York: Arno, 1980.

Thomson, David. *A Biographical Dictionary of Film*. Rev. ed. London: André Deutsch, 1994.

Williams, Anne. *Art of Darkness: A Poetics of Gothic*. Chicago: U of Chicago P, 1995.

WILLIAM VEEDER

The Nurture of the Gothic, or How Can a Text Be Both Popular and Subversive?

What I want to do in this essay is offer a contribution to one of the longest ongoing enterprises in fiction studies—the attempt to define the nature of the gothic in literature. Nearly two hundred years ago, vexed reviewers struggled to explain the amazing, perverse, inescapable, loathsome, irresistible phenomenon of *The Monk* by contrasting the narrative practices of Matthew Gregory Lewis and Anne Radcliffe. From the controversy over *The Monk* came the first tools for defining gothic fiction—the distinction between terror and horror. The inadequacy of these useful terms has driven students of the gothic for the past two centuries to offer other terms, to devise other distinctions.

A distinction common in recent gothic studies is my starting point. Critics frequently create a binary opposition between inside and outside, between gothic as an exploration of the unconscious and gothic as a concern for and even an intervention in social reality. In refusing this binary of Freud versus Marx, I want to define a gothic praxis that involves—necessarily—the interplay of psychological and social forces. This interplay has determined both the title and the subtitle of my essay.

My title, the nurture of the gothic, plays obviously on the phrase "the nature of the gothic" already old by John Ruskin's time, because I believe the nature of the gothic is to nurture. This belief derives from what I take to be a basic fact of communal life: that societies inflict terrible wounds upon themselves *and at the same time* develop mechanisms that can help heal these wounds. Gothic fiction from the late eighteenth century to the present is one such mechanism. Not consciously and yet purposively, Anglo-American culture develops gothic in order to help heal the damage caused by our embrace of modernity. Thus my title: gothic's nature is the psychosocial function of nurture, of healing and transforming.

To define this healing process, I will begin with the work of a physician, the British pediatrician and psychoanalyst D. W. Winnicott. His notions of potential space, transitional objects, and play will help me produce a general definition of gothic that I can then historicize and contextualize, drawing upon such thinkers as Michel Foucault, Michael Taussig, Ross Chambers, and Peter Stallybrass and Allon White. This will bring me to the question posed in my subtitle: how can a text be both popular and subversive? Why do we hug closest what threatens us most? This is another way of asking, How does gothic nurture?

A MODEL FOR GOTHIC

D. W. Winnicott's view of human function enabled him to discuss both infant development and cultural life in *Playing and Reality*. Essential to his view are three concepts: potential space, transitional objects, and play. Potential space is what Winnicott calls "the third space." It is not the internal psychological or the external social; it is the space between, where we are "when we are . . . enjoying ourselves" (105, 106). Our need for this third space begins soon after birth. "The baby has maximally intense experiences *in the potential space between the subjective object* [the maternal introject] *and the object objectively perceived* [the mother]" (100).

What occurs in this third space between the psychological and the social is, for Winnicott, the paramount human action— play. For play to occur, the child abiding in the space between psyche and society must be in touch with an object which is also characterized as in-between. "I have introduced the terms 'transitional objects' and 'transitional phenomena' for designation of the intermediate area between thumb and teddy bear, between oral eroticism and true object relationship" (2). Winnicott is careful to establish precisely the peculiar ontology of the transitional object. It "is related both to the external object (mother's breast) and to internal objects (magically introjected breast), but it is distinct from each. . . . it is a possession. Yet it is not (for the infant) an external object" (14, 9). Practically speaking, the transitional object is something soft—the edging of a blanket, a strip of flannel, even a string. But we must not let any particular object obscure the ontological peculiarity that Winnicott specifies for all such objects. Paradoxically, "the baby creates the object, but the object was there waiting to be created" (89).

Creativity is play of a momentous type. "It is in playing and only in playing that the individual child or adult is able to be creative" (54). Winnicott's belief that play is constitutive of human being means that he sees us continuing to play our whole lives. "Health here is closely bound up with the capacity of the individual to live in an area that is intermediate between the dream and the reality, that which is called the cultural life" (150). Many theorists of play posit, of course, a continuity between childhood and adulthood; what attracts me to Winnicott is that he defines play in a way that confirms our life-long continuity as creatures in-between.

All three notions of Winnicott—potential space, transitional objects, and play—are useful in defining how gothic may be experienced by readers and how it is positioned in culture. What I cannot proceed immediately to do, however, is to map Winnicott directly onto gothic. Such a mapping would fail to engage the historical specificity of gothic, its temporality, the fact that Anglo-American culture produced it at a moment of specific needs. I will, therefore, begin with Winnicott's first concept, potential space, and proceed historically.

What makes gothic fiction a potential space is its commitment to the simultaneous exploration of inner and outer, the psychological and the social. Now I'm fully aware that the same thing can be said for other genres and for the various modes of fiction. I make no claim for absolute uniqueness, for any rigid opposition between gothic and, say, the novel of manners. All fiction engages some psychological factors and social forces.

Granted, however, that any difference will be a matter of degree, I believe gothic is, of all fiction's genres, the one most intensely concerned with simultaneously liberating repressed emotions and exploring foreclosed social issues, since gothic presents most aggressively the range of outré emotions conventionally considered beyond the pale—incest, patricide, familial dysfunction, archaic rage, homoerotic desire.

HISTORICAL CONTEXT

Emphasis on the social as well as the psychological aspects of gothic introduces the question of context. Why did gothic not *flower* at the time of its inception in 1764? Why did all the major gothic texts—with the exception of *Otranto*—appear *after* the French Revolution? Answers of an expressly political nature have been offered by Paulson and others for British gothic and by various students of Brockden Brown in America. Enlightening as this political approach is at its best, it can neither account for nonpolitical features of the texts in question nor, more importantly, explain the *ongoing* force of gothic, the endurance of the tradition after the issues of revolutionary politics had ceased to inflame and frighten. Likewise, a too-exclusive focus on the specific social issues dramatized in postrevolutionary gothic texts—economic exploitation, racial and gender discrimination, religious intolerance—makes it difficult to achieve a coherent, overall perspective on the diverse social issues and the different decades in which each issue produced particular upheaval. What I propose is a contextualization of my earlier theory about social healing. Granted that societies simultaneously inflict terrible injuries upon themselves *and* develop ways of healing those injuries, the severest injury suffered by the Anglo-American middle-class readership in the late eighteenth and nineteenth centuries was, I believe, inflicted by a force that drew strength as never before from every site of conflict in every decade of the period. This force of injury is repression.

REPRESSION AND PLEASURE

The mention of repression evokes the figure of Michel Foucault, whose attack upon "the repression hypothesis" in the first volume of his *History of Sexuality* constitutes one of the influential arguments of our time. What Foucault establishes beyond question is that the nineteenth century was *not* an era when sexuality was unilaterally silenced; the period was characterized by what he famously calls "the multiplication of discourses."

What I want to go on to say is that Foucault's book-long argument functions finally to *confirm*, rather than to *refute*, the repression hypothesis, once we understand "repression" to mean the identifying and policing of sexuality. To view Foucault this way allows us a purchase on the question of how gothic heals through pleasure.

My discussion of repression has three parts. First, in the process of demonstrating beyond question that the nineteenth century spoke about sexuality obsessively, compulsively, Foucault acknowledges again and again what is simply true—that silencing was prevalent and intimidating: "[w]ithout question, the rules of propriety screened out some words: there was a policing of statements" (17–18). Thus, Foucault attempts to rebut the repression hypothesis not by denying that the nineteenth century engaged in silencing but by insisting that the nineteenth century did *more* than silence. Concomitant with silence was a great deal of talk.

Second, these discourses were—by Foucault's own admission—dualistic. As silencing coexisted with the multiplying of discourses, so discursive formations themselves had two functions. They policed society, and they produced pleasure. Before focusing on the phenomenon of pleasure (difficult to define in Foucault and absolutely essential to my view of gothic), I must indicate how the policing function of discourses damaged persons by damaging language.

The taxonomic regimes of medicine, law, anthropology, ethics, criminology, demography, pedagogy, and psychology were all agents of repression, insofar as they all functioned to control the sexuality they helped produce. I'll take as an example of medical discourse Dr. William Acton's book *The Functions and Disorders of the Reproductive System*, which appeared in fourteen editions (eight in Britain, six in America) between 1857 and 1897. Acton uses language to police sexuality, both thematically and rhetorically. Thematically, his purpose is to deny that "normal" women experience sexual desire. "Any susceptible boy is easily led to believe, whether he is entirely overcome by the syren or not, that she, and therefore all women, must have at least as strong passions as himself. Such women, however, give a very false idea of the conditions of female sexual feeling in general" (62). Notice the binary oppositions here: susceptible boys versus knowledgeable professionals like Acton; a few promiscuous sirens versus the majority of sexless ladies. These judgmental oppositions rigorously foreclose the intricate complications of human desire and the diverse social forces that encourage "female sexlessness." Functional versus dysfunctional, healthy versus diseased—ultimately, good versus bad. These binaries are, in turn, constitutive of both Acton's class and his profession. As the bourgeoisie defined themselves by means of denial (neither dirty, ignorant, and noisy like the lower orders nor effete, irresponsible, and arrogant like the aristocracy), so nineteenth-century medicine founded its emergent but still precarious status upon difference. Doctors were well trained, unlike midwives, responsible, unlike quacks, scientific, unlike faith healers. By deploying in their syntax the judgmental oppositions foundational for society, the discourses of sexual science functioned to police both desires and self-understanding.

Denial is also at work rhetorically in the implicit contract between Acton and his readers. There is an obvious erotic charge to Acton's materials, particularly the numerous case studies in which patients confess sexual secrets. We readers are repeatedly made privy, for instance, to anxieties that early contamination by masturbation has had or will have dire consequences for the marriage bed. Readers' affective involvements in these intimate materials Acton cannot acknowledge. Here and throughout the nineteenth-century discourses on sexuality, what tantalizes must be mediated through its opposite, through scientific objectivity, social concern, even disgust and indignation. The result is prurience. Only by lying to oneself—only by denying one's desire and thus one's place in the community of desiring and desirable creatures—can the reader experience desire.

In claiming that gothic fiction works differently, I want to avoid any easy polarization. Mediation operates in fiction as well as in discourses, but in fiction the mediation is effected not through denial but through displacement. In *The Monk*, for instance, it is indispensable that Ambrosio is Italian, not English, and Catholic rather than Protestant. In *The Scarlet Letter*, issues of female sexuality and independence that are volatile with Hawthorne's Victorian readers are projected back upon early American history. Without the mediation of these or other types of distancing, readers could not engage in that empathic relationship with literary characters which is the ground and precondition of novelistic art in the nineteenth century. Given such distancing, however, readerly desire can operate through—rather than in denial of—the desires represented in the text. Reading Hawthorne is not a prurient experience; reading Acton is.

This brings me back to the question of pleasure and my third point about repression. Foucault defines two types of pleasure produced by the discourses of sexuality. One is the polarized pleasures experienced by the powerful and the disempowered: "[t]he pleasure that comes of exercising a power that questions, monitors, watches, spies, searches out, palpitates, brings to light; and on the other hand, the pleasure that kindles at having to evade this power, flee from it, fool it, travesty it" (45). Among several intriguing lines of speculation that I haven't time now to pursue is whether Foucault is actually championing these pleasures, espousing them as compensation for the damage done by repression. It's impossible to tell for sure. What is unquestionable—and here is my focus—is that nowhere in *The History of Sexuality* does Foucault explore the negative consequences of a discursive situation that restricts people to the pleasures of spying and hiding. Granted, in the Victorian period spying and hiding did yield some pleasure—to those affiliating with the dominant position by writing and reading hegemonic tracts like Acton's and to those submissives who enjoyed their abjection. What's crucial is how these pleasures of spying and hiding relate to the damage done by repression itself. The polar enterprises of spying and fooling leave both the powerful and the disempowered caught in a dialectic of slavery that infantalizes. The pattern of punishing parent and guilty devious child is never matured beyond. In turn, since infantilization is another type of silencing, the discursive pleasures of spying and hiding function to exacerbate rather than to heal the wounds caused by repression.

Foucault defines a second type of pleasure by contrasting the *ars erotica* of India and China with the *scientia sensualis* of modern Western culture. In the *ars erotica*, pleasure produces truth; in the *scientia sensualis*, truth produces pleasure. Focusing on the *scientia sensualis*, Foucault maintains that we have "invented a different kind of pleasure: pleasure in the truth of pleasure, the pleasure of knowing that truth . . . a pleasure that comes of knowing pleasure, a knowledge-pleasure" (71, 77). Since Foucault is discussing the *scientia sensualis* in terms of its pleasure-producing truths, we can fairly ask to what extent nineteenth-century Anglo-American readers did indeed experience as pleasurable the "truths" of scientific discourse.

Consider, briefly, two "scientific proofs" of women's intellectual inferiority. One was that female brains are smaller than male brains. When someone inconveniently noted that since women's bodies were, on average, smaller than men's their brains would of course be smaller proportionally, many of the scientists engaged in weighing and measuring switched to other body parts, especially the thigh bone, compared femurs from each sex, and concluded resoundingly that, even proportionally, female thigh bones were smaller. Women were indeed inferior intellectually. A second controversy involved menstruation. Assuming that the amount of blood allotted to the reproductive system during the catamenial period meant that only a dangerously small amount of blood remained in the brain, scientists argued that sustained intellectual work at this time of the month could seriously threaten young women's health. College was not for them.

My point in foregrounding the menstruation and brain weight controversies is not of course to deny that serious men and women throughout the nineteenth century devoted estimable effort to seeking the truth about our gendered selves. These scientists' methods of research and modes of argument were, however, anything but "disinterested" and "objective." As for the femur measurers, since the effect (and maybe the intent) of their experiment was to confirm conventional biases, we can surely inquire whether most of the victims of bias experienced pleasure. Women denied admission to college because of discursive systems that judged their brain power in terms of their thigh bones and utterly misunderstood their cardiovascular system— these women and their partisans were made to suffer, both practically and psychologically, as a result of the policing function of discourse.

Foucault thus enables us to establish three things about Anglo-American society in the nineteenth century. Repression in the form of direct silencing was a powerful force; discursive structures exacerbated repression by policing desire rigorously; and the pleasures generated by scientistic discourses made things still worse.

How gothic fiction produced a different type of pleasure in this same epoch, pleasure that could potentially heal, I'll now try to explain. Gothic can help heal the wounds of repression by putting into play what silencing, denial, and infantilization tried to police. Through its thematic and representational insistence upon outré desires, gothic acts as a counterdiscursive formation that fosters pleasure in terms of both psyche and society by the release of repressed affects and by the exploration of foreclosed topics. As counterdiscursive, gothic works in a manner quite opposite from the *scientia sensualis* and much more like the *ars erotica*. In gothic, it is not truth that produces pleasure but rather pleasure that produces truth.

How this truth-producing pleasure gets generated is suggested by the opening sentence of Poe's "The Cask of Amontillado": "[t]he thousand injuries of Fortunato I had borne as I best could, but when he ventured upon insult I vowed revenge." My guess is that most readers of this sentence's first clause would agree that Montresor intends to say: "the thousand injuries inflicted by Fortunato I had endured as best I could." Montresor, in other words, defines himself as the victim of Fortunato's malice. In the process of making this point, however, Montresor's initial eleven words generate three puns. "The injuries of Fortunato," for instance, deploys the genitive in a way which suggests not only the injuries *by* Fortunato but also the injuries *of* Fortunato, *to* Fortunato. "I had borne" suggests "I had birthed, I had produced," as the obvious alternative phrasing, "I had endured," does not. And then there is "as I best could" rather than "as best I could, as long as I could." Montresor is justifying his counterattack by insisting that he retaliates only after he held out to the limits of his endurance. "As I best could" does not *say* this, however. "As I best could" says that no one could have suffered as well as Montresor.

What do these three plays on words add up to? The puns, I believe, create a latent level to Montresor's sentence, a subtext that dramatically opposes the manifest meaning. At this subtextual level, Montresor is the victimizer and Fortunato the victim: "[i]njuries were inflicted upon Fortunato as only Montresor can." This is precisely what the story goes on to dramatize, of course. Fortunato, who imagines himself dominant, is reduced to the submissive position, while lowly Montresor reigns untouchable. What Poe's puns provide us readers is an experience like that of the *ars erotica*. We move from pleasure to truth. From the pleasure of engaging with verbal artistry so elegant, we come to insight into human motivation. We see how conveniently an aggressive will to power can mask itself as victimization. We see how suspect an emotion socially sanctioned indignation is.

To be clear: my point is not simply that the initial three puns enable us to see in advance what the narrative goes on to make plain; we see in fact a moral/psychological truth that never finds articulation in the text because Montresor never comes to recognize it. He never learns that converting from victim to victimizer—and thus simply reversing a binary—does not undo wrong and produce happiness. The story's initial puns cue us to the underlying truth of Montresor's situation so that we can be alive to the myriad other pleasure-producing revelations that abide at the latent level of the text.

In focusing on puns I may seem to be praising in gothic what I've faulted in Acton: a bileveled textuality which produces contradictory perspectives. What comparing Acton and Poe reveals, in fact, is a basic difference of procedure, a difference which highlights the pleasure-producing capacities of gothic fiction. In

both Acton and Poe, denial operates to repress unwelcome affect
and awareness from the manifest level of the text. At issue is the
question, unwelcome to whom? Unwelcome to Acton and unwelcome to . . . Montresor. In Poe's story, denial proceeds from
the narrator, not from the author. Poe's text allows us to see
through what Acton's text wants to restrict us to. In effect, Poe's
text thematizes nineteenth-century discursive procedures, even
as it offers an alternative to them.

In addition to language play and unreliable narrators, gothic
fiction fosters its pleasure through its handling of denouements
in ways particularly important to the engagement of readerly desire. I believe (it can be shown) that all major gothic novels are
open-ended to an extent unmatched in other modes and that this
mobility is fundamental to their pleasure-producing capability.
Immediately, however, I must make a qualification: most gothic
texts allow us to read them as Acton's text insists on being
read: as an indictment of outré behavior and an affirmation of
orthodoxy. Victor Frankenstein, the Wielands, Captain Ahab,
Carmilla, Dr. Jekyll, Dorian Gray, Count Dracula, Thomas Sutpen are all exterminated. To take pleasure in stopping here, however, to enjoy a unilateral satisfaction in the defeat of evil and
madness, is to refuse many of the pleasures of reading. Everything about great gothic texts encourages us to see their characters—and thus human desire—as more implicating and pleasure
producing. My belief is this: gothic texts provide us readers with
pleasures as multiple and intense as our desires. The pleasure of
gothic involves, therefore, the adaptation of textual materials to
readerly needs. Gothic allows each individual reader to discover
the quality and intensity of pleasure most useful at the particular
moment of this reader's life.

Take as an example *Dr. Jekyll and Mr. Hyde*. In addition to seeing it as a righteously resolved tract that exposes the dangers of
transgressive medicine, we can also find diverse affects and issues
for which Stevenson's denouement provides no comparably orthodox resolution. We can, for instance, find a novel about compulsion, about how difficult it is to desist from whatever passionate pursuit we're driven to by desire. We can go further and see
compulsion as a dilemma of professionalism, one of the difficul-

ties of the medical and legal caste that had joined with the House of Commons to control British society in the late nineteenth century. Going on, we can see in professionalism a drama of male sociability—there are *no* major women in the story. And further still, we can see that beneath this homosocial conviviality rage homicidal urges. Killing in turn shows itself both patricidal and fratricidal. Looked at differently, the homosocial reveals ties to the homoerotic world of night stalking and "unspeakable" desire.

How much each individual reader participates in the desires loosed by Stevenson's plot depends upon that reader's particular relationship with those desires. One reader may focus on the homicidal and worry that England is destroying itself from within, since the murder of the MP is perpetrated not by a foreigner or a proletarian but by an eminent London physician. This worry, in turn, may or may not be associated by the reader with the increasing anxiety about Britain's fate that was surfacing throughout the culture, an anxiety that H. Rider Haggard had already dramatized in *She* and that Bram Stoker would soon mobilize in *Dracula*. This same reader might not, however, engage the text's homoerotic elements. Details such as "Queer Street," "by-street," "favorite," and rear entry might not receive from this reader the attention necessary to engage with their connotations and to link them to other details such as Utterson's dream of Hyde entering Jekyll's bedroom and the fact that Utterson's relation with Hyde is called "bondage."

Gothic texts thus do in hyperintense fashion what all literary art does to some extent: provide individual readers with diverse materials that can be experienced according to the individual's desires. No genre of fiction goes so far as gothic, however, in encouraging each reader to produce an understanding that gives this reader the quantity and quality of outré pleasure appropriate to immediate needs. For myself, I saw fairly early in my work on *Jekyll and Hyde* the operation of patricidal rage, the "old war in the members" that Stevenson referred to. It wasn't for several years, however, that I realized there was a pun here on "members," that sexuality was also at stake in the homoerotic features of the novel. Last came my recognition that the word "members" in its familial sense was not restricted to fathers and sons and that fratricidal rage, the story of Esau against Jacob, was also being enacted. Why did I "see" some things early and some much later? I was a close reader throughout my work on Stevenson, but only quite late did I notice the "hairy hands" of Edward Hyde and thence his connection with Esau.

What I'm offering for your consideration is a general phenomenon of reading that has special relevance for gothic—why we see some things and not others at any one time, and why we see various things at various times. I believe that as literary critics we tend to be strikingly uncurious about our commitments—why we specialize in a particular author, genre, period, and why we "see" different things at different stages of a project and a life. Obviously, diverse factors will contribute to so overdetermined a phenomenon as scholarly "seeing." But one of these factors, a crucial factor I believe, is the way pleasure relates to repressed desire. Gothic fiction aggressively encourages what all art allows—that we build our own artifact out of the materials provided by the object.

This brings me back to D. W. Winnicott and the relevance to gothic fiction of his concepts of potential space, transitional object, and play. A gothic text positions its reader in a potential space where the psyche's repressed desires and the society's foreclosed issues can be engaged and thus where healing can occur. The gothic text itself functions as a transitional object. It is created by the reader, yet it is already there. We produce a novel that has never before existed, though a century old. By engaging in the creative play of reading, the individual experiences the pleasure that indicates the extent to which he or she has experienced desire. Desire is in fact what is produced by the reader's healing play with the text.

HEALING

Winnicott is not very clear about how healing actually occurs— in the psyche and in society. While no one (including Freud) has ever managed to define this process precisely, I've found helpful the work of anthropologist Michael Taussig, literary critic Ross

Chambers, and the cultural analysts Peter Stallybrass and Allon White.

Healing psychic wounds has been and remains in many cultures the responsibility of the shaman. Michael Taussig's book *Shamanism, Colonialism, and the Wild Man* is subtitled "a study in terror and healing." How terror heals is his theme. Like Winnicott, Taussig recognizes the importance of space, in this case "the space of death" where colonizer and colonized have killed for centuries. While the death space is not identical to Winnicott's potential space, Taussig is defining a place in-between, "a threshold that allows for illumination as well as extinction" (4). The shaman in turn functions more like a transitional object than like a Western physician, since healing is produced not by him but through him. The shaman with his chanting and powerful *yage* drink enables a creative play through which the patient cures himself in ways that help explain the play of gothic healing.

Today in Guatemala, white people can go for healing to Indian shamans whose power is presumed by the whites to be indigenous, a consequence of the Indian essence as dark Other. What Taussig establishes, however, is that the shaman's demonic power derives from the white Spanish missionaries who came to Guatemala in the sixteenth century and "believed firmly in the efficacy of sorcery, which they supposed Indians to be especially prone to practice on account of their having been seduced by the devil. . . . the magic of the Indian is a colonial creation" (142–143, 445). Taussig is not simply recycling here the banality that conquerors project their fears onto the lowly, who then come back to terrorize them. What occurs with the Guatemalan shaman is not the return of the repressed to haunt but the return of the projected to heal. The healing is self-healing, for what the whites encounter in the shaman is white magic, not black; not his power, but theirs displaced. The colonizers had been injured by projecting onto the colonized a puissant part of their own being, those desires that were unacceptable to the European orthodoxy of their time. The wound that lingers in the Guatemalan whites today is self-division. They can therefore be healed only by regaining contact with their own puissant desires through the mediation of the terrifying Other. They can be healed only by themselves.

This is what gothic does—self-healing through terror—though with a difference which I must specify immediately. That white Guatemalans receive great benefit from shamans is largely fortuitous. Projection of terrifying desires onto the dark Other was originally a tactic of imperialist conquest, "facilitating the legalities of enslavement and the use of military force. . . . the colonizers provided the colonized with the left-handed gift of the image of the wild man—a gift whose powers the colonizers were blind to" (Taussig 142, 467). What was inadvertent with colonialism is constitutive of gothic. In reading, we avoid that denial of the terrible which repressive culture enacts. Reading gothic fiction parodies this repressive process, displacing onto characters and scenes those terrifying desires which are thereby positioned so that we can call them back to us in creative play. What Taussig makes clear is that engagement with the projective Other means reengagement with our own *power*, our own *magic*. In the projective Other of shamanism and the displaced Other of gothic we regain contact not simply with forbidden desires but with desires forbidden because of their terrifying—and thus potentially therapeutic—power.

How reengagement with our desires can help heal the wounds of society is the next question. Ross Chambers in *Room for Maneuver* states with brilliant simplicity that a change in desire can cause a desire for change. (Reading, for Chambers, involves "the possibility of a conversion in the reader from a form of desire assumed to be consonant with the structures of power to an 'other' form, more congenial to textual oppositionality and simultaneously constituting a shift that is a *conversio ad se*" [243]. Although a "conversion" model seems to me too oppositional and manipulative to represent how most fiction—and particularly gothic—fosters self-healing, I do agree with Chambers's view of the social aspects of changes in individuals' desires.) "What I am influenced by . . . changes 'my' sense of the desirable. And to that extent . . . my production of the real" (236). Since social reality is not natural and essential but constructed and thereby contin-

gent, cultural forms are forms of desire and thus are subject to
changes in desires.

Chambers's ahistorical discussion leaves unanswered the
question of how social change could occur in the specific context
of gothic's heyday, nineteenth-century Anglo-American culture.
An answer can be developed through Stallybrass and White.
They start from a fact of cultural history—during the nineteenth
century, carnival was increasingly suppressed. Concurrently,
there appeared three phenomena—hysteria, psychoanalysis, and
the ghost story revival—which exemplify in a European context
the general cultural mechanism I've posited: society's wounding
itself and then developing ways to heal the wounds. In the later
nineteenth century, the wound of choice was hysteria. Stallybrass and White relate the outbreak of hysteria to an aspect of
cultural life that Bakhtin emphasizes: "post-romantic culture is,
to a considerable extent, subjectivized and interiorized and on
this account frequently related to private terrors, isolation and
insanity rather than to robust kinds of social celebration and
critique" (Stallybrass and White 180). Stallybrass and White
demonstrate that a carnival confined to the private theater of the
psyche is hell on earth.

> It is striking how the thematics of carnival pleasure—eating,
> inversion, mess, dirt, sex and stylized body movements—find
> their neurasthenic, unstable and mimicked counterparts in
> the discourse of hysteria . . . It is as if the hysteric has no
> mechanism for coping with the *mediation* of the grotesque
> body in everyday life except by violent acts of exclusion.
> (182, 184)

Where mediated self-recognition can occur for hysterics is in
a space provided by an institution which appeared as carnival was
disappearing: psychoanalysis.

Freud uses the resonant term "agencies of disgust" to describe
the forces arrayed against him in the struggle to cure hysterics. Those "agencies of disgust" are the same agencies which,
in their public form, mobilized religious and civil authorities

against carnival. . . . Carnival allowed the society involved to
mediate into periodic ritual the culturally structured "otherness" of its governing categories. We might call this process
of periodic mediation *active reinforcement*. . . . This contrasts
strongly with the mechanism of hysteria which Freud called
reactive reinforcement. . . . "Contrary thoughts are always
closely connected with each other and are often paired off in
such a way that the *one thought is exaggeratedly conscious while its
counterpart is repressed and unconscious*." (Stallybrass and White
188, 189)

Psychoanalysis was one mode of active reinforcement that the
fin de siècle developed. "Periodic" in the regularity of the
analysand's "hour," psychoanalytic ritual utilized the potential
space of the couch, as carnival utilized its site, to actively facili-
tate both the mediation of repressive categories and reengagement with denied desire. To what extent does gothic fiction also
provide active reinforcement—in America as well as Europe?

The years when hysteria proliferates and Freud begins his
major work are also the time of the ghost story revival. *Jekyll
and Hyde*, "The Phantom Rickshaw," "The Yellow Wallpaper,"
Dorian Gray, "The Monster," *The Turn of the Screw*, *Dracula*, plus
the best short stories of Robert W. Chambers and M. R. James
all appear between 1885 and 1914. What gothic and psychoanalysis share importantly is their utilizations of potential space.
Gothic too is a site where human beings can forgo reactive
reinforcement and can actively reengage with "component"
thoughts that have been repressed into the unconscious.

Moreover, gothic, like psychoanalysis, has its strikingly carnivalesque features. These become clear in light of Bakhtin's claim
that "carnival celebrates temporary liberation from the prevailing truth of the established order" (7). "The Cask of Amontillado" is a carnival story that enacts the carnivalesque capabilities of all gothic fiction, since Poe's story stages a temporary
liberation even as it questions whether liberation is possible.
Montresor uses the potential space of carnival for killing. His is,
in effect, a countercarnival where suppressed rage is vented, but
repression is not escaped. Montresor utilizes rather than abjures

the binaries of good/bad, victim/victimizer which undergird social orthodoxy; his carnival is a reactive reinforcement disguised
in motley. In turn, Poe's story is a true carnival, an active reinforcement. His readers experience the carnivalesque because
we can escape Montresor's binaries and encounter the "grotesque" as defined by Stallybrass and White: "a boundary phenomenon of hybridization or inmixing in which self and other
become enmeshed in an inclusive, heterogeneous, dangerously
unstable zone" (193).

   This process of grotesque hybridization is particularly prominent in fin de siècle gothic. Dorian Gray exemplifies the "grotesque body" which carnival celebrates and which "transgres-
sions of gender, territorial boundaries, sexual preference, family
and group norms are transcoded into" (Stallybrass and White).
Grotesque bodies recur in *Dracula*, in which the Count grows
physically younger every day he threatens Britain; in *The Monster*, in which a black man already effaced politically and socially
in a racist culture is literally effaced by a fire that burns his face
to a cinder; in "The Yellow Wallpaper," in which pregnancy so
distorts the protagonist's self-image that she sees herself reflected in wallpaper patterns of "bloated curves" that "go wad-
dling up and down in isolated columns of fatuity" (Gilman 9). In
these and other carnivalesque masterpieces of the fin de siècle,
"hybridization . . . produces new combinations and strange in-
stabilities" (Stallybrass and White 58). Gothic is reborn at the
moment when psychoanalysis is born and carnival is dying,
thus helping to assure that healing remains available to repression's many.

SUBVERSION/TRANSFORMATION

How does healing become subversive? My answer to the question posed in my subtitle is formulated in terms of "transformation" rather than "subversion," because the repression that damaged the Anglo-American middle class in the nineteenth century
and that continues to dog us today was not imposed by some
despot or oligarchy. It was taken on gradually, for reasons that
seemed good or at least necessary at the time. Change therefore
involved not a simple opposition and overthrow, as in a dicta-

torship, but a gradual alteration in desire and perception. This process is particularly difficult to chart in instances which produce no signal moment like the storming of the Bastille or the election of Nelson Mandela. There are no guarantees with gothic as with any other site of potential transformation. Insofar as the plight of women and gays and blacks and religious minorities is certainly less arduous in Anglo-American society today than in, say, 1820, I have no great difficulty believing that gothic has made a contribution, has helped effect changes in individual desires that produced a longing for change throughout the society. But there are no guarantees. The March sisters in *Little Women* are reading sensation novels, but when the sisters close the covers of their books they go back to the sentimental life, just as their author wrote *Jo's Boys* long after the gothic thrillers of *Behind a Mask*. Gothic fiction is a *potential* space precisely because actualization depends upon each individual reader and, especially given the private nature of reading, is anyone's guess.

What does seem clear is that gothic constitutes a site which readers return to generation after generation. Gothic has surely contributed more than its share of imagoes to our permanent memory (Frankenstein, Jekyll and Hyde, Dracula above all, but the scarlet letter and the white whale too), images that proffer to each citizen in the terrifying privacy of readerly quiet the same healing question, Why are you so afraid? The teeth of Heathcliff shining in death, the necrophilic bedroom of the Emily to whom Faulkner offered a rose, the rusty sawblade that Sethe passes across the throat of Beloved—why are we so afraid? I asked at the beginning of this essay how a popular text could be truly subversive. I end by asking, How could transformation occur any other way?

WORKS CITED

Acton, William. *The Functions and Disorders of the Reproductive System.* Quoted from vol. 2 of *The Woman Question.* Ed. Elizabeth K. Helsinger, Robin L. Sheets, and William Veeder. New York: Garland, 1983, rpt. Chicago: U of Chicago P, 1989.

Chambers, Ross. *Room for Maneuver*. Chicago: U of Chicago P, 1991.

Foucault, Michel. *The History of Sexuality: An Introduction*. New York: Random House, 1978.

Gilman, Charlotte Perkins. "The Yellow Wallpaper." *The Charlotte Perkins Gilman Reader*. Ed. Ann J. Lane. New York: Pantheon, 1980.

Stallybrass, Peter, and Allon White. *The Politics and Poetics of Transgression*. New York: Cornell UP, 1986.

Taussig, Michael. *Shamanism, Colonialism, and the Wild Man*. Chicago: U of Chicago P, 1987.

Winnicott, D. W. *Playing and Reality*. London: Tavistock Publications, 1971.

MAGGIE KILGOUR

Dr. Frankenstein Meets Dr. Freud

Since Mary Shelley's *Frankenstein*, the mad scientist has been one of the most popular of the gothic's bag of tricks, a figure whose descendants include Dr. Jekyll, Dr. Moreau, and now countless horror and science fiction villains (see Svilpis, Goodrich, Baldick). Twentieth-century readings and revisions of Shelley's work often turn the story into a moral cautionary tale that teaches the evil consequences of using technology and science to dominate nature (see Mellor 89–114). More generally, however, the figure seems central to the gothic's critique of the ideology of the Enlightenment (faith in individualism, progress, reason, and its partner, science), which has made the genre of recent critical interest (see Punter 425; Miles 224; Kilgour 5–6, 10–15, 218–223). Moreover, today the gothic is a dominant popular genre, especially if we define it loosely, as it really must be defined, for it is always a boundary breaker which erodes any neat distinction between formats and modes, combining sentimentality and the grotesque, romance and terror, the heroic and the bathetic, philosophy and nonsense. This promiscuous generic cross-breeding is part of the gothic's "subverting" of stable norms, collapsing of "binary oppositions," which makes it appropriate for a postmodern sensibility. It appears to offer both a critique and an alternative to our Enlightenment inheritance: as it warns us of the dangers of *repressing* energies, natural, social, psychic, textual, or sexual, the gothic offers itself a means of *expressing* otherwise taboo forces. The gothic draws on the modern assumption that it is dangerous to bury things (which always return, as *Pet Semetary* shows); by bringing the unspoken to light, it acts as a potential corrective.

There may be some irony here, however, as in many ways it has been the increasing demand to model literary theory on the sciences that has helped revive the gothic's previously unsavory reputation. More specifically, the application of psychoanalytic methods to the gothic, beginning early in this century with the surrealists, taught readers to see the gothic not as superficial sensationalism but as the revelation of repressed dark cultural secrets. Freud's theories of repression and the uncanny have been fruitful for reading the gothic, not the least in simply bestowing a greater profundity on a form previously trivialized as superficial. But there is also some circularity here between subject and object—a kind of gothic doubling between the object under analysis and the scientific method. Freud himself noted, in discussing the nature of the uncanny, that "I should not be surprised to hear that psycho-analysis, which is concerned with laying bare these hidden forces, has itself become uncanny to many people" (151). Ian Watt thus claims further that "Freudian theory can itself be seen as a Gothic myth. It presents the individual, much as the gothic does, as essentially imprisoned by the tyranny of an omnipotent but unseen past" (167). William Patrick Day, who rightly reads Freud as a late gothic writer, suggests that the gothic and analysis have a common source: "the two are cousins, responses to the problems of selfhood and identity, sexuality and pleasure, fear and anxiety, as they manifest themselves in the nineteenth and early twentieth centuries" (6). Both reveal the dark truth that the autonomous subject is not a unified whole but fragmented and dismembered, internally ruptured so that it is alienated not only from nature and others but from itself.

As Day notes, however, the goal of the Freudian analyst, like that of Victor Frankenstein, is to re-member the dismembered parts of our fragmented selves, to cure us by making us whole. To do so he must achieve a delicate balance of scientific objectivity and sympathetic identification, remaining detached from the patient, even as he tries to understand his (or usually her) mind (186). For Day, this makes the analyst similar to the gothic

detective, who, since Sherlock Holmes, has often been represented as an amateur scientist (97, 177–190). In *Dracula*, he is
even a medical doctor whose specialty is diseases of the brain.
The detective is an outsider, an analytical observer, whose ability to solve the crime depends upon this detached perspective of
scientific objectivity. However, it contradictorily also depends
upon his identification with the criminal. The detective story
thus usually requires a simultaneous identification and opposition between detective and criminal. They are opposites in that
the detective is good and the criminal bad; the criminal hides
and the detective seeks. However, the detective's mode of exposure depends upon an underlying similarity between the
two minds—an almost symbiotic understanding between them
which enables the detective to intuit the criminal's moves. Like
Victor and his creation, good and evil, innocence and guilt, pursuer and pursued are thus complex doubles of each other, locked
together in a complex identity.

The doubling of the detective and criminal and their mutual
relation to Freudian models is central to Thomas Harris's bestseller and Jonathan Demme's Academy award–winning film *Silence of the Lambs*, to which I now wish to turn to suggest further
some of the meanings of the gothic for us today. Hannibal
Lecter is a version of the gothic mad scientist who contains elements of his ancestors, Frankenstein, Dr. Jekyll, Dr. Moreau,
transgressive experimenters who tamper with nature and whose
exploits have also been recently revived and revised on film.[1] As
a literally cannibal ego, Lecter is also the most exaggerated version of the modern Hobbesian individual, governed only by will
and appetite, detached from the world and other humans, whom
he sees simply as objects for his own consumption.

As a mad doctor, however, Lecter has even more delicious
resonances. In an ironic twist of *Totem and Taboo*, in which cannibalism was posited as the hidden originating moment of civilization, cannibalism becomes the dark truth *psychoanalysis* conceals. While analysis could be seen as the most benevolent and
civilized form of science, because it dissects the mind rather than
the body, in Harris's work the pretense of refinement masks a
secret and increased appetite for flesh. Cannibalism is Lecter's

cure for neuroses, or at least his way of putting an end to analysis interminable; he kills and eats one patient when "[t]herapy wasn't going anywhere" (Harris, *Silence* 54). By making the head-shrinker a cannibal, the story suggests that, as one critic has argued, "stripping the mind is no less a violation than stripping the body" (Halberstam 48).[2] Analysis and cannibalism thus form a continuum, differentiated only by degree, not kind, as to see into the hearts of others is an act of aggression which leads to a physical consumption.

Like many other gothic works, the novel depends upon a pattern of doubling which establishes similarities between apparently different activities and figures. In Harris's earlier novel, *Red Dragon*, Lecter and the other psychopath, the tooth fairy, who has his own oral obsession, are pitted against a male scientist-detective, Will Graham. The novel raises the classic gothic problem, given the underlying similarity, of distinguishing pursuer and pursued, detective and criminal; Lecter tells his antagonist, "[W]e're just alike" (Harris, *Dragon* 67), and part of Graham's goal is to reassure both himself and others that they're *not*—that there *is* a way of telling the two apart. In *Silence*, Lecter's counterpart is Clarice Starling, whose bond with him is apparent from their first meeting, when she notes that "he was small and sleek; in his hands and arms she saw wiry strength like her own" (Harris, *Silence* 16). The two opposites are working together, exchanging knowledge, "quid pro quo," analyzing each other, trading secrets so that it's difficult to tell who's who. Both are detective and analyst and also patient under analysis. Both are interpreters, each reading the other for clues to the secret knowledge they desire.

Starling's motive for meeting Lecter is to harness psychic surveillance, which threatens to consume society for social surveillance—to turn literal cannibalism into a more socially acceptable form. To lure him into helping her against another criminal, Buffalo Bill, she offers herself as bait, gradually revealing to him her own secrets. Motives then provide one means of differentiating between the two doubles: Clarice serves society, while Lecter serves society to himself. In the classic gothic dualism, altruism is pitted against selfishness, the community against the ravenous ego. Moreover, Lecter alone is the criminal. Clarice's secret, the clue to the meaning of the title, is not one of real guilt, nor is it of a sexual nature (a family romance), as orthodox Freudianism would lead us to expect. In general, the secrets revealed by the story are not explained in terms of sexuality, even in the case of Buffalo Bill (see Tharp). Clarice's uncanny past consists of some traumatic experiences—the brutal death of her father, her subsequent exile to first relatives and then an orphanage, and, especially, her terrifying experiences at her aunt's slaughterhouse—which explain the title of the story but which also link her to Lecter, as, growing up around an abattoir, she "from early life had known more than she wished to know about meat processing" (Harris, *Silence* 27).

The titular lambs reinforce patterns of religious imagery in the text which introduce the central themes of change, renewal, and rebirth. Most of the patterns are parodic: the image of the "floaters," which suggest a demonic baptism; the burial and resurrection of the girls as part of Bill's gruesomely literal conversion, in which he will put off the old man to put on the new girl. Lecter's cannibalism appears as a perversion of communion, and Lecter is surrounded with twisted icons—his drawings of Golgotha and the Christ on his crucifixion watch (onto whose body he has superimposed Clarice's head), as well as his crazy neighbor, Sammie, descendant of both *Dracula*'s Renfield and gothic tales of religious enthusiasts. Clarice's story, in contrast, suggests a potential norm of change and development, as the novel charts her growth and liberation from her traumatic past.

In this plot, Clarice's role is that of the patient, whom Lecter helps to cure. Her narrative is a version of Freudian analysis in which gender often guarantees the difference between doctor and patient necessary to effect the cure. The male scientist cures the female patient by exposing a previously buried past that, because it was hidden, had haunted her. The last paragraph of the novel focuses on a breaking with Clarice's past, suggesting that even her subconscious has been purged of its demons, as she falls asleep and "sleeps deeply, sweetly, in the silence of the lambs" (Harris, *Silence* 367).

The film also foregrounds Clarice's metamorphosis but to

bring out a slightly different narrative model: the gothic scenario, which itself lurks beneath the analytic relation. In the gothic, too, the heroine has to be freed from a haunting past in order to grow up and attain adult female identity. The film begins with a scene in which Starling is running through the woods. We first read this as a conventional gothic scene of pursuit, only to slowly realize that she is on an FBI training course. The opening scene indicates self-consciously how Clarice plays the role of gothic heroine, whose experiences enable her to confront and come to terms with a past that haunts her, associated with her father's murder but also, beyond that, with her ancestors, invoked at several points as a primitive race.[3] As a modern woman, she tries to separate herself from these barbaric origins, wanting to change, as Lecter recognizes when he mocks her for being, like all gothic heroines, "[d]esperate not to be like your mother" (Harris, *Silence* 22). As a woman, too, she is identified with the murder victims, who are images of a self she might have been if she hadn't "evolved." Like the traditional male scientist, she detaches herself from this identity through forensic analysis. In so doing, she disassociates herself also from the traditional figure of the gothic heroine, who is usually passive and incapable of separating herself physically and emotionally from her family. Clarice Starling, whose name evokes the sentimental Richardsonian model of femininity which influenced the gothic, is a new type of woman and part of a current vogue for female detectives. In the course of the film and book we see her evolve into this type before our eyes, battling not only against the killer of women but against the feudal sexism that still haunts the system.

In *Silence*, Clarice's sexual identity might offer one obvious difference between the two central characters. At the same time, however, as critics have noted, all the characters are sexually ambiguous. Becoming an agent, Clarice enters the male world of the FBI, so that she appears an androgynous figure (whose sexuality is unclear in the movie, though not in the book), while Lecter is given some feminine traits. His homosexuality is suggested, though never made explicit; in this world, cannibalism is certain and direct, while sexuality, and the difference between male and female, is murky and hard to determine. The slipperiness of gender as a mark of difference is literalized in the figure of Buffalo Bill, who further intensifies the identification between Clarice and Lecter. Bill plays Renfield to Lecter's Dracula, serving as a kind of perverted double of an original perversion. To Lecter's Dr. Jekyll, he is "Mr. Hide" (a name which takes on a whole new meaning in this context, as it is his alias). If Lecter is a descendant of Victor Frankenstein, Bill "combines both Frankenstein and the monster; he is the scientist, the creator, and he is the body being formed, sculpted, stitched and fitted" (Halberstam 46). Lecter and Bill have complementary methods of incorporation which break down the opposition between self and other, inside and outside: where Lecter takes others inside himself, Bill puts himself inside others.[4] As skin is the border between the self and the world, the place where inside and outside meet, his appropriation of others' surfaces is a further parodic version of more traditional ways of encountering the world. By merging his own body with women's, Bill blurs the boundaries between male and female in a literalization of the marriage ritual in which man and woman become symbolically one flesh. Like cannibalism, Bill's crime is also a weird parody of a consumer mentality which enables him to objectify his sexual Other in order to "suit" himself and subsume her. But Bill's real goal is to be a complete constructionist who can "fashion" for himself a new female self, turning male into female and thus transcending gender differences. By seeking to transform himself, he thus appears to be a distorted version of Clarice. As she flees the limits of traditional femininity, he seeks, through more direct means, a way out of orthodox masculinity. Yet he also understands the symbolic nature of his attempt at self-transcendence, as the presence of a moth in the mouths of his victims indicates. It suggests that Buffalo Bill's motives are renewal and change; like Clarice, he is trying to free himself from a past self limited by conventional ideas of sexual difference.

Both Bill's and Clarice's stories of development and self-transformation, of attempts to transcend the confining boundaries of their natural gendered identities, relate back to the story of Lecter. While logically a peripheral figure, brought in ostensibly simply to help the good guys against the bad, like most gothic villains the chilling Lecter becomes the central figure. We never learn anything about Lecter's past, what caused this monster, which makes him all the more unsettling. If Bill is the evil that can be reduced, as it is by reporters, to an "unhappy childhood" (Harris, *Silence* 357), Lecter is a larger evil that contemporary society both creates and denies. When Clarice asks her superior, Jack Crawford, what Lecter is, Crawford replies, "I know he's a monster. Beyond that, nobody can say for sure" (Harris, *Silence* 6), suggesting that he is the uncanny thing that normal language cannot define. His intelligence is "not measurable by any means known to man" (Harris, *Silence* 199). He has a nice sense of poetic justice; as he tells her, "A census taker tried to quantify me once. I ate his liver with some fava beans and a big Amarone" (Harris, *Silence* 24). Instead of being contained by the system, he swallows it—a truly subversive element. The analyst resists analysis, reduction in terms of his own theories, which cannot contain him any more than the prison system (whether the prison house of language or a jail) or census taker can. Even his motives are never clearly defined: part revenge, part perverse pleasure and an aesthetic appreciation of murder as one of the fine arts. We cannot analyze him scientifically to say, reassuringly, what the cause of his evil is. He mocks Clarice when she comes with her questionnaire: "[y]ou'd like to quantify me" (Harris, *Silence* 22); "do you think you can dissect me with this blunt little tool? . . . You can't reduce me to a set of influences. You've given up good and evil for behaviorism, Officer Starling. You've got everybody in moral dignity pants—nothing is ever anybody's fault . . . Look at me, Officer Starling, can you stand to say I'm evil? Am I evil, Officer Starling?" (Harris, *Silence* 21). Lecter suggests that he is a deeper moral evil unleashed by a relativistic world which reads good and evil only in terms of social conditioning. He is created by and feeds upon a world which no longer believes in absolute differences.

Like Clarice, Lecter is free in the end. For him, identity can be simply remade as he first literally takes a new face in order to escape, then uses plastic surgery as a method for conversion, which affords him the Frankensteinian power to construct himself as a new man. In the novel, the exposing of Clarice's demons seems an exorcism that enables her to sleep silently in the arms of her lover. The happy romantic ending, which suggests that the banishing of a demonic past leads to the attainment of heterosexual love, is somewhat troubled by the resonances of the last lines, which echo the title. Moreover, if the demons have been exorcised, that may not mean that they have been successfully contained but rather that they, in the form of the cannibal, are now free and uncontrolled. The film ends with the figure of Lecter, whose break and reconstruction of identity also become a parodic version of Clarice's, in which, further, the parody subversively usurps the place of the norm. In the film, the last scene is of Lecter pursuing his real nemesis, the odious and lecherous Dr. Chilton, who had harassed Clarice. Reasserting his bond with her against a common foe, Lecter calls her to say, "I'm having an old friend for dinner." The movie thus ends neatly with a cute pun. Poetic justice triumphs, as one bad doctor eats another. While in one sense the ending is left open (allowing for a lucrative sequel that fleshes out the further madcap adventures of Hannibal the Cannibal), in another it is resolutely shut, through the projected union of the two opposites. Cannibalism itself becomes a tidy image for closure—a quick, if cheap, resolution of differences which both seems provocatively witty and subversive and yet also satisfies the audience's craving for a neat and, in some sense, happy ending.

The end of the film suggests further the possible dissolution of the difference between Clarice and Lecter, not only by focusing on their common enemy but by juxtaposing scenes of their respective liberty.[5] The penultimate scene focuses on Starling's graduation, which marks the climax of her quest as the attainment of autonomy and independence when she becomes literally an "agent." Elizabeth Young argues that the relation between the final scenes reveals that while Clarice's development may distance her from her former self, it identifies her further with Lecter; it suggests that while she becomes an agent, it is of the state, and she is "now fully trained to enforce the power of the state through modes of invasion, surveillance, entrapment, discipline, and punishment that not only parallel but literalize, as Freud's work helps to remind us, the operative modes of psychoanalysis itself" (Young 25). The psychic scrutiny of the analyst feeds into and makes possible the social scrutiny of the FBI; the two are not opposites after all but simply different stages of the same force. The movie thus could be read as showing the transformation of the detective into the criminal she was pursuing, eradicating the difference between good and evil.

In its implicit final identification of detective and criminal the film picks up the theme of Harris's earlier novel. At the end of *Red Dragon*, the good guy is left wondering if he is indeed any different from the criminal as he faces his own destructive nature, musing "that he contained all the elements to make murder" (*Dragon* 354). Harris seems to imply that the dark truth of civilization is that what is most highly civilized is most savagely cannibalistic—a message that Conrad conveyed with somewhat more style and subtlety. The film appears to want to make us confront our own insatiable appetites—at the same time, of course, as it feeds them. The scene of Clarice's final pursuit by Buffalo Bill, which repeats and literalizes the opening episode, gives us a real scene of gothic pursuit, shot from the perspective of the pursuer, with whom the viewer therefore becomes identified. The film also leaves us siding with Lecter, rooting for him as he sets out for dinner, and so suggests our own identification with the cannibal, who becomes our gothic double. This replicates, more graphically, the way in which in the novel the readers' reading is slyly mirrored back to them. Reading is a form of consumption too; Lecter's ambiguous analysis within the text is analogous to the activity of analyzing the text itself. The text's moral might then be "caveat Lectorem"—not reader beware, but beware of the reader. Critics, readers, interpreters, those who consume what others have produced are cannibals after all (see Young 27, 28n6).

This is a favorite theme of contemporary gothic and horror films—Pogo's famous warning, "I have seen the enemy and it is us." One reason that the gothic and film today go so successfully together is the fact that horror films often work to implicate the viewer in the crime committed (aside from film's essential uncanniness, it has the ability to revive the dead and blur the line between fact and fiction). In its origins, the gothic offers itself

as a vehicle for an emerging bourgeois ideology; today it provides an even more urgent means of cultural self-analysis, a way
of scrutinizing the desires and appetites which propel what is
now the status quo.

As a form of cultural analysis, moreover, the gothic provides
an important model for criticism in general today as it strives to
achieve more rigorous scientific theories of the relationship between literature and life. Critics are like gothic detectives as we
try to free ourselves from the mysteries of ideology through
reading, which enables us to criticize cultural motives and impulses. Like the gothic and psychoanalysis, criticism today is
conceived of as a way of revealing the hidden, making the uncanny canny, freeing ourselves from the past through detachment and objectivity. The analogy also feeds into contemporary
criticism's concern with its social relevance and political engagement. In their anxious relations to a political reality, the
progress of the gothic and criticism have mirrored each other,
which may explain in part why the gothic is now so central to
criticism in general. In its early career, the gothic was often dismissed as an escapist form, isolated from the world in its ruined
castle or laboratory and so ridiculously out of touch with life. An
unreal genre, it has always been aware of and nervous about its
own dubious status. While often reveling in its own artificiality,
one of its central themes is the instability of the difference between fiction and reality. A common convention within the
gothic is that of a work of art that comes to life. For Rousseau,
one of the gothic's bad fathers, this "Pygmalion theme" suggests
the power of art to revolutionize the world (see Kilgour 8,
85–87, 156–158, 160). Such a topos might suggest the gothic's
own aspiration to a more material substance: its desire to imagine itself as real and powerful. The (usually corrupting) influence
of art is often thematized within gothic novels: *Dorian Gray*,
Frankenstein contain fantasies of how literature constructs identity, claiming for art a power over life. The form that was accused
of irrelevance overcompensates by asserting vigorously its own
power, even if it can only imagine that as a power that is ultimately not creative but destructive.

Criticism today also wants to assert the gothic's place in the "real" world, even as that category itself seems problematized. Early gothic criticism was largely apologetic for expressing interest in such a superficial and irrelevant genre. Again, psychoanalysis helped give the gothic respectability and profundity and thus made possible the recent social and cultural readings which have been fruitful for an understanding of its appeal. Like the gothic, criticism in general is haunted by accusations that it is irrelevant and escapist, and it still often appears anxious to detach itself from the hideous specter of New Criticism, demonized as a big bogeyman we have just barely managed to vanquish in order to assert our power in the world.

However, the gothic also reveals to us the dangerous side of our own claims for power. The gothic will not let us simply see ourselves as heroic liberators as it reminds us of the affinity between the detective and the criminal, the healer and the mad doctor, the cure and the disease. The gothic critic is always a version not only of the detective but also of his or her necessary nemesis, the villain—especially the cannibalistic mad scientist Lecter. Like psychoanalysis, criticism is a gothic genre, involving dismemberment, necromancy. As Fred Botting suggests, critics may merely extend Victor Frankenstein's quest as they rip apart old texts "to produce new and hideous progenies that have lives of their own" (3, 4). The critic searching for the reading that will reform the world can always look like a mad scientist. The gothic thus gives us a way of ironically distancing ourselves from our own endeavors, of scrutinizing our own scrutinization (something I'm taking to an even further degree here too, of course—a sobering reminder that gothic paranoia is the natural state of our profession). The mad scientist is *our* dark double who reveals our current deep suspicion that all motives, including our own and especially any that lay claim to aesthetic detachment, disinterest, or scientific objectivity, are dark and sinister, weighted with power, Oedipal strife, propelled by self-interest. We know too well that the dream of using art or even theory to deconstruct the world and remake it in a better form too often turns into a Frankensteinian nightmare.

NOTES

1. In recent years there has been a remarkable rash of films focusing on this particular type of gothic villain: Kenneth Branagh's *Frankenstein*; *The Island of Dr. Moreau* with Marlon Brando; the revision of "Dr. Jekyll," *Mary Reilly*; as well as Francis Ford Coppola's *Bram Stoker's Dracula*. Interestingly, all have been utter disasters.

2. Halberstam 48; Young also sees cannibalism, flaying alive, and therapy as symbolically the same.

3. See Harris, *Silence* 290, 325 for her meditations on her ancestors as a doomed race of backward hillbillies from whom she needs to differentiate herself. Earlier, in her first encounter with one of Bill's victims, her background earns her a privileged status with the West Virginia police, who accept her as "heir to the granny women, to the wise women, to the herb dealer, the stalwart country women who have always done the needful, who keep the watch and when the watch is over, wash and dress the country dead" (82). Her exploitation of her past here and her "special relationship" with the victim enable her to enter the male realm from which she had just been excluded—by playing on her identification with other women, she distances herself from them.

4. Laura Killian pointed out to me the precise nature of this analogue, in which the two are neatly reversed images of each other.

5. The novel creates a similar effect by juxtaposing the final scene of Clarice's apparently innocent sleep with a scene in which Lecter writes to her. While the letter reveals their geographic separation (we don't know where Lecter is now), it also shows their continuing communication and sympathy, suggested both by Lecter's proposing a pact with her ("I have no plans to call on you, Clarice, the world being more interesting with you in it. Be sure you extend me the same courtesy" [366]) and by his closing remark that, though they are in different places, "[s]ome of our stars are the same" (367).

WORKS CITED

Baldick, Chris. *In Frankenstein's Shadow: Myth, Monstrosity, and 19th-Century Writing*. Oxford: Oxford UP, 1987, 141–162.

Botting, Fred. *Making Monsters: 'Frankenstein', Criticism, Theory*. New York: Manchester UP, 1991.

Day, William Patrick. *In the Circles of Fear and Desire: A Study of Gothic Fantasy*. Chicago: Chicago UP, 1985.

Freud, Sigmund. "The Uncanny." *On Creativity and the Unconscious*. New York: Harper and Row, 1958.

Goodrich, Peter H. "The Lineage of Mad Scientists: Anti-Types of Merlin." *Extrapolation* 27 (1986): 109–115.

Halberstam, Judith. "Skinflik: Posthuman Gender in Jonathan Demme's *The Silence of the Lambs*." *Camera Obscura: A Journal of Feminism and Film Theory* (Fall 1991): 37–52.

Harris, Thomas. *Red Dragon*. New York: Bantam, 1982.

———. *The Silence of the Lambs*. New York: St. Martin's P, 1988.

Kilgour, Maggie. *The Rise of the Gothic Novel*. London: Routledge, 1995.

Mellor, Ann. *Mary Shelley: Her Life, Her Fiction, Her Monsters*. New York and London: Routledge, 1989.

Miles, Robert. *Gothic Writing 1750–1820: A Genealogy*. London: Routledge, 1993.

Punter, David. *The Literature of Terror: A History of Gothic Fiction from 1765 to the Present Day*. London: Longman, 1980.

Svilpis, J. E. "The Mad Scientist and Domestic Affections in Gothic Fiction." *Gothic Fiction: Prohibition/Transgression*. Ed. Kenneth W. Graham. New York: AMS P, 1989, 63–87.

Tharp, Julie. "The Transvestite as Monster: Gender Horror in *The Silence of the Lambs*." *Journal of Popular Film and Television* 19.3 (1991): 109–113.

Watt, Ian. "Time and Family in the Gothic Novel: *The Castle of Otranto*." *Eighteenth Century Life* 10.3 (1986): 159–171.

Young, Elizabeth. "*The Silence of the Lambs* and the Flaying of Feminist Theory." *Camera Obscura: A Journal of Feminism and Film Theory* (Fall 1991): 5–35.

PART II

Psychoanalysis and
the Gothic

DAVID R. JARRAWAY

The Gothic Import of Faulkner's "Black Son" in *Light in August*

> How much does it cost the subject to be
> able to tell the truth about itself?
>
> MICHEL FOUCAULT, *Foucault Live*

> I think that no one individual can look at truth. It blinds
> you . . . It [is], as you say, thirteen ways of looking at a blackbird.
> But the truth, I would like to think, comes out, that when the reader
> has read all these thirteen different ways of looking at the blackbird,
> the reader has his own fourteenth image of that blackbird
> which I would like to think is the truth.
>
> WILLIAM FAULKNER, *Faulkner in the University*

No revisionary thinking about America's national narratives can overlook William Faulkner's version of southern gothic. *Light in August* (1932) is perhaps exemplary of the traditional gothic tale of mystery, horror, and violence in America that I suggest, in its modernist inflection, might profitably be reread alongside the theorizing of Julia Kristeva and her devotion to the psychodynamics of subjectivity. To move, however, from a classically gothic tale of mystery and horror, on the one hand, to the ultra-contemporary post-Freudian ruminations of Kristeva, on the other, as a means of providing one plausible method of illuminating William Faulkner's modernist intervention in the American canon seems almost to invite the construction of an "ontological gothic" in order to account for Faulkner's extraordinary renovation of a genre, if not an entire tradition.

"Ontology" may sound like a rather odd term to use in connection with the modernist, post-Freudian reinvention of subjectivity. But I'm thinking here of Slavoj Žižek's conception of such a subject which, inaugural with the modernism of Kant and Hegel, can no longer be thought of as "'part of the world' but is, on the contrary, correlative to 'world' as such and therefore *ontologically constitutive* [since] 'world,' [and] 'reality,' as we know them, can appear only within the horizon of the subject's finitude." In this sense, Žižek goes on to explain, subjectivity as the "black space of the [Kantian] Thing" becomes "something extremely dangerous to approach if one gets too close to it, 'world' itself loses its ontological consistency, like the anamorphotic stain on Holbein's *Ambassadors*: when we shift our perspective and perceive it 'as it is' (as a skull), *all remaining reality loses its consistency*" (137). The several shifts in perspective, in world, in reality that Žižek attaches to the sea-change in the modernist treatment of subjectivity invite us to think that something parallel might be detected in the long-standing and ostensibly well-grounded tradition of gothic storytelling as well. If so, could it be that what we eventually come to discover is *less* an "ontology" but something rather more like the "temporality of gothic" in the general renovation of tradition in America? In terms of the way subjectivity may be redeployed in that tradition, therefore, in an important sense William Faulkner's modernism might be thought of as a highly evolved experimentation with gothic temporality.

As both Žižek's "black space" just mentioned and my title playfully suggest, Julia Kristeva's *Black Sun: Depression and Melancholia* (1989) furnishes the means for a fresh, critical reappraisal of the tragic career of Joe Christmas, the problematical "black son" of Faulkner's novel. If the trajectory of southern gothic is mobilized by mystery, then the problematic identity of Faulkner's black son takes us very near the heart of that narrative trajectory. For as we shall see, Christmas's uncertain lineage, traceable equally through a heritage of either black or white blood, is never readily decidable—"the embrace of a chimaera," as Faulkner describes it near the end.[1] A line, however, from Gérard de Nerval's "Chanson gothique"—"Fair-haired or dark / Must we choose?"—suggests a quite similar undecidability for Kristeva with respect to the determination of identity in poetic discourse. In fact, in the gothic context of Nerval's poetry, the truthful determination of identity may be well nigh impossible: "[i]f the 'persons' that have been named belong to the same world of love and loss, they suggest . . . a dispersal of the 'I' . . . among a constellation of elusive identities." Hence, as Kristeva concludes, "[t]he litaneutical, hallucinatory gathering of their names allows one to suppose that they might merely have the value of signs, broken up and impossible to unify, of the lost Thing."[2]

The gothic import that bilaterally infuses the texts of Faulkner and Kristeva through the join of the black son focuses much of our attention, then, upon the vexatious identification of human subjects. Before proceeding with this brief intertextual reading of their handling of identity, particularly with respect to its overlading with the issues of gender and race, I first want schematically to outline what we might consider to be the "structure" of gothic identity in their writing (extrapolated largely from Kristeva). This will then allow me later to differentiate between two "forms" of gothic (extrapolated largely from Faulkner) that are perhaps best foregrounded in the byplay of their titles—the difference, say, between "black" and "light"—and thereby address the issue of the "constant ambiguity" (*BS* 152) that might be said to attend the issue of identity in both their works.

A brief citation from Kristeva's chapter entitled "Holbein's Dead Christ" will begin to suggest the problematic nature of identity we are likely to encounter in its gothic context when, following Hegel, Kristeva writes:

Gothic art, under Dominican influence, favored a pathetic representation of natural death; Italian art, under Franciscan influence, exalted . . . the glory of the beyond made visible through the glory of the sublime. Holbein's Body of the Dead Christ in the Tomb is one of the rare if not a unique realiza-

tion located at the very place of the severance of representation of which Hegel spoke . . . What remains is the tightrope . . . a severance that is represented by death in the
imagination and that melancholy conveys as a symptom[.]
Holbein's answer is affirmative. Between classicism and man-
nerism his minimalism is the metaphor of severance: between
life and death, meaning and nonmeaning, it is an intimate,
slender response of our melancholia. (*BS* 136–137)

In this extraordinarily resonant passage, which suspends the
gothic on a tightrope between nonmeaning and death on one
side and meaning and life on the other, severe and pathetic as opposed to sublime and transcendent representation, we should
first begin to comprehend the gothic within the psychic space of
"melancholy." Kristeva, to a certain extent, follows Freud in
making a clear separation between the pathos of "melancholy"
here and a more life-affirming, life-sustaining "mourning" elsewhere. In the latter case, a loss is grieved and put by or negated
through the transcending process of symbolization. Mourning
thus assures that the loss of an essential object like "mother" will
come to be recovered, once again, in "signs" or "language" (*BS*
43). Not so, however, with melancholy. At the center of its
gothic pathos lies the *disavowal* of negation. Like tightrope
artists, melancholiacs would suspend negation or, much worse,
cancel it entirely "and nostalgically fall back on the real object
(the Thing) of their loss, which is just what they do not manage
to lose, to which they remain painfully riveted" (*BS* 43–44).[3]
The result of this negation-of-negation inevitably leads us back
to that state of nonmeaning associated with death mentioned
previously: in Kristeva's further elaboration, "the setting up of a
fundamental sadness and an artificial, unbelievable language, cut
out of the painful background that is not accessible to any signifier" (*BS* 44).

Within the gothic context, then, identity treads a constant
line of disavowal and negation, precariously structured between
what it cannot know enough of, at the level of Things, and what
it can know only too well, at the level of Symbols. In other related theories of Kristeva's, gothic identity becomes "the subject

in process/on trial," tactfully negotiating a semiotic path of rhythmical force and energy along a "thetic" threshold or rim between maternal abjection, on the one hand, and paternal order, on the other (*Revolution* 22, 48; *Powers of Horror* 22–24). Endeavoring to foment "a rhythmic reverberation in the symbolic" (Lechte 27), the gothic subject in *Black Sun* is thus brought "to the threshold of naming, to the edge of the unsymbolized": "[b]y representing that unsymbolized as a maternal object, a source of sorrow and nostalgia, but of ritual veneration as well, the melancholy imagination sublimates it and gives it a protection against collapsing into asymbolism . . . [through] the temporary triumph of that genuine arbor of names hauled up from the abyss of the lost 'Thing'" (*BS* 165). This relentless fixation on an impossibly nonrepresentable maternal perhaps explains the perennially nostalgic cast of the gothic imagination and the childlike character of romance more generally. "There has never to my knowledge been any period of Gothic English literature," Northrop Frye has observed, "but the list of Gothic revivalists stretches completely across its entire history, from the *Beowulf* poet to writers of our own day" (186). Frye, of course, is thinking mostly of British literature in formulating this insight. In America, what perhaps takes obsessive hold of the melancholy imagination more than the maternal itself is the experience of *being separated* from the maternal, as in the colonies' historical separation from the motherland in the War of Independence, or the American South's constitutional separation from the North in a mother country wracked by civil war, or, in more recent times, the multicultural dissolution of a mother tongue, since "the pluralism that characterizes American democracy depends on [its] devotion to an *unvermögender* Other," that is, a "(m)other without qualities" (Copjec 33, 41 n8), and so forth.

If pressed to characterize definitively the sort of identity we are likely to encounter in structures of gothic discourse, along tightropes or thresholds or rims where their subjects are invariably constituted or put on trial, can there be any coincidence in Kristeva's lighting upon Holbein's dead Christ and Faulkner's choosing the name "Joe Christmas"? In the view of John Lechte, the figure of Christ would appear to be the very type of the gothic melancholiac, that is to say, the "imaginary subject (ego) forming the border between the real (Mother) and the symbolic (Father)."[4] Accordingly, both Kristeva and Faulkner point, theoretically, to a quite similar "scenario" within which to position their travailing egos, a scenario that Lechte describes as follows:

> to transcend death (which is also the death of the symbolic) it is necessary to identify with it for all we are worth, expanding our imaginary capacities, and thereby overcoming the unnameable basis of our depression. "To enter heaven, travel hell," as Joyce put it. We need to put hell into the symbolic, to describe it, name all its aspects, experience it in imagination, and so constitute ourselves as subjects, with an identity. We will become . . . somebody and this, through transcending nothingness: the void, the unrepresentable. (37)

Switching our attention now to Faulkner's gothic narrative, we can readily envision the subjectivity of Joe Christmas in the process of formation between two counterposed spheres of psychic investment-heaven and hell-rehearsed once again for us here. At least, that is the presentiment we get in Gail Hightower's concluding reminiscence of Faulkner's protagonist: "[t]his face alone is not clear. It is confused more than any other . . . [for] he (Hightower) can see that it is *two faces* which seem to strive . . . in turn to free themselves one from the other, then fade and blend again" (*LA* 491–492, my emphasis).

Through the course of Faulkner's novel, then, we find one face of Joe Christmas continually turned back upon the maternal, the sphere of loss, separation, and abjection. In Faulkner's words, "[i]t was as though he and all other manshaped life about him had been returned to the lightless hot wet primogenitive Female," a maternal space not unlike the "black pit" from which Christmas, while on the run from the law, at one point mysteriously emerges: "black, impenetrable, in its garland of August-tremulous lights . . . the original quarry, abyss itself" (*LA* 115, 116).[5] In endeavoring to fathom Christmas's facing backward in this way, we need to remind ourselves precisely of the extent to which he suffers, over and over again, the experience of maternal loss throughout the novel: in his abandonment by his real mother, Millie Hines, who dies while giving him birth, in his desertion by twelve-year-old Alice and rejection by the dietitian, Miss Atkins, during his stay at the Memphis orphanage, and in his subsequent betrayals by Bobbie Allen and Joanna Burden at crucial points, as we shall see later, in his sexually active youth and early adulthood. In his riveting rearward fixations, therefore, Joe Christmas conceivably becomes the type of Kristeva's "depressed narcissist" who fails to negotiate primal loss "on the basis of which the *erotic Thing* might become a captivating *Object of desire*" in the procession to maturity and sociosymbolic acculturation (*BS* 13, 14), and never more so than in his frequent misogynistic outpourings against females and their "periodical filth" and "Woman's muck": "[i]t was the woman: that soft kindness which he believed himself doomed to be forever victim of and which he hated worse than he did the hard and ruthless justice of men" (*LA* 185, 238, 168–169; also on 109, 157, 189, 198, 225, 234, 265, and passim).

But there is, conceivably, in Faulkner's tale another face of Joe Christmas that looks to the future rather than the past, a side of him that *can* perceive an identity for himself as a kind of reward in heaven for having withstood so many of the torments of hell. The fifteen-year purgatory interposed between Christmas's confrontations with Bobbie early and Joanna later on, "where beneath the dark and symbolical archways of midnight he bedded with the women and paid them when he had the money, and when he did not have it he bedded anyway" (*LA* 224)—this period in Christmas's life would appear to match that "untiring quest for mistresses" which, according to Kristeva, theoretically "points to the elusive nature of that *Thing*—necessarily lost so that [the] 'subject,' separated from the 'object,' might become a speaking being" (*BS* 145). When Joe Christmas finally *does* speak, he constructs for himself the subject position of a black man, telling several of his paramours that "he was a negro" (*LA* 224). In so doing, however, he inserts himself within a circle of symbolic ideology that demands that this representation of himself be taken naturally, peremptorily, unalterably. The woman, for instance, who thinks Joe Christmas "just another wop or something" experiences horrifically just how murderous such essentializing ideologies can be, and at the hands of Christmas himself: "[i]t took two policemen to subdue him. At first they thought that the woman was dead" (*LA* 225).[6] So that while it might seem possible for Christmas finally to have become "somebody" through transcending no-thing-ness, his inclination to exclude rather than cultivate maternal difference in so doing would appear to have made him as much a victim of the future as of the past. As Christmas himself admits just prior to his arrest for the murder of Joanna Burden, "I have been further in these seven days than in all the thirty years," and yet "I have never got outside that circle. I have never broken out of the ring of what I have already done and cannot ever undo" (*LA* 339).

Exactly who, therefore, is Faulkner's tragic hero: the son of Milly Hines? the public ward of a Tennessee orphanage one day at Christmas? the foster-child of the Bible-punching McEacherns? Under the "Gothic force" (Kristeva's term) of melancholy "that turns out to be the source of the mysterious silence that striates writing" (*BS* 242), Kristeva would perhaps argue that Joe Christmas was *all three*, and maybe even more. Yet the true horror of Faulkner's gothic narrative would appear to lie not so much in his melancholy subject's inability to locate for himself a fixed identity in either the maternal or the paternal sphere. Rather, its frightfulness lies in that subject's complete lack of tolerance for, and perhaps skepticism about, experience in both spheres—a tolerance and skepticism that he ideally acquires from his earliest years by being able imaginatively *to withstand* primal separation or abjection rather than indifferently pathologizing it or aggressively attempting to overcome it. We're on the thin edge of the gothic wedge here, back once again on the suspenseful tightrope, as it were. For as Elizabeth Grosz remarks, "the abject is both a necessary condition of the subject, and what must be expelled or repressed by the subject in order to attain identity and a place within the symbolic" (88). Who's to say, then, that pathologizing or masterfully overcoming abject Otherness are not those very forms of expulsion and repression through which the subject comes to constitute itself as a fully functioning agent within the symbolic order?

My response to this line of reasoning would simply be to observe that overcoming abjection, in whatever form, presents to identity an equilibrium where none actually exists. The mysterious darkness and horrific suspense of the gothic narrative tells us that, in a sense, we never do get past our depressive melancholy, that the reality of abjection will always exceed even our best imaginative efforts to symbolize it (why, perhaps, we are so fixated on our separation from it), and that abjection, as such, through its eternal provocation of identificatory attainment, will always leave open for us the process of subjective construction to continuous and repeated articulation. "Even at times of its strongest cohesion and integration," as Grosz quite rightly explains, "the subject teeters on the brink of this gaping abyss which attracts (and also repulses) it," for "[t]his abyss is the locus of the subject's generation and the place of its potential obliteration" (89). I think, however, the difference between attraction and repulsion will largely depend upon whether or not, in expecting to extract a final equilibrium from the abyss, one might become outraged to discover, in its place, an abject excess as a threat to complacent self-adequation. For only at that overwhelming moment is attraction likely to turn into repulsion and, at that moment, is identity likely to slip helplessly from the tightrope and find itself spiraling uncontrollably downward into an abyss of complete and utter self-annihilation:

It seems to [Joe Christmas] that the past week has rushed like a torrent and that the week to come, which will begin tomorrow, is the abyss, and that now on the brink of cataract the stream has raised a single blended and sonorous and austere cry, not for justification but as a dying salute before its own plunge, and not to any god but to the doomed man in the barred cell within hearing of them and two other churches, and in whose crucifixion they too will raise a cross. "And they will do it gladly," he says in the dark window. He feels his mouth and jaw muscles tauten with something premonitory, something more terrible than laughter even. (*LA* 368)

The "something" premonitory and terrible in this ghastly description of the doomed protagonist reveals how subtly the tightrope, in gothic fiction, can modulate into a lynch rope, when the infinitizing of subjectivity (see Minow-Pinkney 158–159) turns murderously into its mere finalizing or, to borrow some recent phrasing of Judith Butler, when "the melancholy recesses of signification" can so unwittingly become exchanged for "the permanent pathos of symbolization" (*Bodies that Matter* 71, 207). And American gothic we may perhaps find fascinating in particular for its reenacting "a crisis of subjectivity which is the basis of all creation, one which takes as its very precondition the possibility of survival" itself (Kristeva qtd. in Lechte 25).

Earlier, I alluded to the ambiguity about which identity is hedged in gothic discourse and suggested that it might be useful to make a distinction between two of its "forms" in order to understand better the paradoxical nature of both Kristeva's and Faulkner's black sun/son. In what remains of this paper, I don't aim to systematize a typology for American gothic. Like Gail Hightower, I merely want to prize apart "two faces" of gothic textuality that I fully believe are both present in Kristeva's and Faulkner's work—accorded somewhat different emphases, however, as suggested by their titles—before these faces "fade and blend again." Faulkner, I have no doubt, would be in complete agreement with Kristeva's observation that "serious depression or paroxysmal clinical melancholia represents a true hell for modern individuals," especially so when "Christly dereliction presents that hell with an imaginary elaboration" that can so easily and so frighteningly come to naught (*BS* 133). Kristeva wants to draw out of this "dereliction" in *Black Sun*—and brilliantly so in the work of Dostoyevsky and Duras, in addition to that of Holbein and Nerval—"those unbearable moments when meaning was lost, when the meaning of life was lost," as a consequence of what she elsewhere refers to as "an actual or imaginary razing of symbolic values" (*BS* 133, 128). John Lechte's call, cited earlier, "to put hell into the symbolic" (37) captures more accurately the significant shift in emphasis in Faulkner's own gothic agenda, and I would like to turn briefly to three additional characters in *Light in August* to show, finally, how this may be so.

To this point in our discussion, an analogous paraphrase for putting hell into the symbolic might read: "put the maternal into the paternal." As I have argued elsewhere, however, it would be quite misleading to construe such an injunction strictly as an argument for feminism (Jarraway esp. 144–146). Hell, in its association with the maternal, we should more accurately construe as a trope for what we are given to think might be *possible* to emerge in heaven in the Name-of-the-Father, that is to say, in the day-to-day world of meaningful, practical, and regulated discourse. In terms of human identity, the chief focus of this rereading of gothic narrative, we view hell as a possible sign for a kind of characterological "polymorphism" (Kristeva, *Revolution* 156), knowing full well that even in heaven, choices do have to be made and that, as I noted earlier, an infinitized subjectivity ultimately *does* have to resolve itself into some form of finalized identity in order for us to take control of, and to get on with, our lives. Heaven, therefore, in its association with the paternal, is perhaps best construed as a trope for that very control—a control well beyond the realm of possibility now and more in touch with ideas like probability, necessity, inevitability. Kristeva is sometimes dismissed by feminists because her work is so often focused upon male writers, on modernists like Mallarmé, Artaud, and Joyce, for example. But clearly, hers is not a "paternal" attraction. She is most often drawn to figures such as these mainly because they are writers who are completely *out of control* ecstatically, exuberantly, extravagantly and, for this reason, are perhaps more characteristically "maternal," in the counterhegemonic sense we have been using this term, than any social or cultural assignment of gender could ever possibly account for. And undoubtedly, there was perhaps something of a similar uncontrollable quality that drew Faulkner to a character like Joe Christmas: "'My God,' [Christmas] thought, 'it was like I was the woman and she was the man'" (*LA* 235).

Although she acknowledges a debt to Claude Lefort and not Julia Kristeva, nonetheless Joan Copjec makes the very useful suggestion that in a radical democratic context, it will be "the contributions of detective and Gothic fiction" from which we can expect "a 'mutation of the symbolic order'" (41n6). I would like to think that Faulkner had conceived *Light in August* as making a similar contribution and, in somewhat of a departure from Kristeva, shifted much of the burden of the melancholiac's dark and depressive mutations onto the slightly more lightened plane of maternal intervention, with a view to paternal renovation. This is not to take anything away from much of the gothic import of what Faulkner himself described as the "tragic view of life" he consciously attempted to develop for his doomed hero, particularly in a novel that the author moreover once contemplated titling "Dark House" (Faulkner, *Faulkner* 96–97). But the shift in emphasis is there nevertheless. And the characterization of Joanna Burden gets us started thinking about Faulkner's discursive alterations.

The gossip in Jefferson concerning Joanna Burden as "a lover of negroes" (*LA* 46), exemplified most notably in her erotically charged though ultimately fatal attachment to Joe Christmas, suggests the possibility of deregulating egregiously paternalistic and racist attitudes entrenched in the cultural life of the hierarchically ordered South. However, the sense of Joanna's maternal disruption of white, patriarchal ideologies is considerably belied by her masculine portrayal ("[i]t was as if [Christmas] struggled physically with another man for an object of no actual value to either" [*LA* 235]), a portrayal that figuratively reveals the enormous extent to which Joanna has unwittingly internalized the rank prejudices of her father (and grandfather). "What I wanted to tell him," she admits to Joe, "was that I must escape, get away from under the shadow" of the black man. "'You cannot,' he said. 'You must struggle, rise. But in order to rise, you must raise the shadow with you. But you can never lift it to your own level . . . The curse of the black race is God's curse'" (*LA* 253). Joanna's subsequent schemes to mother a child with Joe and later have him take over her various integrationist projects are the typical manifestations of control, remarked previously, that we expect to find on the paternal "level" to which her father refers. And her "praying over" Joe (*LA* 105, 282) and, when he refuses, her taking a defective cap-and-ball pistol to him are the final vestiges of control that inevitably convert themselves into lethal violence,

to Joanna's horrific misfortune. Joanna and Joe's incendiary pre-
dicament, of course, had all along been anticipated in Christmas's tempestuous relationship with the male-nominated Bobbie
Allen fifteen years earlier. Yet by comparison, the latent sexual aggression that Faulkner carefully locates in Bobbie's "big-
knuckled hands" prominently arrayed across her lap (*LA* 193,
192, 199, and passim) receives only a slight workout when Bobbie's pimps, characteristically, are allowed to fight her battles for
her, beating Joe senseless for getting their moll "into a jam with
clodhopper police" (*LA* 218).

Our second character, Gail Hightower, moves us a bit closer
to the light at the end of Faulkner's very long, gothic tunnel. The
femininity of Hightower's first name that seems conspicuously at
odds with his domineering last name rather ingeniously cor-
roborates what Judith Butler refers to as "the impossibility of a
full recognition" in socially symbolic discourse, "that is, of ever
fully inhabiting the name by which one's social identity is inau-
gurated and mobilized," thus forever pointing to "the instability
and incompleteness of subject-formation" ("Critically Queer"
18). Indeed, Hightower's appearance in Jefferson as a "shabby,
queer-shaped, not-quite familiar figure" to the workmen of the
town's planing mill, and one among those thought not incapable
of "tak[ing] their pants down" to Joe Christmas, reveals a gendered existence potentially wide of the normative mark (*LA* 413,
464). This skewing of social identity is enlarged even further by
Hightower's considerable skill at midwifery, most notably in the
birthing of Lena Grove's bastard child, while his penchant for
"Handpainted Xmas & Anniversary Cards" (*LA* 58) and for the
lush lyricism of Tennyson's poetry hovers in the background.
"Gail Hightower" thus presents us with, in Butler's words again,
"the historically revisable possibility of a name," a name that has
"a certain priority and anonymity with respect to the life it ani-
mates" ("Critically Queer" 18). Such revisable possibility, in the
most general sense, promises a significant realignment of social
values, despite the fact (or perhaps because of it) that Hightower
"was not a natural husband, [and] a natural man" (*LA* 71) for pur-
portedly having driven his suicidal wife to an early grave. But

there is a limit to the degree to which even Hightower is able to intervene in the paternal on behalf of the maternal. His refusal, for instance, to provide temporary shelter to the expectant and ailing Lena and, more crucially later, his reprobate fear of helping to stay the descent of Percy Grimm's castrating knife disclose a mind as complacently enmeshed in the toils of the present social order as it once was, a generation ago, among the "quiet and safe walls" of his religious order, beyond "horror or alarm" (*LA* 478). The fact that Joe Christmas should desperately head for Gail Hightower's dark house as a final refuge from arraignment for murder tellingly solidifies the bond between them as obliging victims of objective control rather than revisers of subjective truth.

In the end, then, Joe Christmas seems perfectly to fit Nerval's "El Desdichado" in the gothic refunctioning of identity—"I've twice, as a conqueror, been across the Acheron"—for which Julia Kristeva offers: "[t]here would be no third time" (*BS* 171). Having relinquished the imaginative optativeness of subjective constitution to the expedient choice of either controlling or being controlled—Joanna, on the one side, and Bobbie, on the other, as horrendous embodiments of "[t]he sighs of the saint and the screams of the fay" in Nerval's concluding line (*BS* 172)— Christmas has no third choices by the time he crosses the Acheron of Gail Hightower's haunted threshold, hounded by the hell of Percy Grimm's vengeful bloodlust. But what about us? A third and final character, Faulkner's Lena Grove, I think presents us with an alternative to social control and sexual legislation in the very image of her abjection and the repeated mobilization of subjective articulations that her impossible condition, outside the bourgeois family contract, deploys and sustains: "[m]y, my. A body does get around" (*LA* 30, 507). Abandoned or rejected, in turn, by her lover, Lucas Burch, her stepbrother McKinley, the traveler Armstid, Gail Hightower, and the rest, Lena is perhaps a type of the primogenitive Female "of the old earth and with and by which she lives . . . [and] conquers" (*LA* 27) that the Jefferson community cannot do anything with but cannot do without either.

In the final chapter, Lena Grove's continued pursuit of someone *like* Lucas Burch, though surely not Burch himself, and her refusing the sexual advances of Byron Bunch, though surely not Bunch himself, both suggest for her character a kind of "hiatus, blank, or spacing" that Kristeva herself attaches to "that other unrepresentable . . . the female body" (*BS* 26–27, also on 100, 124, 200, 243, 248, 256) and that raises the issue of the necessary incompleteness of identity formation once again:

> Because do you know what I think? I think she was just travelling. I dont think she had any idea of finding whoever it was she was following. I dont think she had ever aimed to, only she hadnt told him yet . . . And so I think she had just made up her mind to travel a little further and see as much as she could, since I reckon she knew that when she settled down this time, it would likely be for the rest of her life. (*LA* 506)

Why is it we feel that the anonymous furniture dealer in Faulkner's conclusion has everything right about Lena except her final settling down? Is it because Faulkner himself might envision thirteen ways of looking at Lena, as in the epigraph, but could always be provoked to imagine a fourteenth, or perhaps even a fifteenth or sixteenth resistant to allow her to settle on just *one* way? Or, as in the epigraph from Foucault, he could imagine the terrible cost that would have to be paid if, as in the case of the blackbird Joe Christmas, there could only possibly be *one* truth to tell? Toby Miller, who also invokes Foucault on the final pages of his recent *The Well-Tempered Self*, alludes to "a huge crisis" in contemporary life not unlike that period in Europe's shift to modernization, when, according to Foucault, "we must produce something that doesn't yet exist and about which we cannot know." Observes Miller, "To be agile in such a crisis necessitates putting an end to attempts to embrace one's incompleteness in the service of obedience. In order to begin again, we must lose ourselves, and do so in sight of danger" (230–231). The "black son" of *Light in August* clearly puts us in the sight of danger. But its gothic import also shows us how we might swerve past arresting notions of human identity "in the service of obedience," past, that is, the search for "any ultimate self," as Miller else-where puts it, in the service of "an overarching account of the person" (223–224) when the loss, represented by Lena Grove, serves us admirably as our guide. In the end, her loss is our gain. Which ought only to substantiate Lena's final words in Faulkner's gothic tale: "[w]e got another fur piece to go tomorrow" (*LA* 503).

NOTES

1. Faulkner, *Light in August* 449. Hereafter cited as *LA*. The closest we come to a definitive attribution of "nigger blood" to Joe Christmas is Byron Bunch's account of a story told to the ultraracist Doc Hines about Joe's mother's brief affair with a Mexican circus employee who may have been part black. But it is a highly moot attribution, according to Byron: "[m]aybe the circus folks told [Doc Hines]. I don't know. He aint never said how he found out, like that never made any difference" (*LA* 374).

2. *Black Sun* 156, 157. Hereafter cited as *BS*. See also *BS* 171.

3. Thus, as Charles Bernstein recently observed, "[d]enial marks the refusal to mourn: to understand what we have lost and its absolute irreparability" (216).

4. Eve Sedgwick's doctoral dissertation of 1976 only *slightly* verges on the notion of a transmigrant ego here in her linking of gothic conventions to an "insidious displacement of the boundaries of self" that she elsewhere and more generally attributes to "the dilativeness and the permeability of the self" and to "the real shiftiness inher[ing] in the notion of identity" characteristic of a great deal of early gothic fiction (33, 43, 111).

5. "Calvin," Kristeva remarks in "Holbein's Dead Christ," "insists on the *formidabilis abysis* into which Jesus had been thrust at the hour of his death," a passage not unrelated to her characterization of the "maternal object" in terms of "the abyss of the lost 'Thing,'" cited previously (*BS* 119, 165).

6. Faulkner's own judgment on the matter is that Joe Christmas "deliberately evicted himself from the human race because he didn't know which he was" and goes on to add: "[t]hat was the tragedy, that to me was the tragic, central idea of the story—that he didn't know what he was, and there was no way possible in life for him to find out. Which to me is the most tragic condition a man could find himself in—not to know what he is and to know that he will never know" (*Faulkner* 72, also

118). I shall return to this epistemological conundrum at the end of the essay.

WORKS CITED

Bernstein, Charles. *A Poetics*. Cambridge, MA: Harvard UP, 1992.

Butler, Judith. *Bodies that Matter: On the Discursive Limits of "Sex."* New York: Routledge, 1993.

———. "Critically Queer." *GLQ: A Journal of Gay and Lesbian Studies* 1 (Spring 1994): 19–32.

Copjec, Joan. "The Unvermögender Other: Hysteria and Democracy in America." *New Formations* 14 (Summer 1991): 27–41.

Faulkner, William. *Faulkner in the University: Class Conferences at the University of Virginia, 1957–58*. Ed. Frederick L. Gwynn and Joseph L. Blotner. Richmond: U of Virginia P, 1977.

———. *Light in August (the Corrected Text)*. New York: Vintage Books, 1990.

Foucault, Michel. *Foucault Live: Interviews, 1966–84*. Ed. Sylvere Lotringer. New York: Semiotext(e), 1989.

Frye, Northrop. *Anatomy of Criticism: Four Essays*. New York: Atheneum, 1969.

Grosz, Elizabeth. "The Body of Signification." *Abjection, Melancholia, and Love*. Ed. John Fletcher and Andrew Benjamin. New York: Routledge, 1990, 80–103.

Jarraway, David R. "To Hell with It: Modernism in a Feminist Frame." *Rereading Modernism: New Directions in Feminist Criticism*. Ed. and intro. by Lisa Rado. New York: Garland Publishing, 1994, 137–157.

Kristeva, Julia. *Black Sun: Depression and Melancholia*. Trans. Leon S. Roudiez. New York: Columbia UP, 1989.

———. *Powers of Horror: An Essay on Abjection*. Trans. Leon S. Roudiez. New York: Columbia UP, 1982.

———. *Revolution in Poetic Language*. Trans. Margaret Waller. Intro. by Leon S. Roudiez. New York: Columbia UP, 1984.

Lechte, John. "Art, Love, and Melancholy in the Work of Julia Kristeva." *Abjection, Melancholia, and Love: The Work of Julia Kristeva*. Ed. John Fletcher and Andrew Benjamin. New York: Routledge, 1990, 21–41.

Miller, Toby. *The Well-Tempered Self: Citizenship, Culture, and the Postmodern Subject*. Baltimore: Johns Hopkins UP, 1993.

Minow-Pinkney, Makiko. "Virginia Woolf: 'Seen from a Foreign

Land.'" *Abjection, Melancholia, and Love: The Work of Julia Kristeva.* Ed. John Fletcher and Andrew Benjamin. New York: Routledge, 1990, 157–177.

Sedgwick, Eve Kosofsky. *The Coherence of Gothic Conventions.* New York: Methuen, 1986.

Žižek, Slavoj. *Enjoy Your Symptom! Jacques Lacan in Hollywood and Out.* New York: Routledge, 1992.

STEVEN BRUHM

On Stephen King's Phallus,
or The Postmodern Gothic

There is no group therapy or psychiatry or community social
services for the child who must cope with the thing under the bed or
in the cellar every night, the thing which leers and capers and threatens
just beyond the point where vision will reach. The same lonely battle must
be fought night after night and the only cure is the eventual ossification
of the imaginary faculties, and this is called adulthood.
STEPHEN KING, *'Salem's Lot*

The peculiarity of the acts [of violence] *seems to rise in direct
ratio to the intelligence of the man or woman so afflicted.*
STEPHEN KING, *The Dark Half*

Horror is epistemological. Ever since the Enlightenment, the
definition of horror has been intimately bound up with the
representation of the thinking subject. But while nineteenth-
century writers like Matthew Lewis, William Godwin, and
Charles Robert Maturin locate the source of repression in the
social institutions of church, state, and the family, for Stephen
King the repression seems much more inevitably and universally
psychological in nature. My first epigraph from *'Salem's Lot* argues that horror is an infantile affliction that can be overcome
only with maturity, with the "ossification of the imaginary faculties" in adulthood. Yet the quotation from *The Dark Half* suggests that the standard marker of adulthood—the development
of sophisticated intelligence—may itself be a cause of horror.
While the child of *'Salem's Lot* will seek out knowledge (in ther-

apy, psychiatry, social services, or common sense) to allay his fears, the adult of *The Dark Half* will be terrorized by precisely that knowledge. How are we to make sense of this apparent contradiction? What epistemological basis can be ascribed to horror as it is defined by Stephen King?

The contradictory implications of the search for knowledge are specifically rendered in King through the figure of the author. Hotel caretaker and playwright Jack Torrance of *The Shining*, for example, believes that the cabin fever which drove his predecessor to murder his family and himself was the result of boredom, too much television and solitaire during the long winter at the isolated Overlook Hotel, whereas he absorbs himself in novels, has a play to work on, and will teach his young son to read (9). And it is this same Jack Torrance who will later try to ax-murder both wife and son. Indeed, the function of articulateness in making one vulnerable to horror is an idée fixe for King: those characters most susceptible are males on the threshold of some crisis with the world of language. They are writers—Jack Torrance in *The Shining*, Ben Mears in *'Salem's Lot*, Thaddeus Beaumont in *The Dark Half*, to name a few—undergoing a block or crisis of productivity, or they are boys on the cusp of full emergence into the symbolic order—Danny Torrance is learning to read, Mark Petrie of *'Salem's Lot* is just coming to understand the meaning of words, and young Thad Beaumont, who came to writing at age eleven, generates the murderous George Stark, a pseudonym who comes to life and commits the atrocities he writes about. Despite King's own prolificacy, he connects the desire to write to the fearful repressions instituted by the act of writing itself.

This fixation on the vicissitudes of verbal productivity—its relation to madness and self, its pleasures and horrors—suggests an almost uncanny resemblance to the fixations of another theorist of language and desire, Jacques Lacan, who theorizes many of the same complexities and fixations of King's postmodern gothic. It should become evident through the course of this essay that King is (or at least appears to be) remarkably in line with contemporary theories of psychoanalysis as he depicts the writing psychology. In a world after Lacan, the ego is no longer

given the verbal mastery over the ineffable repository of instincts that is the id, but rather the id itself, that locus classicus
of gothic activity, contains "the whole structure of language"
(Lacan, *Écrits* 147). And as a definitively verbal site, this unconscious registers a crisis in the production of the self—and in particular the male self—that is documented in King's fiction. Thus,
I want to argue two things here: first, that Stephen King employs
the anxieties over language as articulated by Lacan to discuss a
postmodern condition, and second, that this deployment signals
in King's characters, as in Lacan, a crisis of male self-definition
that throws into question the very category of male heterosexuality.

THE WRITING ON THE WALL

Just as Schreber's psychosis is, for Lacan, primarily a question of
grammatical shifts between the verbs love/hate and the pro-
nouns I/him,[1] so do the horrors surrounding King characters
appear as formal, linguistic problems. King's is a universe where
the seemingly clear contests of good and evil have become questions of linguistic formulation: Father Callahan of *'Salem's Lot*
bemoans, "[T]here were no battles. There were only skirmishes
of vague resolution. And EVIL did not wear one face but many,
and all of them were vacuous and more often than not the chin
was slicked with drool. In fact, he was being forced to the conclusion that there was no EVIL in the world at all but only evil—
or perhaps (evil)" (150). And while this (evil) makes itself clearly
known in the real world as those "phobic pressure points" that
King says are virulent in postwar America (divorce, child abuse,
isolation, superstar writers and their fans) (*Danse* 4), his fiction presents them as problems of material signifiers. From
The Shining: "[t]he greatest terror of Danny [Torrance]'s life was
DIVORCE, a word that always appeared in his mind as a sign
painted in red letters which were covered with hissing, poison-
ous snakes" (27), and hell for this six-year-old is "a blackness
where one sinister word flashed in red: REDRUM" (57; "MURDER"
presented backward on the mirror of his consciousness). Or
from *'Salem's Lot*: "the trees . . . were half denuded now, and the
black branches were limned against the gray sky like giant letters

in an unknown alphabet" (378), and Ben Mears, visiting author and vampire slayer, "could almost see the word 'vampire' printed on the black screen of his mind, not in scary movie-poster print, but in small, economical letters that were made to be a woodcut or scratched on a scroll" (326). Lacan's insistence that analysis recognize "what function the subject takes on in the order of the symbolic relations which covers the entire field of human relations" (*The Seminar* 67) opens up a means of understanding King's fascination with the writer in horror and begins to meld the feared imagination with the anxiety about the discourses of intelligence itself.

"Ask the writer," charges Jacques Lacan, "about the anxiety that he experiences when faced by the blank sheet of paper, and he will tell you who is the turd of his phantasy" (*Écrits* 315). Ask Thad Beaumont about the anxiety he experiences, and he will locate it in George Stark. Stark is the pseudonym under which Thad produces financially successful horror schlock, and in that sense he is a thermometer for what contemporary readers desire in fiction. But as a literary creation who becomes flesh and blood, Stark is also the projection of Thad's own fear: fear of writing as an addiction and as something that will fragment us, alienate us from our families and ourselves. As Thad begins to realize that "[p]en names [can] come to life and murder people," he decides, "*I will call it my William Wilson complex*" (*The Dark Half* 135), a complex which, like that in the Poe story, must lead to a fight to the death. But while Thad spends most of the novel being horrified by his own literary creation, what is really at stake in *The Dark Half* is what Lacan calls the agency of the letter in the unconscious, the way self-referentiality inscribes the self only by doubling, fragmenting, and killing the self: "Thad Beaumont did not keep anything resembling an organized journal, but he did sometimes write about the events in his own life which interested, amused, or frightened him. He kept these accounts in a bound ledger. . . . Most were strangely passionless, almost as if part of him was standing aside and reporting on his life with its own divorced and almost disinterested eye" (82). This self-splitting is replicated near the end of the novel when Thad realizes that it is not George Stark who is the agent of hor-

ror but Stark's own fictional creation, Alexis Machine, the sadistic villain of the Stark novels (*The Dark Half* 447). In this novel,
horror is the result of a *chain* of signifiers, a veritable lexis machine. If the Enlightenment gothic documents a self-splitting
that is the result of the repression of desires, King's postmodern
gothic documents the fear of self-splitting that is the result of
documentation, of the act of writing, and of representing the
self. If the earlier genre knew what Freud knew—that monsters
are the products of our repressed and projected fears and desires
("The Uncanny" 241)—then Thad Beaumont knows what Lacan
knows: "[w]ords on paper made him [Stark, the psychotic other],
and words on paper are the only things that will get rid of him"
(*The Dark Half* 430). Like a Lacanian case study, Thad is ripped
apart by the symbolic order.

This incipient madness, this source of great terror, is, as for
Lacan, a voice of Otherness that produces flickers of signification unintelligible to the analysand: "[s]ince Freud the unconscious has been a chain of signifiers that somewhere (on another
stage, in another scene, he wrote) is repeated, and insists on in-
terfering in the breaks offered it by the effective discourse and
the cogitation that it informs" (*Écrits* 297). That "somewhere,"
that inevitable space that Lacan calls the Other, is the overwhelming alterity from which the King hero suffers his horror.
Plaguing Beaumont throughout *The Dark Half* is a sentence
written on the wall at the site of each of Stark's murders: THE
SPARROWS ARE FLYING AGAIN. Figuring out who Stark is, how
Thad "made" him, and how Thad can "unmake" him (*The Dark
Half* 341) means figuring out the precise significance of THE
SPARROWS, not merely as signifieds (although actual sparrows do
hover around Thad and George) but as *signifiers*: what precisely
is the meaning of the presence of the words at the murders, and
how can they assist Thad in his own relation to his Other? In a
similar vein, Danny Torrance reads the writing on the wall—and
in his case, the writing on the *mirror*—but with only enough
comprehension to know that he doesn't comprehend. The signifier REDRUM is given to him by Tony, the boy in his bathroom
mirror who shows him "signs," the meaning of which he does
not know but hopes he soon will, as "my mommy and daddy are

teaching me to read, and I'm trying real hard" (*The Shining* 140).
With almost too obvious a precision, King represents Tony as
the discourse of the Other, the barely intelligible voice that proceeds from the space opened up in the mirror stage. Danny explains an early trance in which he sees Tony: "I was brushing my
teeth and I was thinking about my reading. . . . Thinking real
hard. And . . . I saw Tony way down in the mirror. He said he had
to show me again . . . he was in the mirror" (*The Shining* 127).
While Danny cannot exactly remember what Tony has to show
him (the unconscious is, after all, unconscious), he knows it has
something to do with "that indecipherable word he had seen in
his spirit's mirror," a verbal chain comprised of "Roque. Stroke.
Redrum" (*The Shining* 34, 125). ("Roque" is the mallet with
which his father will try to stroke and redrum/murder him at the
end of the novel.) Danny may not know the meaning of his
Other's discourse, but he does know its content. "Signs," he tells
his doctor. "He's always showing me stupid old *signs*. And I can't
read them, hardly ever" (*The Shining* 140).

Danny's frustration over the "stupid old signs," like Thad
Beaumont's impotence in front of the signifying SPARROWS, indeed like the writer's block that prohibits Jack from writing his
play at the Overlook Hotel, proceeds from a castration of verbal
acuity that King places at the heart of his gothic. For Freud, the
uncanny often took the form of a bodily dismemberment that
could be ultimately located in the castration complex. For Lacan,
the phallus that is castrated by the symbolic order is the phallus-
as-signifier, the sense of unity and imaginary wholeness that is
fallaciously granted by one's deployment of language to define
and represent one's self. This symbolic castration appears in
King at the entrance into the symbolic order. The "shining," for
example, is fundamentally the ability to read the signifiers of another's consciousness (or even unconscious), to do "what mys-
tics and mind readers do" (*The Shining* 148). For Danny, "[t]he
most terrifying thing about DIVORCE was that he had sensed the
word—or concept, or whatever it was that came to him in his
understandings—floating around in his . . . parents' heads, sometimes diffuse and relatively distant, sometimes as thick and obscuring and frightening as thunderheads" (*The Shining* 27). But

more to the point, the foreclosed, castrating signification is a sexual castration, effected by the primal scene. Danny explains why he doesn't try to read what his parents are thinking: "[i]t would be like peeking into the bedroom and watching while they're doing the thing that makes babies" (*The Shining* 83). And when Wendy, Danny's mother, does catch him shining her, "[s]he suddenly felt more naked than naked, as if she had been caught in an obscene act," a "masturbatory act" (*The Shining* 201, 297). The sexualization of signification continually points to castration, as Danny is told by one of the hotel's ghostly tenants, one of the shined: "I'm going to eat you up, little boy. And I think I'll start with your plump little cock" (*The Shining* 334). This cannibalistic specter is not the first one Danny has met: his own father is represented to him in a dream as "a tiger in an alien blue-black jungle. A man-eater" (*The Shining* 130): Nor is he the only castrating father in King. Mark Petrie of *'Salem's Lot* allows that his dead father "would have made a very successful vampire. Maybe as good as Barlow [the king vampire], in time. He . . . was good at everything he tried" (382). And perhaps most obvious is the castrating paternity of George Stark, who is horribly on the mark when he declares that he is the father of Thad's successful novel writing: "[m]aybe he knew how to write before I showed up, but I was the one who taught him how to write stuff people would want to read" (*The Dark Half* 413). The written word becomes the father, the real turd of Beaumont's fantasy. And to drive the point home, Stark commits his first murder—of Frederick Clawson, who had threatened to expose Stark as Thad's pseudonym—by cutting off Clawson's penis and stuffing it into his mouth. Thus does the King hero undergo the castration of the Name of the Father, the symbolic commandment that orders, punishes, and frustrates the subject. Yet ultimately, it is also that Name which catapults the subject into a battle for self-definition as it figures the evil to be beaten in the novel.

The conventional gothic double, or doppelgänger, then, is for King not a projection of repressed desire so much as a discourse, the discourse of the Other that is, for Lacan, the language that proceeds from the castrating split that plagues every human subject. And it is the nature of gothic fiction that such doubleness

comes to represent the force of evil against which the protagonists battle: in King, the discourse of the Other becomes the discourse of the other, the seemingly autonomous George Stark, or
the Overlook Hotel, which, like Danny, has the ability to read
others' minds and to absorb the emotions and discourse of the
people who stay there. But whereas for Lacan this Elsewhere
emits only partially intelligible utterances ("[i]t thinks rather
badly, but it does think" [*Écrits* 193], for King, the ability of this
Other to think is startling. George Stark's symbiotic relation to
his literary creator allows him to know exactly where Thad is and
what he is thinking, so that George can stay one step ahead of
him in the murder game, a punishing father at the same time as
a literary son. The Overlook Hotel, that Elsewhere of Danny's
greatest fears of divorce and paternal violence, swims in the
voices of America's literary and cultural past; it is a veritable "index of the whole post–World War II American character"; it is
an ex-writer's school that will commission Danny's father to
write its story like a "large and rambling Samuel Johnson" that
had "picked [Jack] to be its Boswell" (*The Shining* 187, 282).
What is terrifying about the Overlook Hotel is not what is repressed but what is articulated; it is articulation itself. The hotel
echoes with quotations from Eliot's "Prufrock" and Poe; it presents to Danny images of its murderous history "like pictures in
a book" (*The Shining* 87–88). The Overlook is a castrating Father
whose discourses of violence threaten one's ability to move in a
signifying order.

Such articulateness, such jubilantly evil deftness with the
symbolic order, suggest a further erosion in the postmodern
gothic—that boundary between the superego and the id that the
ego is thought to negotiate. Whereas the topography of evil
in *'Salem's Lot* presents us with an obvious Freudian contest between superego and id (Ben Mears's typewriter stands sentinel in
an upstairs room while a vampire sleeps in the basement), in the
Overlook Hotel the basements are full of newspapers, letters,
journals, and various other bits of literary information. That the
id may be the site of an articulate language and thus indistinguishable from the superego is embodied most forcefully in Kurt
Barlow, the child-sucking vampire of *'Salem's Lot* who is both

ravenous murderer and "thoughtful" (144), tasteful, urbane, cultured, literate, a perfect double of the novelist Ben Mears. This casting of the monstrous not only as id but also as superego is a familiar psychic image for Lacan, for whom "[t]he super-ego is at one and the same time the law and its destruction. As such, it is speech itself." Thus it is "identified with only what is most devastating, most fascinating, in the primitive experiences of the subject. It ends up being identified with what I call the *ferocious figure*, with the figures which we can link to primitive traumas the child has suffered." That trauma, moreover, is often "reduced down to a word whose meaning and significance for the child we are not even able to define, but which nonetheless ties him to the community of mankind" (*The Seminar* 102–103)—a word like "vampire," "REDRUM," or "SPARROWS." Such a word alienates the speaking subject in Stephen King yet also comprises the very language of his unconscious. It is projected outward into an other evil, the destruction of which he will dedicate his life to in the service of "the community of mankind."

If the discourse of the Other—the semilucid yet literate register of one's fear of language—represents in its projected embodiments the ultimate terror for a King hero, it also represents the possibilities for triumph over the evil agent. King's plots often turn on the recognition that, by remembering, by bringing some piece of information from silence into speech, the protagonist will be able to disempower the evil other. In *The Shining*, Tony assures Danny that "[y]ou will remember what your father forgot" (420). Thad begins his ascendancy over George by realizing that George does not hear the sparrows and has no idea of their presence. At this revelation, Thad "did not know exactly why, but it was as if his nerve-endings possessed some arcane understanding the rest of him did not have. He felt a moment of wild triumph" (*The Dark Half* 221). This arcane understanding is, in Lacanian terms, a return to the presymbolic imaginary of childhood, a period before the castrating submission to the paternal Law of language (although King's boys are much older than Lacan's mirror-stage child). What Danny remembers—and what Jack forgot—is that if the caretaker does not let off some steam from the old boiler in the basement, it will explode and destroy the hotel. And if this danger sounds allegorical, it is: it parallels other realizations Danny has as he crouches in the hotel hallway, waiting for his father to find and kill him:

> He knew. A long and nightmarish masquerade party went on here, and had gone on for years. Little by little a force had accrued, as secret and silent as interest in a bank account. Force, presence, shape, they were all only words and none of them mattered. It wore many masks, but it was all one. Now, somewhere, it was coming for him. It was hiding behind Daddy's face, it was imitating Daddy's voice, it was wearing Daddy's clothes.
>
> But it was not his daddy. (*The Shining* 420)

As Danny faces "the controlling force of the Overlook, in the shape of his father," "the image of that dark and stumped form," the "mask . . . [the] false face" that Lacan has called the Name-of-the-Father, Danny remembers what his father forgot, that words are "false faces": "[e]verything is a lie and a cheat . . . like the presents they put in the store windows and my daddy says there's nothing in them, no presents, they're just empty boxes" (*The Shining* 421, 422, 426, 427–28).[2] Jack's fatherhood, constructed as it is out of prohibitive utterances, is arbitrary, self-justifying, prone to self-destruction if questioned. Like the child of Freud's *Totem and Taboo* who can gain power only by killing the figure of power (141–142), Danny knows what Lacan says the psychotic forgets, that one's placement in the Name-of-the-Father is self-contested, divisive, disempowering, yet arbitrary. Castration is a metaphor dangerously potent and debilitating but also arbitrary and silly if identified as such. Hence Lacan could be prescribing for Danny Torrance when he writes, "I will not be surprised if the child . . . throws back [*verwerfe*] the whale of imposture, after piercing . . . the web from one end to the other" (and Danny, at the moment of throwing back the whale of imposture, "seemed to be bursting through some thin placental womb" [421]). Then, says Lacan, "the divine voices will make their concert heard in the subject [the shining?] in order to tell the Name-of-the-Father to fuck himself with the Name of

God in his backside and to found the Son in his certainty" (*Écrits* 220–221).

And Thad Beaumont's sparrows? In the novel, they are the mythical agents who escort souls from the world of the living to the world of the dead. But they are also the sparrows that hovered around the young Thad when he learned to write; that attacked the hospital the day the boy-writer was rushed to surgery to remove a brain tumor that turned out to be the body parts of a twin that Thad's fetus had absorbed in utero; and that show up in Thad's fugue states (Danny's shinings) when he unconsciously and automatically writes what George is thinking. And finally, they are the sparrows—the writing—that Thad must wrest back from George and claim as his own language. After the final showdown in which Thad refuses to write the novel George would have him write (George, that self-referential Name-of-the-Father, can write nothing but his own name and the word "sparrows" over and over) and after they have had a physical battle whose weapons are pencils and typewriters, millions of sparrows enter the room, pick the flesh from George's bones, and transport him to the other world. And King is clear as to where these sparrows come from: they are words that Thad writes on a blank sheet of paper (*The Dark Half* 448). They are the signifiers that Thad takes back from George, the Other who has spoken to him, the father who has taught him how to write. The act of writing that had originally split Thad becomes the discourse that can re-empower Thad and give him back some agency.

For Douglas Keesey, the hero's attempt to take back language is ultimately the means by which he is empowered: "by giving fears fictional form, he is able to overcome them" (196). Perhaps, but King also resists the impulse to empower the author precisely by emphasizing the divisive agency of language itself. Jack Torrance is English teacher, writer, conduit for the voices of American literature, and, mostly, father: "I have . . . the *pecker*, my boy. Ask your mother" (426). This same Jack Torrance is told by the son to fuck himself with the Name of God in his backside. And the terror that befalls Thad Beaumont comes as a result of

Thad's dissolving his alter ego and acquiring the imaginary uniformity and wholeness of fatherhood. When his wife is eight months pregnant with their twins, Thad "kills off" George Stark by publicly admitting that he is a pseudonym: "I decided if I was going to be a father again, I ought to start being myself again, as well" (*The Dark Half* 104), a self that is assumed and generated by writing as oneself. Had Beaumont read his Lacan, as King seems to have done, he would know the fallacy of such an assumption and would have understood the agency of *his* letters as he writes (as) George Stark. All authority in language, says Lacan, is established by reference to other language: "[a]nd when the Legislator (he who claims to lay down the Law) presents himself as the phallus that fills the gap, he does so as an imposter" (*Écrits* 311). Indeed, we remember, when Danny Torrance exposes his father as a lie and an empty box, he does so by reference to what "my daddy says"; the son founded in his certainty, as Lacan says, is not so certain at all. Yet the horror of the postmodern Gothic in King is not merely that the law is an imposter—the superego, the Father, discourse itself—but that it is deadly despite its imposture: the power invested in Jack Torrance by his intelligence and his pecker, the power invested in Stark by the popularity of his readership, is a power licensed to kill. As Lacan says, "there is nothing false about the Law itself, or about him who assumes its authority" (*Écrits* 311).

SHINING THE PHALLUS

"Say, you really are a college fella, aren't you? Talk just like a book.
I admire that, as long as the fella ain't one of them fairy-boys. Lots of
em are. You know who stirred up those college riots a few years ago?
The hommasexshuls, that's who. They get frustrated an have to
cut loose. Comin out of the closet, they call it."

KING, *The Shining*

[P]hilosophy, no matter how deconstructive, remains
"discursive," whereas Lacan's writing is "poetic": allusive, contradictory.
The ladies' man is an expert at flirtation. Unlike the man's man,
philosopher or hunter, who spends his time with serious, frank
confrontation, the ladies' man is always embroiled in coquetry: his

words necessarily and erotically ambiguous. The ladies' man is looked
at askance by the "real" man who suspects the flirt of effeminacy.

GALLOP, *The Daughter's Seduction*

Horror in Stephen King is epistemological, but its epistemology
is self-contested: on the one hand, the subject fears the phallus,
the castrating Father who denies the son agency, yet on the other
hand, he nostalgically pines for the phallus, the articulateness
and presence that can overthrow the Father. It is this pining for
the phallus that, as my quotation from Jane Gallop illustrates, offers us access to another of those cultural anxieties that King says
is laid bare in the successful horror story. Such an anxiety is
blurted out by the Overlook's summer caretaker in my first epigraph above. For just as the literate is equated with the horrific
in King, so is it repeatedly associated with the homosexual.
Vampire extraordinaire Kurt Barlow's "face was strong and intelligent and handsome in a sharp, forbidding sort of way—yet,
as the light shifted, it seemed almost effeminate"; indeed, he
keeps his hair "swept back from his high, waxy forehead like one
of those fag concert pianists" (*'Salem's Lot* 352, 144). The significance of this effeminacy is obvious to the town of 'Salem's
Lot: the victims of the vampire attacks are all young boys, boys
like Danny and Ralph Glick who knew "[t]here were no ghosts,
but there were preeverts," "[t]here were preeverts everywhere,"
boys who then fall victim to the dandiacal, urbane Barlow and
his "partner," Straker. These finely cultured, foreign men, the
town decides, are "[p]robably queer for each other," "[l]ike those
fag interior decorators" (*'Salem's Lot* 71, 70, 86). Such queerness
is realized in the ghostly voices of the Overlook Hotel in *The
Shining*. Harry Derwent, the hotel's erstwhile owner, is "AC/
DC, you know," and during the spectral masquerade party that
takes over the hotel and the Torrances' lives, Derwent coyly
pursues Roger, the man in the dog suit. Roger "is only DC,"
the voices tell Jack. "He spent a weekend with Harry in Cuba
once . . . oh, months ago. Now he follows Harry everywhere,
wagging his little tail behind him" (*The Shining* 347). And it is
this same Roger who represents to Danny the threat of castration ("I'm going to eat you up, little boy. And I think I'll start

with your plump little cock") as he equates Danny with his ex-lover Harry. If Danny and the boys in 'Salem's Lot are on the verge of adulthood and the identification with masculinity, the terror is not only, as Freud would have it, the father's castration; nor is this fear of castration, as Lacan would argue, merely the fear of verbal prohibition. Rather, it is specifically homoerotic in its projection. Like the homosexual in these novels, the protagonist demonstrates a desire for verbal acuity that is coded queer. The gay man, like the King hero, both "has" a phallus and wants one. Thus I want now to turn to the second part of my thesis and to suggest that Stephen King's postmodern gothic can be understood not only with reference to Lacan but also in the way linguistics-based psychoanalysis has manifested a certain gender panic in America after Stonewall.

Kurt Barlow's homosexuality may signal rural Maine's fear of pederastic invasion by gay men whose visibility has increased since Stonewall,[3] but it also puts him (like Lacan) in a history that equates urbanity with effeminacy—one that even sees urbanity as the cause of effeminacy. As Peter Schwenger has argued, the very self-referentiality of language forces the seemingly autonomous male into a self-reflection and internal confusion that is coded feminine. And in Stephen King's New England, this "effeminizing" is equated with the homoerotic: Jack Griffen of 'Salem's Lot is a "bookworm, Daddy's pet," while Mark Petrie is a "four-eyes queer boy" accused of a proclivity to "suck the old hairy root"; Ben Mears is, according to Ann Norton, no fitting suitor for her daughter Susan because he is a "sissy boy" whose novel Air Dance contains a "homosexual rape scene in the prison section," "[b]oys getting together with boys"—although why Ben-as-sissy should then be a sexual threat to the daughter is not clear (35, 46, 191, 21). Nor is Ben naive about the depth of suspicion attending unmarried, articulate men: "[j]ust the fact that you're not married is apt to make [the community] believe you've got a screw loose," he warns Matthew Burke, English teacher and fellow vampire hunter as they contemplate making public their theory that 'Salem's Lot is infested with vampires. "And what backup can I give you? . . . [T]hey would just say I was an outsider. They would even get around to telling each other

STEPHEN KING'S PHALLUS   89

we were a couple of queers and this was the way we got our
kicks" (*'Salem's Lot* 176). And Ben has good reason to worry, for
if it is significant that Barlow has an "almost effeminate" face
with "oddly virile slashes of iron gray" in his hair, then it must
upset Ben to have a "sensitive" face on which "[o]nly his hair
seemed virile in the traditional sense" (*'Salem's Lot* 352, 144,
195). Apparently there may be more than one queer couple in
'Salem's Lot. And there is at least one in *The Dark Half*. Despite
Thad's heterosexual credentials embodied in his twin babies, the
local gravedigger imagines him pictured in a magazine "stark
naked" (pun intended?) "with your old hog-leg stuck up a Great
Dane's poop-chute" (*The Dark Half* 45), and George Romero's
film version of *The Dark Half* indicates that Beaumont's novels
prior to George Stark are about "yuppies and faggots." Indeed,
it seems that to play with words is at some level to play homo-
erotically with the phallus.

Thus it is the phallus—authorial and sexual—whose emergence troubles the heroes of King's postmodern gothic. Traditionally, the gothic has been understood as the unveiling of repressed desires that "ought to have remained hidden," as Freud
says ("The Uncanny" 241), and that constitute the social order
by virtue of remaining hidden. For Lacan, what remains hidden
that constitutes order is precisely the phallus, in that it is the
phallus-as-signifier of identity, wholeness, and unity that unconsciously structures the human subject and authorizes his relations with others (*The Seminar* 288). King's gothic, however,
unveils the phallus and brings it out of the closet in terrifying
ways. Liz Beaumont remembers that, in Thad's writing history,
"George Stark was there all along. I'd seen signs of him in some
of the unfinished stuff that Thad did from time to time. It was
just a case of getting him to come out of the closet" (*The Dark
Half* 23). This closet, moreover, is not simply that of an alter ego
or a projected Other; it is the very nature of the phallic signifier
itself. As Thad begins to write, "[t]he words as individual units
began to disappear. Characters who were stilted and lifeless began to limber up, as if he had kept them in some small closet
overnight and they had to loosen their muscles before they could
begin their complicated dances" (*The Dark Half* 264). These

stilted and lifeless characters are, of course, both the stock per-
sonages of gothic convention and the material letters of words
themselves: both selves and signifiers. And this indulgence of the
phallus, this bringing out of the male desire to indulge the phallus of and with another man, is accompanied by no small pleasure. As George and Thad are brought together in their writing
showdown, we sense the homoerotic *jouissance* that *'Salem's Lot*
makes horribly vampiric: "[f]or a moment—and it was only a
moment—there was a sensation of *two* hands grasping two writing instruments. The feeling was too clear, too real, to be anything *but* real . . . a rush quicker and more satisfying than even
the most powerful orgasm" (284). And for Thad, this need to
write with George, to share the pleasure of his instrument, is like
a "trance," a "harsh imperative; there was something which
needed to be written, and he could feel his whole body yelling at
him to get to it, do it, get it done. . . . This itch seemed to be ema-
nating from a place deep in his mind" (*The Dark Half* 317). That
place, obviously, is where the phallus lies veiled, and the desire to
unveil it is both a desire for verbal self-mastery and a homoerotic
desire, a desire for the phallus of the other.

Of all King's novels, *The Dark Half* inscribes most vividly the
ambivalence toward the phallus that Lacan himself outlines in
the (straight male) writer but that he does not, it seems, explore
completely. Lacan, as we know, was adamant that "the phallus
is a signifier, a signifier whose function, in the intrasubjective
economy of the analysis, lifts the veil perhaps from the function
it performed in the mysteries. For it is the signifier intended to
designate as a whole the effects of the signified, in that the
signifier conditions them by its presence as a signifier" (*Écrits*
285). Moreover, Lacan rejects the tendency to psychologize or
biologize this signifier: "the phallus is not a phantasy, if by that
we mean an imaginary effect. Nor is it as such an object (part-,
internal, good, bad, etc.) in the sense that this term tends to accentuate the reality pertaining in a relation. It is even less the organ, penis or clitoris, that it symbolizes" (*Écrits* 285). However,
Lacan's dismissal of the phallus as penis is contradicted elsewhere by his justification of the privilege accorded to the symbol: "[i]t can be said that this signifier is chosen because it is the

most tangible element in the real of sexual copulation, and also
the most symbolic in the literal (typographical) sense of the term,
since it is equivalent there to the (logical) copula. It might also
be said that, by virtue of its turgidity, it is the image of the vital
flow as it is transmitted in generation" (*Écrits* 287). This is worth
considering, for if the phallus-as-signifier displaces/replaces the
penis-as-organ, it also continually signifies the presence of—or
the desire for—the penis *as* organ. While the phallus-as-signifier
in Lacan does not equal the penis, it can never be divested of the
penis; it must always signify the penis at the same time it tran-
scends it. Language, the phallus-as-signifier, has it both ways
(like Harry Derwent of *The Shining*), and its AC/DC nature
troubles the straight male writer, who is, as Thad Beaumont
knows, "*passing some sort of baton*" (437) in a phallic play that is
pleasurable, homoerotic.

What Lacan might be suggesting here—and what Michael
Warner reads in Lacan's first seminar on narcissism (202)—is
that male heterosexuality does not look all that different from
male homosexuality, and precisely because of the elusiveness of
the ever-reified, ever-desired phallus. For Lacan, male heterosexuality is distinguished from homosexuality "by reference to
the function of the phallus" (*Écrits* 289). Straight men seek in the
woman the mirror image of their own phallus, for it is the originary desire of the boy to be the phallus his mother lacks, and so
to want the woman is to want to be that phallus, the phallus she
can never be because she can never have it. The gay man, con-
versely, identifies with the mother's lack of the phallus and con-
tents himself with being the phallus/woman that the straight
man desires. The "perversion" of gayness for psychoanalysis,
then, is the insistence on seeing the phallus not as Phallus but as
penis, as unveiling the phallus and desiring it as penis, as the dedication to being the other man's Other (Lacan, *Écrits* 322). But as
Lacan continually makes clear, the Otherness of phallic repression and splitting constitutes the rupture of *all* identity, so that
the straight man's identification with the woman-as-phallus becomes embattled: if the man does not have the phallus, then it is
he who is inadequate, for she cannot be expected to give him
what she herself does not have. As John P. Muller and William J.

Richardson explain, "[T]he man must avoid impotence if he is to remain busy being the phallus for women, but he must repress his own desire that the woman be the phallus for him in his never-ending quest for the impossible woman-as-phallus" (353). The crisis in heterosexual masculinity, then, is that the man both has the phallus(-as-penis) and desires the phallus(-as-woman) in a display that risks effeminizing him. He must seek the confirmation of his phallic power by identifying with the woman who desires him, and desires him *for his penis*. Hence the "comedy" of gender: heterosexual masculinity is predicated on desiring a phallus while already having one.

Which brings us back to Stephen King. Although Ben Mears suspects that the town sees writers as "either faggots or bull-studs" (106), we might now effect a grammatical shift of our own to "faggots as bull-studs" or, rather, "bull-studs as faggots." For the prowess of phallic signification that characterizes the writer in King also characterizes the villainous vampire, the highly cultured Other who demonstrates the straight author's ambivalence to the phallus. And this ambivalence, I want to conclude, characterizes a particularly postmodern gothic terrorism.

For Eve Sedgwick, homosexual panic in the Enlightenment gothic took the form of a "wildly dichotomous play around solipsism and intersubjectivity" in which the "transmutability of the intrapsychic with the intersubjective" allowed one man's mind to be known by another, resulting in "an epistemologically indissoluble clench of will and desire" (186–187): one man invades another man's space in a way that suggests the terrors of phallic intrusion. In that tradition is Dick Hallorann of *The Shining*, who shines Jack Torrance thus: "[h]e had probed at the boy's father and he just didn't know. . . . Poking at Danny's father had been . . . strange, as if Jack Torrance had something—something—that he was hiding. Or something he was holding in so deeply submerged in himself that it was impossible to get to" (88). This "probing," this "poking," we remember, is a verbal phenomenon: the shining is the ability to read the signifiers of the other's consciousness. What Jack is hiding is not a classic case of homosexual panic but a postmodern one—an ambivalent desire for and rejection of the phallic language of his paternal and cultural past, for the language of masculinity. Similarly, when Thad Beaumont and George Stark awake from their own (intra)psychic clench in which they fall asleep and write together, King describes the "fugue state" thus:

> Stark could vaguely remember dreaming that Thad was with him, in his bed—they were talking together, whispering together, and at first this had seemed both pleasant and oddly comforting—like talking to your brother after lights out.
>
> Except they were doing more than *talking*, weren't they?
>
> What they had been doing was *exchanging secrets* . . . or, rather, Thad was asking him questions and Stark found himself answering. It was pleasant to answer, it was comforting to answer. But it was also alarming. (*The Dark Half* 282)

Asking and answering questions here is "more than talking" only in the sense that the exchange of signifiers—the exchange of the phallus—is both pleasant and alarming. It marks a postmodern gothic homosexual panic, the elements of which are specifically discursive. To speak, to write, to engage the phallus with/of another man is alarming, frightening, invasive. But through a queer male lens, it is also comforting, even pleasant.[4]

When Father Callahan of *'Salem's Lot* catalogs the small skirmishes that constitute the (evil) of the contemporary world as opposed to the EVIL of the ancient one, he employs a useful and instructive diction: "[t]he new priests had theirs [i.e., evils]: racial discrimination, women's liberation, even gay liberation" (150). The qualifier "even" here designates the greatest horror to hit the town of 'Salem's Lot. But it also indicates the queer textuality of these novels; it unveils Stephen King's Phallus. As Lacan reminds us, human needs are made public by demand, by articulating them in discourse, but that demand inaugurates a deeper desire, in that language alienates the subject's needs at the same time that it articulates them. This desire, I have tried to show, arises in Stephen King's authors and speaking subjects who must simultaneously acquire place in the symbolic order and reject that order as evil. But as Lacan points out, discourse itself is also a demand, in that it requires the attention and recognition of the Other who is engaged (or forced) to listen (*Écrits* 58).

It is perhaps this demand, then, that is embodied in subjects as diverse as Roger the Dog Man, Kurt Barlow, and Thad Beaumont who speak in an America marked "even" by gay liberation. If discourse invokes a desire for the phallus even (or especially) among subjects who have a phallus, then the demands of gay men since Stonewall throw into high relief what may be worrying Stephen King's authors. To speak to other men is necessary to constitute the American social order, but it may also demand an exchange of the phallus whose significance—since Lacan, since Stonewall—cannot be divested of the image of the penis. And the implications of this homoerotic demand are alarming: "I be buggered if he ain't hypnotizin me," thinks one of Barlow's victims ('Salem's Lot 146). The ironies here are manifold, for to be hypnotized by one of Stephen King's vampires is to *be* buggered, and what is most alarming is that such hypnotic demand can be *jouissance*, a pleasure which, like the vampire's bite on the male neck, is "as sweet as silver, as green as still waters at dark fathoms" (146).

NOTES

An earlier version of this essay was published in *Narrative* 4 (January 1996), 55–73.

1. For Lacan, Freud's "interpretation of the Schreber case . . . uses the form of a grammatical deduction in order to present the switching of the relation to the other in psychosis, namely, the different ways of denying the proposition, 'I love him,' from which it follows that this negative judgement is structured in two stages: the first, the reversal of the value of the verb ('I hate him'), or inversion of the gender of the agent or object ('It is not I' or 'It is not him, but her'—or inversely); the second, an interversion of subjects ('He hates me,' 'It is she he loves,' 'It is she who loves me')" (*Écrits* 188).

2. Danny is not the only person to know what Jack doesn't about the power of language. George Hatfield was a top student on Jack's debating team at his previous school. However, George allegedly stuttered when nervous, a debator's flaw that infuriated Jack. When Jack finally throws George off the team, the student accuses him of cheating and tells him, "You huh-hate me b-because you nuh-nuh-nuh-know . . . you know" (*The Shining* 113). Jack cannot imagine what George thinks he knows, but clearly it is that George is more articulate than he (not to

mention younger and sexier) and that Jack can evict him simply because he has the power to do so. What George knows—and Jack does not—is that power, here the power to decide what is proper speech (a power that Jack reiterates when he commands Danny not to stutter), is wielded only by those who are arbitrarily granted it.

3. And King makes clear what "real" homophobia looks like. Amid the panic generated by queer men who, by definition, eat little boys, King adds: "[a]t quarter to ten on this Saturday night, two [hospital] attendants were wheeling in the sheet-covered body of a young homosexual who had been shot in a downtown bar" (*'Salem's Lot* 238). This passage is striking for the way it juxtaposes the paranoia of queer vampires with the awareness of real gay persecution.

4. I am not the first to write on homophobia in King. Douglas Keesey argues that King employs scenes of homophobia to satirize social hatred; the fear of Otherness in the self gets projected onto the social other—the gay man—who is sacrificed to purge society. That feared Otherness can range from childhood masturbation between boys to the suspect vocation of novel writing. I find this reading extremely useful, but I resist the assumption that writing can overcome those fears. King uses the gestures of masculinity—phobic violence and phallic signifiers— not to heal masculinity but to deconstruct its very possibility. King's novels are less interesting for their reconciliation of the self to its Otherness than they are for their charting the inescapability of that Otherness. For Keesey, social healing comes from psychological healing; for me, psychological healing is never guaranteed precisely because it requires the very weapons that wound in the first place.

WORKS CITED

Freud, Sigmund. *Totem and Taboo: Some Points of Agreement between the Mental Lives of Savages and Neurotics*. Trans. James Strachey. London: Routledge and Kegan Paul, 1961.

———. "The Uncanny." *The Standard Edition of the Complete Psychological Works of Sigmund Freud*, vol. 17. Trans. James Strachey. London: Hogarth Press, 1957.

Gallop, Jane. *The Daughter's Seduction: Feminism and Psychoanalysis*. Ithaca: Cornell UP, 1982.

Keesey, Douglas. "'The Face of Mr. Flip': Homophobia in the Horror of Stephen King." *The Dark Descent: Essays Defining Stephen King's Horrorscope*. Ed. Tony Majistrale. New York: Greenwood, 1992, 187–201.

King, Stephen. *Danse Macabre*. New York: Berkley Books, 1983.

————. *The Dark Half*. Toronto: Penguin, 1989.

————. *'Salem's Lot*. New York: Doubleday, 1975.

————. *The Shining*. Toronto: Penguin, 1977.

Lacan, Jacques. *Écrits: A Selection*. Trans. Alan Sheridan. New York: W. W. Norton, 1977.

————. *The Seminar of Jacques Lacan, Book I: Freud's Papers on Technique, 1953–1954*. Trans. John Forrester. New York: W. W. Norton, 1988.

Muller, John P., and William J. Richardson. *Lacan and Language: A Reader's Guide to "Écrits."* New York: International Universities P, 1985.

Schwenger, Peter. *Phallic Critiques: Masculinity and Twentieth-Century Literature*. Boston: Routledge and Kegan Paul, 1984.

Sedgwick, Eve Kosofsky. *Epistemology of the Closet*. Berkeley: U of California P, 1990.

Warner, Michael. "Homo-Narcissism; or, Heterosexuality." *Engendering Men: The Question of Male Feminist Criticism*. Ed. Joseph A. Boone and Michael Cadden. New York: Routledge, 1990, 190–206.

PART III

Racial Politics in
Gothic Texts

LESLEY GINSBERG

Slavery and the Gothic Horror of Poe's "The Black Cat"

As Leslie Fiedler put it more than thirty years ago, "the proper-subject" of the "American gothic" is "slavery" (378). In this essay I shall argue that behind the gothic machinery of Poe's "The Black Cat"—with its graphic and "damnable atrocities," its "PERVERSENESS," its murdered corpse, "clotted with gore"—are resounding echoes of antebellum slavery discourses, allusions which allow the story to be read not only as an examination of the narrator's purported "peculiarity of character" but also as an investigation into the peculiar psychopolitics of the master/slave relationship, a bond whose sentimentalized image was at the heart of the South's proslavery rhetoric.[1]

Not only does "The Black Cat" reproduce the struggle between a helpless dependent and an abusive tyrant which figures so prominently in both gothic fictions and abolitionist discourses, but the crumbling edifice of denial exposed by the narrator's confession deconstructs the sentimental strategies of repression so common to antebellum rhetoric. Like many of Poe's gothic tales, "The Black Cat" (1843) cries out for contextualization: critics have shown that the story reflects contemporary sensationalist fictions, parodies the temperance confessional, and critiques the growing acceptance of the insanity defense in antebellum courtrooms (Reynolds, Matheson, Cleman). But the tale also invokes other discourses central to the 1830s and 1840s, including its rehearsal of the scene of pet abuse so often featured in antebellum child-rearing manuals and its

repetition of the obsessive pitting of black against white, dependency against freedom, and animal against human which fueled
contemporary debates over chattel slavery and social reform. As
David Walker famously puts it to his "beloved brethren" (7) in a
phrase which mirrors "The Black Cat's" compulsive iterations of
the domestic battle between a black "*brute beast*" and its human
owner ("a man, fashioned in the image of the High God" [*CW*
856]), the horror of slavery is its dehumanization: while "all the
inhabitants of the earth are called *men*, we and our children are
brutes!!" (Walker 7).

When the *Richmond Enquirer* repeatedly describes Nat
Turner and his accomplices as a gang of "banditti" (qtd. in
Tragle 43, 58, 145), the inaccuracy of this term and its muted
reference to the standard public enemies of British gothic fiction
belie the extent to which southern discourse was all too ready to
conflate the real horrors of slavery and insurrection with the
conventions of Radcliffean cliché. As the *Enquirer* reports, using
imagery which is as conspicuously literary as it is flagrantly removed from southeastern Virginia, these real-life rebels "remind one of a parcel of blood-thirsty wolves rushing down from
the Alps" (qtd. in Tragle 43). In a rhetorical gesture which transforms rebel slaves into wild beasts and dissolves fact into fiction,
the editors of the *Enquirer* participate in the production of a cultural convention: the creation of a national gothic narrative
whose conspicuously fictive framework masks the real horror of
race war at the core of the peculiar institution.

"Why?, Why?, Why?, the papers asked in long and repetitious articles which habitually described those who had revolted
as 'banditti'" (Tragle 4). As historian Henry Irving Tragle notes,
the overwhelming question which vexed southern newspapers,
the riddle which ostensibly impelled Thomas Gray to extract
Turner's confession, was the seemingly unsolvable enigma of
motive. For, as the *Enquirer* muses, Turner acted "without any
cause or provocation, that could be assigned"; the *Richmond
Compiler* concurred when this newspaper submitted that "[t]heir
ultimate object . . . [is] not yet explained." In his teasing introduction to the *Confessions*, Gray commiserates with the frustration of readers who have seen "the insurgent slaves . . . de-

stroyed, or apprehended, tried, and executed . . . without revealing anything at all satisfactory, as to the motives which governed
them." As Gray empathizes with his puzzled patrons, "[p]ublic
curiosity has been on the stretch to understand . . . the motives"
of the "great Bandit" and his gang: "[e]verything connected with
this sad affair was wrapt in mystery, until [Gray adds in a transparent advertisement for his pamphlet] Nat Turner . . . was cap-
tured" (qtd. in Tragle 43–44, 48, 303).

By persistently describing the rebellious slaves as a gang of
thieving banditti, southern reporters have already imputed a
motive, but the repeated assertions that the insurrection was
motiveless betray the poverty of the plunder hypothesis, while
the paltry consolations provided by southern pundits underscore
their failure to mollify white anxiety. As Gray puts it ominously
in his introduction to the *Confessions*, in a characterization of
Turner which seems lifted out of the pages of Charles Brockden
Brown's gothic novel *Wieland*, "whilst every thing upon the surface of society wore a calm and peaceful aspect, a gloomy fanatic
was revolving in the recesses of his own dark, bewildered and
overwrought mind, schemes of indiscriminate massacre to the
whites" (qtd. in Tragle 304).

Yet when he imagines a "society" whose "surface," at least, was
"calm and peaceful," Gray proffers his own version of the familiar fictions surrounding southern plantation life. As if tuned to
the pulse of slaveholding apprehensions, Gray's insistence that
Turner was but a uniquely deranged extremist became the most
popular explanation for the rebellion: like a deadly but incom-
municable disease, the revolt was no more than "a sudden . . .
outbreak of fanaticism and subtle craft," soothes the *Constitutional Whig*. Beneath a headline proclaiming "THE BANDIT–
TAKEN!" the *Enquirer* effectively stifles any nascent debate over
the causes of the insurrection by declaring that "[n]o man" can
read Turner's account of the rebellion "without setting Nat
Turner down as a wild fanatic." If Turner was just a crazed en-
thusiast, slave owners could continue to deny the far more
frightening conclusion that the cause of the revolt was built into
the very structure of the peculiar institution. Gray concludes the
narrative with the ringing judgment of the court: "your only

justification," proclaims the court chairman, as Turner's death sentence is pronounced, is that "you were led away by fanaticism" (qtd. in Tragle 90, 136, 319). But even as the court attempts to give its authoritative answer to the vexing question of Turner's motives, the circulation of his narrative offers at least the possibility that readers could recover another story buried within the *Confessions*, despite its controlling layers of introductions, official documents, and formal dictation supplied by Gray. To paraphrase Poe's later treatment of the paradoxical invisibility of the obvious in his most famous ratiocinative tale, "The Purloined Letter" (1844), in an echo of that document which haunted Turner's rebellion, the Declaration of Independence, perhaps the secret of Turner's motive remained opaque because the answer was just "'A little *too* self-evident'" (*CW* 975).[2]

Nat Turner's revolt prompted fearful southerners to launch a verbal and ideological counterattack which was manifested in an outpouring of proslavery literature as well as a series of debates in the Virginia state legislature on the subject of emancipation, which the legislature predictably deemed impossible, though not without significant opposition. Many delegates, particularly those who represented the western parts of the state, favored either some form of gradual abolitionism or various schemes of deportation and colonization (Leverenz 213–214, Freehling 122–169). Horrified by the implications of these intellectually freewheeling debates, Thomas R. Dew (then a twenty-nine-year-old professor at the College of William and Mary) published a response in the *American Quarterly Review* that reads as a species of proslavery damage control. Soon reprinted with added commentary in pamphlet form, Dew's *Review of the Debate in the Virginia Legislature* (1832) became what Lewis P. Simpson calls "the prototypical document in a literature that was to flow unceasingly from Southern pens for the next thirty years" (169). Indeed, if Dew's treatise can be said to have provided a rhetorical template for the aspiring southern gentleman, his experience also demonstrated that identification with the discourse of white supremacy offered no hindrance to a markedly meteoric rise; four years later Dew ascended to the presidency of the college while concurrently forging a name for himself in the periodical press as a prominent contributor to the *Southern Literary Messenger*—a sideline which coincided with Poe's stint as editor of that magazine. And if Dew's chronicle of the debates can be read as an articulation of some of the South's most cherished fictions, it is worth noting that Dew quotes at least one participant who frames his opinion of emancipation in an argument which explicitly invokes gothic literature:

> To turn ["the negro"] loose in the manhood of his physical passions, but in the infancy of his uninstructed reason, would be to raise up a creature resembling the splendid fiction of a recent romance; the hero of which constructs a human form with all the physical capabilities of man, and with the thews and sinews of a giant, but . . . finds too late that he has only created a more than mortal power of doing mischief, and himself recoils from the monster which he has made. (Quoted in Dew 105)

In an allusion to a novel which sounds suspiciously like Mary Shelley's *Frankenstein* (1818), this Virginian participates in the creation of what could be called a national gothic narrative of slavery. And by invoking Shelley's novel, whose layers of frame narratives enclose the monster's own damning tale at its center, this extraordinary moment in the debates belies the fear on the part of these southern patriarchs that their control over the discourse of slavery was being challenged by the voices of those who were traditionally mute: women, children, slaves, and, by extension, animals.

At the core of proslavery ideology was the equating of slaves with animals. J. K. Paulding's *Slavery in the United States* (1836) asserts that the "woolly-headed race"—that familiar, hackneyed phrase which itself evokes an animal-like image—is burdened with an immutable "inferiority"; blacks are rightly "classed as the lowest in the scale of rational beings" (280). In *The South-West* (1835), Joseph Holt Ingraham approvingly notes that the field slave, whom he ranks as "but little higher than [a] brute . . . the last and lowest link in the chain of the human species," is commonly traded from "one [master] to another" like "a purchased horse." A provincial northerner, as Ingraham remarks, might look upon "a band of negroes, as upon so many *men*. But the planter, or southerner, views them in a very different light" (254, 194, 260). As William Drayton concurs in his vitriolic *The South Vindicated* (1836) in a stunning example of southern repression in the teeth of Turner's revolt, "[t]he slave, besotted, servile, accustomed to degradation, and habituated to regard his master with deference and awe, does not presume to dream of contending with him" (299).

Yet if proslavery advocates were wont to dehumanize blacks, abolitionists would consistently exploit the horror of slavery's challenge to the limit between human and animal. "The Black Cat" appeared two years before Frederick Douglass's *Narrative*, while Douglass toured the North delivering those speeches that culminated in the publication of his rhetorical transformation from the "beast-like stupor" of slavery to the full humanity of freedom, as Douglass famously reiterates the slave's lament, "O, why was I born a man, of whom to make a brute!" (1966–67). Theodore Dwight Weld's encyclopedic *American Slavery As It Is* (1839) documents the sufferings of slaves who are worked like "droves of 'human cattle,'" then "herded at night like swine" (76, 19). In his expert revision of abolitionist tropes, Douglass persistently equates slaves and animals: "horses and men, cattle and women, pigs and children" are all valued as if "holding the same rank in the scale of being" (1958). For Douglass, humanization was inextricably bound to literacy and the authorizing power of his *Narrative*. But like the condemning wail of the *"brute beast"* who convicts his owner with "a voice from within the tomb!" (Poe 856, 858), Douglass narrates his first act of physical resistance in terms that are as gothic as they are Christian: "[i]t was a glorious resurrection, from the *tomb* of slavery" (1971, my emphasis). By imagining the assertion of his humanity as a return from the grave, Douglass allows us to reread the irrepressible voice of the dead in "The Black Cat" as an explicit metaphor for the silences and repressions upon which the peculiar institution was built.

If southern ideology rested heavily on the supposed animal-like nature of black people, proslavery rhetoric was quick to sentimentalize the relationship of master and slave by repeated allusions to the cloying imagery of the bonds between humans and domesticated animals, especially pets. In Ingraham's romantic depiction of slavery, "slave children are pets in the house, and the playmates of the white children in the family" (126). J. K. Paulding (Poe's friend and literary champion during his tenure at the *Messenger*) thought highly enough of Ingraham's sentiments that he reprints this passage in full in his own treatise on slavery (223). Ingraham's much-loved passage is also echoed almost verbatim in "The Black Cat," when the narrator tells us that his cat was his "favorite pet and playmate" (*CW* 850–851).

Though southerners were apt to romanticize dependency, their most potent defense of slavery was the domestic fiction of the happy slaveholding family. As Dew sentimentally affirms, "[T]he slave . . . generally loves the master" (113). And in a stunning passage which conflates slavery and the dependency of childhood, Drayton declares, "We are all, in early life, slaves" (82). As George Fitzhugh puts it, all dependents are slaves: "[w]ives and apprentices are slaves; not only in theory, but often in fact," just as "[c]hildren are the slaves to their parents, guardians and teachers" (though in Fitzhugh's trivialization of slavery, "[t]hree-fourths of free society are slaves") (88–89, 91, 90). But it was not only southerners who represented family government on the antidemocratic model of master and slave. Samuel Goodrich, one of the period's premiere publishers of children's literature, articulates a similar vision in *Fireside Education*, a child-rearing guide popular enough to have gone through six editions by 1841. As Goodrich asserts, familial government is rightly "despotic, giving absolute authority to the monarch parents over their subject children" (26). And in his children's periodical *Merry's Museum*, Goodrich inundates the child reader with stories of loving dependency. The January 1843 edition includes a version of that tale so dear to southern apologists, entitled "Fidelity of a Negro Servant," the story of a vassal who is freed when his white "master" suffers financial disaster. But the grateful "negro" refuses to desert: "'[n]o, master, we will never part.'" The same issue includes a short essay on "EQUALITY" which flatly proclaims: "absolute equality" is "impossible." "Equality does not mean that a woman shall be equal to a man, or a child the same as a man." Though "[i]t is said in our Declaration of Independence, that 'all mankind [*sic*] are created equal,'" this part of the Declaration is not "literally true" (37–38).

While the narrator's alcoholism links "The Black Cat" to the temperance confessional, his struggle with "the Fiend Intemperance" (851) also echoes those ubiquitous antebellum domestic guides whose relentless focus on emotional temperance implicitly highlights the dangers of familial tyranny. But as abolitionists argued, the intoxication of absolute power bred the intemperate abuses for which slavery was infamous—in a corollary to the atrocities in "The Black Cat," both Lydia Maria Child's *Anti-Slavery Catechism* (1835) and Weld's *Slavery As It Is* report incidents of eye gouging as well as outright murder (Child, *Catechism* 5; Weld 20, 77). As Weld puts it, "Arbitrary power is to the mind what alcohol is to the body; it intoxicates." For Weld, power is just as addictive as drink: "the more absolute the power, the stronger the desire for it." Power, Weld concludes, "is such a fiery stimulant, that its lodgement in human hands is always perilous" (115, 116).

At the same time as the abolitionist critique of power circulated on the fringes of respectable middle-class discourse, antebellum domestic guides struggled to justify traditional family government by lauding those parents who wielded their powers with discretion. To illustrate "the happy effects which may flow from firm, yet just and kind treatment of a disobedient child" by his omnipotent but temperate parents, Goodrich's *Fireside Education* includes a version of the scene of pet abuse so familiar to antebellum child-rearing guides, in this case an episode lifted from Catharine Maria Sedgwick's novelistic child-rearing manual, *Home*. In a fit of anger, young Wallace Barclay plunges his sister's kitten into a vat of boiling water; his elder brother first rescues the animal, but, "seeing its misery," he allows it to die in the hot water, a gesture of his "characteristic consideration." Wallace's father banishes him to his room with a curse that emphasizes the humanizing mission of parental absolutism: "'[y]ou have forfeited your right to a place among us. Creatures who are the slaves of their passions are like beasts of prey, fit only for solitude'" (26–27). Guilty of "murderous cruelty to an innocent animal" (Goodrich 26), dehumanized, like the narrator of "The Black Cat," by an act of wanton violence against an "unoffending brute" (852), Wallace finally redeems himself by subduing his temper.[3]

Just as Wallace's father wields his disciplinary power wisely, the relation of the relatively powerful child to his powerless pet may have been central to antebellum household guides because it mirrors the dynamics between parent and child and enables children to act out the adult role by assuming responsibility for a helpless dependent. But as "The Black Cat" warns, the specter of abuse haunted antebellum domestic guides, despite their happy images of familial tyranny, for the unspoken family politics behind the story reveals a tyrant who enjoys the full privileges of any of Goodrich's monarch-patriarchs, while his dependent wife bears the brunt of his growing addiction to domestic power: "from the sudden, frequent, and ungovernable outbursts of a fury to which I now blindly abandoned myself, my uncomplaining wife, alas! was the most usual and the most patient of sufferers" (856). And as Elizabeth Cady Stanton accuses, antebellum legal codes and employment restrictions rendered married women almost as powerless as any dependent slave: a woman's husband was, "to all intents and purposes, her master— the law giving him power to deprive her of her liberty, and to administer chastisement" (92). As if in response to this explosive charge, George Fitzhugh—that tireless defender of the Old Dominion—boldly asserts that spousal abuse is a uniquely northern affliction: "[t]here, wife-murder has become a mere holiday pastime; and where so many wives are murdered, almost all must be brutally treated" (89). But as historian Thomas E. Buckley shows in his study of divorce petitions filed in antebellum Virginia, the South was no stranger to wife abuse: "[t]he greatest percentage of women petitioners requested a divorce on the grounds of battery." And in a finding which further links the source of domestic violence to both legalized gender discrimination and slavery, Buckley argues that while drunkenness played a significant part in episodes of wife beating, alcoholism itself was not the root cause of domestic violence in the Old Dominion: the testimony of battered wives reveals that liquor "tended to release inhibitions rather than cause the battery. . . . In a society based on slavery," Buckley concludes, the "free white male" assumed that he had the right to "absolute power" over "wife and family" (4, 39, 47).[4]

For abolitionists, the keeping of forcibly domesticated animals had uncomfortable echoes of slavery. In *The Mother's Book* (1831), Lydia Maria Child concedes that caring for pets is a key step in the "cultivation of the affections," but Child also admits that she has moral qualms about the ethics of pet keeping: "I cannot think it right to keep creatures that must be confined in cages and boxes." And when Child reports a scene of pet abuse, she emphasizes the specter of parental tyranny: "I once saw a mother laugh very heartily at a kitten, which a child of two years old was pulling backward by the tail. At last, the kitten, in self-defense, turned and scratched the boy. He screamed, and his mother ran to him, and beat the poor kitten." As Child glosses, "the kitten was struck for defending herself; this was . . . a lesson of tyranny to the boy" (*Book* 6–7, 58, 7–8).

More tellingly, Child's abolitionist-leaning children's magazine includes stories which make the link between slavery and pet ownership explicit. In 1831, the *Juvenile Miscellany* offered the child-reader a story called "The Prisoners Set Free," authored by Hannah F. Gould, in which the Elsworth children decide to liberate their beloved caged pets (though as one child complains, in an echo of proslavery sentimentality, "I didn't keep my little Bonny because I was angry with him, but because I loved him"). Their mother affirms there is "no doubt" that her children's "little captives longed for freedom as much as the poor Africans do, who have to live and die in bondage to white men" (206–207). And if this story asserts that keeping formerly wild animals as pets reproduces the conditions of slavery, it is worth recalling that the pet-owning household in "The Black Cat" keeps not only domesticated creatures (like the cat and a "fine dog") but also "birds, gold-fish, rabbits," and, significantly, a "small monkey," whose position as a captive reads as a clear echo of slaveholding ideology, which, as David Walker complains, routinely classed blacks with "the tribes of *Monkeys*" and "*Orang-Outangs*" (*CW* 850; Walker 10).

As Shawn Rosenheim points out, the etymological root of the word orangutan—so central to both "The Murders in the Rue Morgue" (1841) and Poe's grim "Hop Frog" (1849), in which a formerly fawning servant ("forcibly carried off" in his youth from a home in "some barbarous region") summarily immolates his oppressors after symbolically reversing roles by costuming them as "orang-outangs" in "chains" (*CW* 1346, 1350)[5]—signifies not merely an animal but a "*wild man*" (Rosenheim 159), or, as the OED has it, an uncivilized "man of the woods." In Rosenheim's terms, what separates orangutans from humans "is less biology than culture, epitomized by the possession of language" (159); in other words, the dynamics of domestication is a model in miniature of the enslavement of the uncivilized Other (as well as the transformation of speechless, unsocialized infancy into adulthood). Further, representations of pet keeping trope those missionary impulses which were typically invoked to gloss involuntary servitude with a patina of sacredness; if (as Dew puts it in a telling syllogism) "the acquisition of dominion over the inferior animals" is "a step of capital importance in the progress of civilization," it "may with truth be affirmed, that the *taming* of man . . . is more important than the taming and using the inferior animals [*sic*], and nothing seems so well calculated to effect this as slavery":

> There is nothing but slavery which can . . . eradicate the character . . . which mark[s] the independent savage. He may truly be compared to the wild beast of the forest—he must be broke and tamed before he becomes fit for labor. . . . There is nothing but slavery which can effect this—the means may appear exceedingly harsh and cruel—and, as among wild beasts many may die in the process of taming and subjugating . . . but in the end, it . . . consequently speeds on more rapidly the cause of civilization. (Dew 29–30)

Six months after Turner's revolt, the *Juvenile Miscellany* included another story by Gould which explores the dangers of dependency as well as the horror of confounding animals with humans. In "The White Kitten with a Black Nose" (a figure which itself blurs the lines of racial difference), young Caroline makes the mistake of doting too heavily upon a domesticated animal. In a parody of the proslavery position, Caroline asserts that her kitten needs "as much care as a child." But Caroline's mother warns her daughter that she has gone too far: "'you must not confound persons and animals. Your excessive fondness for your kitten is too much like what is felt for human creatures for me to approve'" (297, 300).

If the relationship of pet to pet owner was understood by antebellum Americans as a trope for both slavery and domesticity, in the early 1840s *Graham's Magazine* was stuffed with the sentimental iconography of this bond. And while *Graham's* published such abolitionist sympathizers as Longfellow and Sedgwick, it also featured well-known southern advocates like Paulding, so that the magazine embodied a meeting ground for these opposing ideologies. When Poe was an editor at *Graham's*, the November 1841 edition confronted the reader with an engraving called "The Pet Lamb" (fig. 1). Though this engraving is an antebellum pop-cultural take on the traditions of early-eighteenth-century Anglo-American portraiture, the poem which accompanies the image firmly situates this engraving in its sentimental, nineteenth-century context.[6] Written from the point of view of a man who has "paused to gaze" upon the young woman and her pet, the poem narrates a drama conspicuously absent from the engraving, which culminates in the speaker's marriage to the sitter—but only after her pet lamb has been "murdered" in a freak accident. The speaker enters the scene when a "shot re-echoed through the wood," and, in the poem's most macabre moment, the speaker sees the lamb "bleeding in her lap," an image with undeniably hymeneal connotations. Emotionally devirginized, the young woman discovers a "void where once she loved." But by "sooth[ing] her fears" and "mingl[ing] tears with tears," our sympathetic hero wins his place in his lover's sentiments. While the engraving evokes the specter of female sexuality through its reproduction of the conventional imagery of Madonna and child, the poem further sexualizes the act of pet keeping, since

1. *The Pet Lamb.*
Engraving by H. S. Sadd, New York. In *Graham's Magazine,*
November 1841.

the speaker cannot woo or wed his lady love until a "void" has been created through the murder of her lamb. Read in light of its narrative trajectory, the poem suggests that the relationship of pet to owner was viewed as a training ground for the mutual dependencies of marriage. Though the speaker replaces the lamb as the object of the young woman's affections, by "yielding" to the speaker's "side" and by allowing him to take her "passive hand," the sitter is simultaneously transformed into the petted wife of her fond husband (94). But as "The Black Cat" suggests, dependency can be dangerous: the story's "hideous murder" is the horrifying evidence of what might happen when a man confuses persons and pets (*CW* 856).

Poe claimed that he resigned from *Graham's* in April 1842 in "disgust with the namby-pamby character of the Magazine," a quality which was manifest in its "contemptible pictures" (Poe to Frederick W. Thomas, *The Letters* 197). But *Graham's* understood that much of its appeal lay in these cloying images of domestic bondage. The November 1842 edition offers a dreamy young woman holding a rabbit while a child reaches out to stroke the rabbit and perhaps usurp its place in his mother's attentions (fig. 2). But the eight-line poem which accompanies "The Pet Rabbit" avoids mention of this child altogether, and in a substitution thick with overtones of the Freudian family romance, the poem instead presents the piqued perspective of her conspicuously absent husband, who mournfully concludes: "[s]he scorns her husband, but—*adores her rabbit*" (261).[7] Set off with a dash, our husband's complaint revives the specter of a different form of sexual jealousy as well, since the metonymic link between child and rabbit not only reads as a visual metaphor for the wife's implicit fecundity, but her enervated, self-satisfied air also suggests that the soft, furry, well-petted creature nestled between thighs and breasts could be symbolic of a proclivity toward auto-eroticism—a preference which might intimidate the insecure husband, who enviously narrates from behind the scene, shut out of the closed circle of his wife's affection.[8]

If "The Pet Rabbit" (like "The Pet Lamb") comes freighted with textual explorations of sexual jealousy, the following edition of *Graham's* presents a soothing image of blissful dependency, entitled "True Affection" (fig. 3). The glaring doubleness at the sentimental heart of this engraving—as mother touches baby to her cheek, so daughter touches her pet—reinforces the argument laid out by both antebellum domestic guides and proslavery advocates that pet keeping is an accurate model for the bonds of domesticity. But the circularity of the engraving also implies that all the figures—woman, child, daughter, and dog—are equal, be-

2. *The Pet Rabbit.*
Engraving by H. S. Sadd, New York. In *Graham's Magazine,*
November 1842.

cause they are all equally dependent upon the conspicuously absent father.

Though the cruelty of the husband in "The Black Cat" can be read as a cynical response to these sentimental representations of the pleasures of domestic subservience, in September 1844 *Graham's* published an engraving based on the British painter William Mulready's popular *The Wolf and the Lamb*

3. True Affection.
Engraving by Rawdon et al. In *Graham's Magazine*, December 1842.

(1820) (fig. 4). Accompanied by an explanatory essay, *Graham's* asserts that the print contains a lesson for "our young readers. Let them study it, and beware lest the unhappy fruits of ungoverned passion embitter their lives." The image offers up a narrative of domestic distress, complete with a cowering pet dog and a child fleeing from the older boys lurking behind a tree, one of whom has his fists clenched (a "young tyrant," as *Graham's* glosses). An unsheathed arrow dropped in the bottom right corner points to the threat of violence yet to come. Though the en-

4. *The Wolf and the Lamb.*
Engraving by J. N. Gimbrede, Rawdon, et al., New York.
In *Graham's Magazine*, September 1844.

graving evades the specter of pet abuse, the enormous tree trunk
in the middle of the image links the human creatures which
surround it to their counterparts in the natural world, while
the shape of the birdcage to the right of the woman's porch is
doubled by that of the nearby dwellings. But in a rhetorical gesture which highlights the dangers of domestic dependency, the
accompanying essay offers a dramatic departure from the engraving by way of a terrifying anecdote: "[a] drayman was cruelly
treating a noble horse. No one interfered, till a pretty woman

went up to the brute (not the horse) and, shaking her finger in his face, said—'You cruel monster! you beat your wife—I know you do!'" ("The Wolf" 140). Here the slippage between animal and human invokes the Hegelian horror of slavery, a dialectic which finally reduces the master to a "brute" or a "monster" and which is ironized in "The Black Cat" when the narrator remarks that the disappearance of his black dependent made him feel like a "freeman" (*CW* 858). Yet this anecdote not only mimics the climactic murder scene in "The Black Cat," when the narrator's wife offers that fatal gesture of "interference" in an attempt to spare the family pet (*CW* 856), but the commentary in *Graham's* also reproduces the same warning as "The Black Cat," for, as our editor grimly concludes, the outraged woman above "reasoned from very good premises, for a man who will be cruel to one dependent, will be to another" ("The Wolf" 140).

Like the southern version of Turner's revolt, "The Black Cat" seems to give us a terrifying example of a crime which challenges the logic of causality and a murderer whose criminality appears mysteriously motiveless. Like Turner, the narrator expresses no remorse, and by offering a confession which crazily collapses the murder of his wife with the slaying of his cat, the narrator begs to be dismissed as a lunatic. Yet this narrative quirk structurally reproduces the rhetoric of inversion and denial which allowed the *Enquirer* to describe rebel slaves as banditti and enabled southerners to indulge their wish that the insurrection was the motiveless work of "a complete fanatic" (Tragle 317). Further, when the narrator attempts to spook us with a black nemesis whose identity is tantalizingly obscure (is the second one-eyed cat a different pet, one of Poe's creepy undead, or the literal return of a shell-shocked creature who failed to die in the first place?), this narrative gesture mimics the dynamics of racial essentialism, which sometimes risks the destruction of individual particularity by predicating the self upon the oft-artificial category of race.[9] At the same time, the cat's mysterious subjectivity mocks the agitation of southerners who feared that every black could suddenly turn (to pun badly) into another Nat Turner; politicians admitted that Turner "had only furthered the 'suspicion attached to every slave,' the 'withering apprehension' that an 'insurgent' might lurk in any neighborhood, in any household" (Freehling 156). But if the South was haunted by Turner, the gothic exaggerations of the narrator's drama with a dark animal whom he owns allow his story to be read as the nightmarish return of the South's inescapable repressions: "I started, hourly, from dreams of unutterable fear, to find the hot breath of *the thing* upon my face, and its vast weight—an incarnate Night-Mare that I had no power to shake off—incumbent eternally upon my *heart*!" (*CW* 856). Figured as both a "creature" and a "*thing*," the cat, like a slave, is variously a beloved "pet," a "beast," a "child," and a "black object" (*CW* 854, 856, 850, 855, 859, 854). While the narrator's bouts of "unutterable fear" invoke the aesthetics of the gothic sublime, his hyperbole recalls that other antebellum "Night-Mare," the one which was embodied "incarnate" in the brutalized body of the slave and inscribed in the condemning words of the slave narrative (*CW* 856). Just as the "informing voice" of a formerly mute creature is that which consigns the narrator "to the hangman" (*CW* 859), the proliferation of slave narratives throughout the antebellum period threatened masters with the accusing voices of their previously muzzled "beasts of burden," in Garrison's metonym for the slave (Douglass 1933). Finally, the "pen-knife" (*CW* 851) which the narrator uses to cut out his pet's eye not only links "violence and the act of writing" (Benfey 36) but also suggests that the narrator imagines his black dependent as a discursive competitor.

Not only is Ingraham's oft-quoted proslavery formula repeated when the narrator tells us that "Pluto—this was the cat's name—was my favorite pet and playmate," but in a devastating mockery of southern sentimentality the narrator adds that "[t]here is something in the unselfish and self-sacrificing love of a brute, which goes directly to the heart of him who has had frequent occasion to test the gossamer fidelity of mere *Man*" (*CW* 850–851, 850). Even the name Pluto recalls one of the few black people to appear in any of Poe's tales—"the old negro called Jupiter" (*CW* 807), who provides a bit of blackface humor in one of Poe's most popular antebellum stories, "The Gold-Bug," published less than two months before "The Black Cat." Like the hero of Goodrich's "Fidelity of a Negro Servant," Jupiter could not be "induced to abandon his young 'Massa,'" though he had previously been "manumitted" (*CW* 807). Further, the associative link between Jupiter and Pluto suggests that Poe may have been reviving the problem of dependency which lies dormant within "The Gold-Bug," but "The Black Cat" radically undermines the sentimental vision of paternal masters and grateful slaves which Poe invokes in this other, only minimally gothic tale. The pet owner in "The Black Cat" degenerates from a child caretaker "noted" for his "docility and humanity" (*CW* 850) to a torturer and a murderer, while the happy dependent of the proslavery imagination not only bites the hand that feeds it, as Pluto first "inflicts a slight wound" upon the narrator's "hand with his teeth" (*CW* 851), but the brutalized animal, like Jupiter's dark double, finally condemns his owner by giving voice to the deeper horrors perpetrated by his master.

With its psychodramas of power and helplessness, "The Black Cat" reproduces the structural inequalities of the antebellum family, a doubling which is manifest when the protagonist is undone by the "scream" of a boughten creature, a dependent whose "cry" sounds suspiciously "like the sobbing of a child" (*CW* 859). As Poe's foray into that most stubborn of "sentiments"—the "spirit of perverseness"—implies (*CW* 852), the romance of dependency can so easily devolve into a horror story of abuse. In accordance with the abolitionist/feminist critique of absolute power, "The Black Cat" highlights the implicit dangers of familial tyranny: "I grew, day by day, more moody, more irritable, more regardless of the feelings of others. I suffered myself to use *intemperate language* to my wife. At length, I even offered her personal violence" (*CW* 851, my emphasis). Drunk with the thrills of petty domestic tyranny, the narrator immediately shifts his attention from wife to pet in a sequence whose crazy logic constitutes a confession that all dependents risk conflation within the brutal hierarchies of antebellum racial and sexual conventions: "[m]y pets, of course, were made to feel the change in my disposition. . . . I made no scruple of maltreating the rabbits, the monkey, or . . . the dog. . . . even Pluto began to experience the effects of my ill-temper" (*CW* 851). And when read against abolitionist children's literature, the hyperbolic description of Pluto's murder in "The Black Cat" convicts the narrator of the same error made by young Caroline in the "The White Kitten with a Black Nose"—the confounding of persons and animals. To kill a cat with "tears streaming" and with "the bitterest remorse at . . . heart," to frame this act as "a sin—a deadly sin" which forever bars the perpetrator from the gates of heaven, is to reenact the deeper sin of slavery—the equating of humans with animals (*CW* 852).

Juxtaposed to the narrator's maudlin account of Pluto's death, his cold-blooded report of his wife's murder reads as an indictment of the dehumanizing effects of both domestic slavery and antebellum family government. In a final gesture of identification, his wife attempts to ward off the fatal ax originally "aimed at the animal," but "[g]oaded by the interference," the narrator "burie[s] the axe in her brain" (*CW* 856). Never graced with a name, the murdered woman dissolves with terrifying speed from a "wife" to a "body" to an "it": the narrator toys with the possibilities of "packing it in a box, as if merchandize," an image which implicitly recalls slavery's commodification of human worth (*CW* 856). In a haunting perversion of the happy positivism of child-rearing manuals, the narrator's early training as a loving pet owner seems to have failed, though these guides insist that pet keeping teaches lifelong "kindness" (Sigourney 35). But as the abolitionist critique of this child-raising formula suggests, the act of keeping a pet may only transform pet owners into tyrannical domestic monsters. While the narrator's putative search for causality seems both gratuitous and perverse, "The Black Cat" needs no Dupin to unravel its secrets, for the cause of the narrator's brutality is walled up within the very structure of inequality upon which antebellum domesticity—and its dark double, domestic slavery—were built.

Like one of Poe's revenants, the specter of racism continues to haunt the Poe canon; even the most tentative perusal of Poe's oeuvre reveals a plethora of racist asides and bigoted formulas. From Robert Carter's angry letter to the *Liberator* denouncing Poe's unabashedly prosouthern puff of the *Southern Literary Messenger* (Thomas and Jackson 521, 520) to the nuanced assessments of contemporary critics, the debate over Poe's relation to proslavery ideology remains one of the most hotly contested issues in Poe scholarship. While the subject demands scrutiny (one more thorough than I can possibly present within the limits of this essay), I invoke this critical specter to suggest not only that "The Black Cat" invites us to deconstruct racist codes as they devolve into sheer horror but that the struggle between absolute dependency and absolute power so central to Poe's gothic fictions might also allow us to reconstruct Poe's vexed affiliation to the rhetoric of the antebellum southern elite. If, as David Leverenz remarks, Poe's work consistently attacks what he calls "gentry fictions of mastery" (212)—and here Leverenz skillfully conflates both the literature of the South as well as those gentry ideologies of aristocratic privilege predicated on the "starkly binary opposition" of "'black' and 'white'" (223)—I would argue that to examine the psychosocial dynamics of race in Poe's fiction is not merely to display the "postabolitionist expectations" (218) of a hopelessly "Yankee" (214) naïveté. Rather, I suggest that the dilemma of race is at the core of Poe's gothic as well as his markedly conflicted attitude toward his own equivocal status as a literary professional.

Take, for example, Poe's distressing praise for Ingraham's *The South-West*, articulated in a review written for the *Southern Literary Messenger*. When confronted by Ingraham's renditions of subhuman, animal-like slaves, Poe asserts that Ingraham "has spoken of slavery as he found it" and "discovered, in a word, that . . . the slave himself is utterly incapable of feeling the *moral* galling of his chain" (122).[10] Yet as unpardonable as this proslavery cliché may be, Poe's pronouncement must also be read in terms of the pressures under which it was produced. In a coincidence which invites us to rethink the strain of writing for the *Messenger* (Poe joined the magazine in August 1835), Thomas Dew's infamous *Review* was published by one T. W. White of Richmond—probably the same T[homas] W[illis] White who would soon launch the *Messenger*. The power struggles between Poe and White which led to Poe's abrupt dismissal from the magazine are notorious; further, the *Messenger* derived much of its support from some of slavery's most prominent apologists, including Dew, Paulding, and Nathaniel Beverley Tucker. When reviewing *The South-West* (a work which Paulding had already singled out for praise in his *Slavery in the United States*), Poe would have known that to be silent about Ingraham's portrait of the South's most crucial institution would be tantamount to professional suicide. As a conspicuously hired hand at the *Messenger*, our insecure young critic obligingly played out his role as mouthpiece for the slaveholding status quo.

At the same time, the act of entering into the editorial persona gave Poe the opportunity to identify with his putative father, John Allan, as well as Allan's circle of Richmond merchant-aristocrats, a class which enthralled Poe throughout his life even as it continued to reject him. And as the disinherited, never legally adopted son of this member of the Virginian elite, Poe was intimately acquainted with the limits of southern paternal benevolence, despite the wishful prose of slavery's apologists. Yet if Poe put up with the indignities of poverty and a marginal social reputation, the daily humiliations of writing for hire continued to chafe. In a letter to Judge Robert T. Conrad soliciting patronage for his ill-fated *Penn Magazine*, Poe takes care to mention that though he imagines his new magazine will be modeled "somewhat on the plan of the Richmond 'Southern Literary Messenger,'" the Poe of the *Messenger* was a counterfeit Poe: "I have been led to make the attempt of establishing it [the *Penn Magazine*] through an earnest yet natural desire of rendering myself independent. . . . So far I have . . . been forced to model my thoughts at the will of men whose imbecility was evident to all but themselves" (Poe, *The Letters* 153–154). Though Stephen Rachman might argue that Poe's plaint is merely a confession of his artistic method (what Rachman convincingly shows is often the practice of plagiarism), I cite this letter for its more prosaic value as an example of the financial burdens under which Poe labored throughout his career (Ostrom, Whalen) and the concomitant ideological encumbrances which clogged the very politicized atmosphere of the antebellum periodical industry.

Further, in Poe's puff of the *Messenger* (*Broadway Journal*,

22 March 1854)—that notice which would so enrage the abolitionist Robert Carter—it is difficult not to hear the sneering
tones of cynicism if not outright parody: Poe outrageously asserts that the *Messenger*'s "subscribers are almost without exception the *élite* . . . of the Southern aristocracy, and its corps of contributors are generally men who control the public opinion of
the Southerners on *all* topics" (qtd. in Thomas and Jackson 520).
While Carter alights on the political threat to "Northern democratic freemen" inherent within Poe's naked appeal to elitism
(Poe is guilty of using "contemptible cunning" in the "alluring
statement, that the supporters of the Messenger are 'the elite of
the Southern aristocracy'"), Carter ignores the parodic implications of Poe's notably overdetermined language, including the
obvious hyperbole contained in Poe's claim that the *Messenger*
"controls" public opinion "on all topics." As Poe's one-time
partner in the *Broadway Journal*, Charles Briggs, would joke
about Carter's complaint: "[t]he Southern Lit[erary] Messenger . . . is as innocent of meaning of any kind as a blank sheet of
paper" (both qtd. in Thomas and Jackson 521–522). Yet when
Carter attacks the *Messenger* for its proslavery slant ("[i]ts principles are of the vilest sort, its aim being to uphold the 'peculiar
institution,' to decry the colored race, [and] to libel abolitionists"), his critique also suggests that Poe may well have had to
conform to the magazine's reigning ideology, an ideology which
for Poe was already fraught with psychological temptation because the assumption of such views was a clear prerequisite to
adoption by the southern elite. I do not mean to excuse Poe's
racism or to force it, still breathing, back into its late unquiet
grave; rather, I wish to suggest that the disjunction between
Poe's proslavery pronouncements and the writer who produced
fiction which plays out the proslavery agenda to its most horrifying conclusions might allow us to imagine a Poe whose relation to race was far more complex than it might at first appear.

Finally, when the narrator invites us into the gothic interior of
his "most wild, yet most homely narrative" (*CW* 849), he does so
in terms which presage the very linguistic contradictions that
enabled Freud to develop a theory of the uncanny.[11] As Freud la-

boriously demonstrates, the word *unheimliche* means both home-like and unhomelike (221–227)—wild yet homely, to paraphrase Poe. "The Black Cat" has already undergone a Freudian analysis of sorts by critics, most notably Marie Bonaparte, and the narra-tor's misogyny seems tailored for Freudian treatment; the vacant eye sockets iterated throughout "The Black Cat" recall Freud's definition of castration anxiety ("the fear of damaging or losing one's eyes"), while Freud's assertion that "the *unheimlich* place" of female sexuality is really the familiar "entrance to the former *Heim* [home] of all human beings" throws the narrator's sexual fears into sharp relief (231, 245). But I make brief reference to Freud's treatment of the uncanny because I'd like to suggest that "The Black Cat" can also be read as the reflection of a collective form of psychosis, a manifestation of what could be called the political uncanny. In Freud's terms, the uncanny is inextricably linked to repression: he defines it as "that class of the frightening which leads back to what is known of old and long familiar" (220). The repeated southern renderings of Turner's revolt as the strange and inexplicable eruption of one person's craziness can thus be read as a form of the political uncanny, whereby southerners turned the event into a gothic horror story precisely because they were actively engaged in repressing the deeper hor-rors at the heart of the peculiar institution, a "familiar" fact of southern life walled up in the cellar of the collective antebellum psyche. To put it another way, when Poe dedicates his *Tales of the Grotesque and Arabesque* (1839) to Colonel William Drayton, au-thor of *The South Vindicated from the Treason and Fanaticism of the Northern Abolitionists* (1836), Poe almost invites us to link the psychological machinery of the American gothic to the political machinations of American racism.[12] Further, if we accept that what often appears to be uncanny is really well known, the seem-ingly uncanny and compulsively repeated scenes of domestic violence throughout "The Black Cat" reveal nothing less than that familiar story of familial abuse, a tale which has its double in the model of domestic slavery. But like the murdered body at the center of "The Black Cat" which refuses to stay buried, the nar-rative itself fails to hide the gruesome remains of antebellum repressions. Thus "The Black Cat" both reproduces and critiques the cultural work of the American gothic.

NOTES

1. Poe, *The Collected Works* 851, 852, 857. Hereafter cited as *CW*. See Marchand, Rosenthal, Sisney, Nelson (90–108), Rowe, and Dayan.

2. Turner had originally planned the revolt for "the 4th July" (see Tragle 310).

3. I am indebted to Marianne Noble for pointing out that the very scene which Goodrich reprints from Sedgwick's *Home* reappears in the opening pages of Maria Cummins's bestseller *The Lamplighter* (Sedgwick 14–27; Cummins 10–12). See also Merish (28–29n9).

4. Quoted with permission of the author.

5. See also Dayan ("Amorous Bondage" 258) and Leverenz (232–233).

6. Compare John Smith's mezzotints (after Kneller); see Belknap (plate XL fig. 48, plate XLI fig. 48A).

7. For more on gender and hairstyles, see Worrell (95).

8. This reading was suggested to me in conversation with Bill Veeder. See also Bonaparte (458–485) and Crisman.

9. For a different yet illuminating treatment of the tension between the universal and the particular as they are played out within and through "The Black Cat," see Elmer (156–64).

10. Attributed to Poe in Thomas and Jackson (185).

11. Compare Madden.

12. Poe's biographers appear quietly baffled by his decision to dedicate the volume to Drayton; Quinn notes the dedication and mentions that according to Drayton family tradition, Poe and the Colonel were friendly. Though Silverman's biography offers an otherwise complete discussion of the prefatory pages to the *Tales of the Grotesque and Arabesque* (the epigraph from Goethe on the title page, the preface by Poe), Silverman oddly omits any mention of the dedication, nor does Drayton appear in his index (see Quinn 129, 275; Silverman, *Edgar A. Poe* 153–154, 175, 545).

WORKS CITED

Belknap, Waldron Phoenix. *American Colonial Painting: Materials for a History*. Cambridge: Belknap Press of Harvard UP, 1959.

Benfey, Christopher. "Poe and the Unreadable." *New Essays on Poe's*

Major Tales. Ed. Kenneth Silverman. Cambridge: Cambridge UP, 1993, 27–44.

Bonaparte, Marie. *The Life and Works of Edgar Allan Poe*. Trans. John Rodker. London: Imago, 1949.

Buckley, Thomas E. "Battered Wives in Antebellum Virginia." Unpublished essay, 1994.

Child, Lydia Maria. *Anti-Slavery Catechism*. 1835. 2nd ed. Newburyport: Charles Whipple, 1839.

———. *The Mother's Book*. 1831. Rpt. New York: Arno, 1972.

Cleman, John. "Irresistible Impulses: Edgar Allan Poe and the Insanity Defense." *American Literature* 64.4 (1991): 623–640.

Crisman, William. "'Mere Household Events' in Poe's 'The Black Cat.'" *Studies in American Fiction* 12 (Spring 1984): 87–90.

Cummins, Maria Susanna. *The Lamplighter*. 1854. Rpt. ed. Nina Baym. New Brunswick: Rutgers UP, 1988.

Dayan, Joan. "Amorous Bondage: Poe, Ladies, and Slaves." *American Literature* 66.2 (1994): 239–273.

———. "Romance and Race." *The Columbia History of the American Novel*. Ed. Emory Elliott et al. New York: Columbia UP, 1991, 89–109.

Dew, Thomas R. *Review of the Debate in the Virginia Legislature of 1831 and 1832*. Richmond: T. W. White, 1832. Rpt. Westport: Greenwood, 1970.

Douglass, Frederick. *Narrative of the Life of Frederick Douglass, an American Slave, Written by Himself*. 1845. Rpt. in *The Norton Anthology of American Literature*. Ed. Nina Baym et al. 4th ed. Vol. 1. New York: Norton, 1994, 1932–1995.

Drayton, William. *The South Vindicated from the Treason and Fanaticism of the Northern Abolitionists*. 1836. Rpt. New York: Greenwood, 1969.

Elmer, Jonathan. *Reading at the Social Limit: Affect, Mass Culture, and Edgar Allan Poe*. Stanford: Stanford UP, 1995.

"Equality." *Merry's Museum and Peter Parley's Magazine* (January 1843): 37–38.

"Fidelity of a Negro Servant." *Merry's Museum and Peter Parley's Magazine* (January 1843): 4.

Fiedler, Leslie A. *Love and Death in the American Novel*. New York: Criterion, 1960.

Fitzhugh, George. *Sociology for the South, or the Failure of Free Society*. 1854. Rpt. in *Antebellum Writings of George Fitzhugh and Hinton*

Rowan Helper on Slavery. Ed. Harvey Wish. New York: Putnam's, 1960.

Freehling, Alison Goodyear. *Drift toward Dissolution: The Virginia Slavery Debate of 1831–1832.* Baton Rouge: Louisiana State UP, 1982.

Freud, Sigmund. "Das Unheimliche" (The uncanny). 1919. *The Standard Edition of the Complete Psychological Works of Sigmund Freud.* Ed. and trans. James Strachey and Anna Freud et al. Vol. 17. London: Hogarth Press, 1962, 218–252.

Goodrich, Samuel G. *Fireside Education.* 6th ed. London: William Smith, 1841.

G[ould], H[annah] F[lagg]. "The Prisoners Set Free." *Juvenile Miscellany* (May–June 1831): 201–210.

———. "The White Kitten with a Black Nose." *Juvenile Miscellany* (January–February 1832): 288–304.

Ingraham, Joseph Holt. *The South-West. By a Yankee.* Vol. 2. New York: Harper, 1835. Rpt. Ann Arbor: University Microfilms, 1966.

Irvine, Alexander. "The Pet Lamb." *Graham's Magazine* (November 1841): 194.

Leverenz, David. "Poe and Gentry Virginia." *The American Face of Edgar Allan Poe.* Ed. Shawn Rosenheim and Stephen Rachman. Baltimore: Johns Hopkins UP, 1995, 210–236.

Madden, Fred. "Poe's 'The Black Cat' and Freud's 'The Uncanny.'" *Literature and Psychology* 39 (1993): 52–62.

Marchand, Ernest. "Poe as Social Critic." 1934. Rpt. in *Edgar Allan Poe: Critical Assessments.* Ed. Graham Clark. Vol. 4. East Sussex: Helm Information, 1991, 104–116.

Matheson, T. J. "Poe's 'The Black Cat' as a Critique of Temperance Literature." *Mosaic* 19.3 (1986): 69–81.

Merish, Lori. "Sentimental Consumption: Harriet Beecher Stowe and the Aesthetics of Middle-Class Ownership." *American Literary History* 8.1 (1996): 1–33.

Nelson, Dana. *The Word in Black and White.* New York: Oxford UP, 1992.

Ostrom, John Ward. "Edgar A. Poe: His Income as Literary Entrepreneur." *Poe Studies* 15.1 (1982): 1–7.

Paulding, James Kirke. *Slavery in the United States.* New York: Harper, 1836.

The Pet Lamb. Engraving. H. S. Sadd, New York. *Graham's Magazine* (November 1841): frontispiece.

The Pet Rabbit. Engraving. H. S. Sadd, New York. *Graham's Magazine* (November 1842): facing 260.

"The Pet Rabbit." *Graham's Magazine* (November 1842): 260.

Poe, Edgar Allan. *The Collected Works of Edgar Allan Poe*. Ed. Thomas Ollive Mabbott. 3 vols. Cambridge: Belknap-Harvard UP, 1969–1978.

———. *The Letters of Edgar Allan Poe*. Ed. John Ward Ostrom. Vol. 1. New York: Gordian, 1966.

Quinn, Arthur Hobson. *Edgar Allan Poe*. New York: Appleton, 1941.

Rachman, Stephen. "'Es lässt sich nicht schreiben': Plagiarism and 'The Man of the Crowd.'" *The American Face of Edgar Allan Poe*. Ed. Shawn Rosenheim and Stephen Rachman. Baltimore: Johns Hopkins UP, 1995, 49–87.

Reynolds, David S. "Poe's Art of Transformation: 'The Cask of Amontillado' in Its Cultural Context." *New Essays on Poe's Major Tales*. Ed. Kenneth Silverman. Cambridge: Cambridge UP, 1993, 93–112.

Rosenheim, Shawn. "Detective Fiction, Psychoanalysis, and the Analytic Sublime." *The American Face of Edgar Allan Poe*. Ed. Shawn Rosenheim and Stephen Rachman. Baltimore: Johns Hopkins UP, 1995, 153–176.

Rosenthal, Bernard. "Poe, Slavery, and the *Southern Literary Messenger*: A Reexamination." *Poe Studies* 7.2 (1974): 29–38.

Rowe, John Carlos. "Poe, Antebellum Slavery, and Modern Criticism." *Poe's Pym: Critical Explorations*. Ed. Richard Kopley. Durham: Duke UP, 1992, 117–138.

Sedgwick, Catharine Maria. *Home*. 15th ed. Boston: James Munroe, 1841.

Sigourney, Lydia Huntley. *Letters to Mothers*. 6th ed. New York, 1845.

Silverman, Kenneth. *Edgar A. Poe: Mournful and Never-ending Remembrance*. New York: Harper Perennial, 1992.

Simpson, Lewis P. "The Mind of the Antebellum South." *The History of Southern Literature*. Ed. Louis D. Rubin, Jr., et al. Baton Rouge: Louisiana State UP, 1985, 164–174.

Sisney, Mary F. "The Power and Horror of Whiteness: Wright and Ellison Respond to Poe." *College Language Association Journal* 29 (September 1985): 82–90.

"The South-West." *Southern Literary Messenger* 2 (January 1836): 122–123.

Stanton, Elizabeth Cady. "Declaration of Sentiments." 1848. Rpt. in

Antebellum American Culture. Ed. David Brion Davis. Lenox: Heath, 1979, 91–93.

Thomas, Dwight, and David K. Jackson. *The Poe Log: A Documentary Life of Edgar Allan Poe, 1809–1849*. Boston: G. K. Hall, 1987.

Tragle, Henry Irving. *The Southampton Slave Revolt of 1831: A Compilation of Source Material*. Amherst: U of Massachusetts P, 1971.

True Affection. Engraving. Rawdon Wright et al. *Graham's Magazine* (December 1842): frontispiece.

Walker, David. *Appeal . . . to the Coloured Citizens of the World*. 1829. Rpt. in *David Walker's Appeal*. Ed. Charles M. Wiltse. New York: Hill and Wang, 1965.

Weld, Theodore Dwight. *American Slavery As It Is: Testimony of a Thousand Witnesses*. 1839. Rpt. New York: Arno, 1968.

Whalen, Terrence. "Edgar Allan Poe and the Horrid Laws of Political Economy." *American Quarterly* 44.3 (1992): 381–417.

The Wolf and the Lamb. Engraving. J. N. Gimbrede et al. *Graham's Magazine* (September 1844): frontispiece.

"The Wolf and the Lamb." *Graham's Magazine* (September 1844): 140.

Worrell, Estelle Ansley. *Children's Costume in America, 1607–1910*. New York: Scribner's, 1980.

ROBERT K. MARTIN

Haunted by Jim Crow
Gothic Fictions by Hawthorne and Faulkner

In his now somewhat outdated but still influential formulation, Harold Bloom argues for an agonistic relationship between the "strong poet" and his predecessors. The task for the belated writer is simultaneously to express admiration and filiation and to mark off difference. The model does not allow for collaboration and simple indebtedness, presumably the characteristic only of weak poets. More importantly, the model assumes the centrality of the heroic individual author without allowing for a larger cultural process of self-creation and citation.

I want to examine two well-known and important American gothic texts, to suggest the ways in which the later text, Faulkner's *Absalom, Absalom!* rewrites the earlier text, Hawthorne's *The House of the Seven Gables*. Of course one way of looking at them might be simply to place them both in the context of the gothic. Indeed, Faulkner's gothicism is often remarked on. As Eric Sundquist has put it, "Which of Faulkner's major works is not an American gothic?" (44). Hawthorne's gothicism, once a commonplace of criticism, is less acknowledged these days, although it is crucial to *The Marble Faun* as well as to *House*. My argument here will be that Hawthorne's drama of "class warfare," as Richard Brodhead has called it (79), conceals other, more troubling conflicts of race and gender that are expressed through gothic elements. In Leslie Fiedler's well-known words, American gothic expresses national "obsessive concerns," especially "the ambiguity of our relationship with Indian and Negro" (xxii), constantly rewriting a masterplot of cultural authority and guilt. Faulkner's reworking of this material (whether taken as a personal or as a cultural act) places into relief the submerged texts of Hawthorne and their significance for the writing of an American history.

The gothic, it seems to be generally agreed, is most often a politically conservative form that gives expression to the anxieties of a class threatened with violent dissolution. On the other hand, the gothic can allow for the voice of the culturally repressed and hence act out a resistance to the dominant culture. This function is particularly striking in African-American adaptations of the genre, where the voice of the dead slave can act as a means of insisting on the presence of history. The references to blackness in *The House of the Seven Gables* are a reminder of that which the new generation wants to forget as it moves away from the house to begin life over again. Hawthorne's gothic text works against his dominant text to recall the anxiety over race and gender in midcentury America, writing a countertext of guilt and endless expiation in the midst of a narrative of redemption.[1] Hawthorne's use of the gothic form is no mere borrowing of its trappings, although they are certainly present. Even if *The House of the Seven Gables*, with its haunted house, doomed family, mysterious lost documents, and hereditary curse, cannot help reminding us of gothic texts such as *The Fall of the House of Usher*, its tensions could suggest a reversal of Poe's famous remark, for *Gables* is distinctly about the terrors of America, if not of Germany. Indeed, it is in part the role of Hawthorne's texts in defining American history that has rendered them so susceptible to rewriting and reinterpretation, from Henry James to John Updike. Hawthorne's gothic enacts the presence of the past, even as his text seeks to deny that past. If the motif of the haunted house central to the gothic is maintained, it is now situated in the heart of commercial Salem, not in a grotesque landscape of the imagination. Among the secrets it conceals is a racial history of slavery which at least in part shifts the novel's theme away from family guilt to national guilt or uses the family as a synecdoche of the nation. The gothic is associated with the past, with the house itself, its gothicism exaggerated as a way of attempting to escape from that tradition. Hawthorne's novel attempts to reclaim the gothic wizard for a new harmonious future, but the very gothic elements he both calls upon and mocks retain a power to haunt.

What links the two texts by Hawthorne and Faulkner is the centrality of the house that stands for a fallen family, the failure of an attempt to inscribe the self in history through possession. Both houses contain a secret, the Indian deed as well as the dead Judge Pyncheon, in Hawthorne's case, and the physical body of Henry Sutpen, standing in for the entire history of forbidden desire and aggression, in Faulkner's. In both cases, the secret of the house is the secret of the family and the sign of the family's participation in a primal crime. Faulkner's reference to Ikkemotubbe, the displaced Indian king (50), makes it clear that Sutpen's claim is as flimsy as that of the Pyncheons. If Faulkner indeed thought of Hawthorne's example as he wrote *Absalom* (and it is of course not necessary to my argument that he should have), it was not, I believe, such generic similarities that would have attracted him most.[2] Rather, what Hawthorne's text reveals, as its own secret, is the story of race in America and of the power of the phallus.

Hawthorne's text was written in the midst of a national—even international—debate over the right to property: private property as opposed to communal property, the right to hold and sell slaves, and the connections between the enslavement of women and that of black Americans.[3] Although the propertyless, like Uncle Venner, are threatened by the poorhouse, *Gables* offers a view of property that suggests the need for better management rather than any radical change, indeed, for a management that can forestall revolution. Holgrave, the Fourierist, will become a wealthy man inheriting, or marrying, property and possessing the woman by a now domesticated phallic power. Although Holgrave is the successor to Hawthorne's scientist/rapist figures, Hawthorne asks us to see him as a new-tamed phallus, domesticated by his "little housewife" (136). It is not that Holgrave lacks the power of the practitioners of black magic from whom he descends but that he chooses not to use it or to accept its service of a new domestic economy. But Hawthorne's text suggests some of the ways in which this shift to a new masculinity would not be total. Hawthorne identifies only two kinds of property—that obtained by legal means, by land grant or purchase, and that obtained by labor. The Maules base their claim to the house on the original work of clearing and building (Maule has "hewn" his land "out of the primeval forest" [7]), but that claim has come to seem weak in mid-nineteenth-century America, where property is bought and sold without any claim to "natural" possession. Even the Pyncheons, rich as they are, find themselves losing out in the new economic marketplace, and the Judge, like the Colonel his ancestor, seeks to find the original land claim. The Colonel had offered to give the Maules back their house in Salem if he can repossess his lands in Maine—his willingness to do so indicates the growth of a capitalist economy in which inheritance plays an increasingly marginal role and is supplanted by colonial mercantilism. That the almost mythic lands in Maine (an "unmeasured tract of eastern lands" [18]) can be claimed only through a missing Indian deed underlines the role of national theft and genocide. These "vast," "unexplored and unmeasured" lands are what remains of the colonial dream of America, the imposition of European property rights on native peoples; they are also a fantasy of the wealth of the "East" that awaits the merchants of Salem.

It is the cultural work of the text to resolve the dilemma of the stolen land, and it does so in a way that evades the issue of the Indian lands by staging a conflict between two white families in the absence of the now dispersed and dispossessed Indians. The two modes of property holding, through labor and through abstract ownership, come together in the marriage of Phoebe and Holgrave. If Hawthorne can acknowledge that aristocracy is based on theft, he quickly moves to resolve that guilt. Marriage between the aristocratic family and the working class makes the wealth of the aristocracy guiltless, as well as provides a new phallic potency which purifies the naked aggression of the earlier patriarchs, both Pyncheon and Maule. By marrying Phoebe, Holgrave, the last of the Maules, will inherit the Pyncheon estate (that is, reassert a male line of succession, in which Phoebe as a *female* Pyncheon is disinherited, as Walter Herbert has remarked [103]) and thereby recuperate the old Maule claim. They will have little need of the house, now that they have the money, which carries no deed and no signature. Capital, not real estate, is the key to the future. The marriage that accomplishes the closure of the novel is not only an act of reconciliation, it is an imagined moment of redemption from history. Phoebe's housekeeping activities have accomplished their goal: there is no longer the grime of history in the house, thereby fulfilling Phoebe's ideological role as the exponent of a domesticity (Pfister 161) that partakes of the Gothic of neither Pyncheon nor Maule. But the light that now penetrates the Pyncheon house also reveals its secrets: by opening the shop, Hepzibah exposes the history of slavery and cannot escape its consequences. At such a moment the sharp difference between Hawthorne and Faulkner becomes visible. For Faulkner there can be no redemption from history, only the suspension of time in death. Similarly, for Faulkner there can be no successful domestication, no Phoebe to let in the sunbeams. It is as if he must insist on the burden, or the nightmare, of history precisely to argue against an American tradition that clings to the possibility of eternal renewal, even as it repeats its gestures of exclusion.

It is not as though Hawthorne were unaware of the stakes. He may misrepresent the meaning of Hepzibah's opening of the shop as "the instant of time when the patrician lady is to be transformed into the plebeian woman" (38), thereby eliding the emergence of the mercantile system and the new middle class. (Phoebe knows how to run a shop, but once she is united with Holgrave she will presumably retire from public life to become the domestic wife. The shop will be closed not, as Hepzibah would have it, to preserve an upper-class claim to the invisibility of money's origins but to prevent any intrusion of the public sphere into the private.) However, Hawthorne locates the commercial exchange at the heart of American history. Hepzibah's first customer (she refuses Holgrave's money) is Ned Higgins, of the new Irish lower middle class, whose shabby dress is "owing to his mother's carelessness"—the renewed Pyncheons and

Maules will surely have better dressed children of careful domestic mothers like Phoebe. And the first transaction is the sale
of a gingerbread Jim Crow.

Slavery, we know, was the mainstay of the Salem economy
and the bartering of human bodies the origin of most New England wealth. Hepzibah's own appearance signals her place in
the economies of sex and race. Her turbaned head is not merely
a "droll parody of Oriental splendor" (Luedtke 190) but an indi-
cation of her status as slave woman, for which the turban was the
accepted sign. By the time of *Gables* slavery had been abolished
in Massachusetts, of course, but the fugitive slave law still required complicity from Massachusetts—it was the only thing
that got Hawthorne excited in opposition to slavery (Mellow
409–410), on which he had highly conflicted views. Hepzibah's
sale of Jim Crow to the voracious boy, who will move on to other
exotic animals, repeats the economics of America and reveals the
hidden sources of northern wealth. That it is the body of the
black that is commodified is made clear by the references to Ned
as a "cannibal." The effect of Hepzibah's transaction is dramatic,
as Hawthorne makes clear: the exchange of money gives her a
"copper stain," the indelible mark of participation in the slave
economy, which for sentimental antislavery writers was inimical
to the family. "The little schoolboy, aided by the impish figure of
the negro dancer, had wrought an irreparable ruin" (51). The
boy and the supposedly comic figure of the black serve as a
return of the (national) repressed and give the lie to the claim
of aristocracy, even more than the ostensible cause of financial
transaction: the aristocracy rests its claims on ownership of land
and on the invisibility of the origins of its gains. Selling Jim
Crow to Ned, Hepzibah is found out. She has clearly opened the
wrong door to the Pyncheon house, as to New England moral-
ity and finance, the one that should always be discreetly shut. Jim
Crow is presented comically in the text, as in the minstrel show
tradition from which he arises, but at the same time his dance,
the sign of the culture's ability to accomplish a reduction of race
to the playful, acts as a reminder of that which has been concealed, of the grounding of New England wealth in the slave
trade. The Jim Crow figure evoked here illustrates the presenta-

tion of the black body as a means of asserting white purity; it is consumed (physically, by Ned) by a white population in the minstrel shows that create a public space for the black and simultaneously contain that black within the confines of an agitated body.[4] The portrayal of the black body as entertainment serves to conceal the black body as labor.

The Jim Crow episode is paralleled by the scene of the street musician. Although it is commonplace to read this scene as an allegory of money or a commentary on popular art and Hawthorne's anxiety about his own declining cultural authority, such a reading, while usefully reminding us of the commercial nature of art despite claims to its purity, also effaces the way in which racial paranoia is built into the urban landscape. Like Ned Higgins, the boy musician is an immigrant set off from the world of the rival New England families, representing another, less idyllic future than that acted out at the end of the novel. Such boys, the text reminds us, "are rather a modern feature of our streets" (162), both a sign of liveliness and activity against the deadly world of the Pyncheon House and too vulgar to be taken seriously. Although it is the immigrant who produces the first level of cultural anxiety in this episode, the text simultaneously raises the stakes by linking the organ grinder and his monkey with the dancing black, Jim Crow. The monkey holds out a "small black palm" in which he receives the "copper coin," virtually the same one that Ned used to buy his Jim Crow. It is not necessary to insist on the monkey as a displaced figure of the black, since such connections were conventional in the period and long after, expressing as they did dismay over theories of evolution.[5] Hawthorne underscores this anxiety by depicting the monkey's "strangely manlike expression" and links it with a new degraded capitalism, "the grossest form of the love of money." Particularly striking about Hawthorne's account is its association of the black/monkey figure with a dangerous and disturbing masculinity, a link already common in the minstrel shows and songs. The obscene play on the monkey's tail and its "preposterous prolixity," which is "too enormous to be decently concealed under his gabardine" (164), gives expression to a fear of cultural and physical impotence (Clifford is a man of "merely delicate endowments" whose tears once again show his femininity) as well as to a possible homoerotic attraction to the phallic black alongside a panic over his possible revolt, what Lee Edelman has memorably called "the essentializing white fantasy of the black male's intensified biological potency and virility, which makes possible the racist reduction of black man to the status of genital part" (Edelman 67). It is not merely that the street musician represents the triumph of a vulgar art of the marketplace, threatening the existence of higher cultural values, but that the musician's monkey insists on the bestiality of such public art, of the display of that which should be private, not only private domestic space but private parts. The dilemma of the text is how to find a new masculinity and fertility that are not threatening. But to evoke that public world of new values and loss of class privilege is, inevitably in the American 1850s, also to evoke the specter of slave revolt imagined in terms of a panicked response to the black phallus. The scene of fascination and horror is one that is repeated throughout Hawthorne's fiction, as the delicate man (Dimmesdale, Coverdale, Owen Warland) watches a display of masculinity with desiring terror.

The gothic embedded narrative in *Gables*, Holgrave's story of Alice Pyncheon, is similarly firmly rooted in the soil of American racism and sexualized power. The story opens with a message from Gervayse Pyncheon to Matthew Maule, brought by Pyncheon's black servant, Scipio. Scipio is not simply an anonymous messenger: the importance of his race is stressed by Holgrave. Scipio speaks in black dialect and identifies himself as that stereotyped "comic" figure, the frightened "poor nigger." Above all, the text insists upon blackness as trope and on Maule's own status as black man, or magician. Scipio says to Maule, "[W]hat for do you look so black at me?" to which Maule replies, "No matter, darkey! Do you think nobody is to look black but yourself?" (188). If Maule employs the derogatory diminutive "darkey," he also sees himself as oppressed, by class if not by race. This claim reminds us that not all whites share the privileges of the Pyncheons (although they can imagine that they could), but at a time before the abolition of slavery (passersby can see "the shining, sable face of a slave" [191] in the windows of the house) a metaphorical reading of "black," like Thoreau's metaphorical reading of "slave," seems problematic. However, the clear analogy between the traffic in slaves and the traffic in women makes the linkage appropriate. Gervayse Pyncheon sells his daughter as he would his slave, and her speech and conduct become the expression of her new mesmerizing master, a voice of the victim seeking revenge, virtually from beyond the grave.

Maule refuses the conventions of class that would have him come to the side door, not the front, and no one is more shocked by this lèse-majesté than Scipio, the servant who, we take it, comes to identify with the masters. Pyncheon himself is willing to accept the lack of manners in the carpenter if only he can obtain the secret of the house, the missing deed. To obtain this he agrees to offer his daughter Alice. The situation is of course similar to that in the main narrative: young Matthew Maule is highly, visibly phallic, with "a long pocket for his rule, the end of which protruded," and a figure that combines "comeliness, strength, and energy" (201). To the declining Pyncheons this new source of power is attractive indeed. Maule the magician can hypnotize the young Alice so that she becomes a creature of his will, just as Holgrave can mesmerize Phoebe. They can become the slaves of love. To be mesmerized is to lose one's self, that is, to be appropriated or dispossessed by a form of possession, much as the slave lost his fundamental property—himself—by being enslaved. Such relations between father and would-be son over the body of a daughter (see the triangular relations in *The Scarlet Letter* and *Blithedale*) were always a source of enormous anxiety for Hawthorne, who worried about Sophia's susceptibility in terms that mark clearly the fear of rape. Hawthorne told Sophia, "[T]he sacredness of an individual is violated by it; there would be an intrusion into the holy of holies—and the intruder would not be thy husband!" (Mellow 190). As Hawthorne's text says of Holgrave, "he could complete his mastery over Phoebe's yet free and virgin spirit" (212). These fears of suggestive power were to be echoed, and rendered more complex, in James's use of the theme in *The Bostonians*, where Selah's control over Verena is then bartered to Olive, who must in turn compete with Basil for the ability to control Verena.

The theme of the two doors, and the refusal to accept one's place, may be fundamental to all stories of class, but the specifics of this story seem clearly echoed in Faulkner's repeated and foundational text of the young Thomas Sutpen as "the boy outside the barred door," the boy who is told "by a nigger to go around to the back" (293). Faulkner attributes much lower-class white prejudice against blacks to such insults, creating a resentment in which the poor whites seek to punish the plantation owners but settle instead on their stand-ins, the servants who execute their orders. Faulkner's rewriting of this primal scene out of the Maules' story thus moves it from a simple tale of class tension by bringing out the racial implications discreetly present in Hawthorne's text. The results, though, are strikingly different: the youngest Maule will seek to marry the last Pyncheon and thus overcome the curse, while the last Sutpens can only yearn for the forbidden black bodies with whose histories they are already intertwined. Faulkner will write no marriage novel in part because the burden of guilt and anger cannot be so easily assuaged and in part because any marriage that can be imagined (Judith and Bon, Henry and Bon, Quentin and Shreve) must be forbidden. It is not that incest is absent in Hawthorne but rather that it is treated (apart from the Beatrice Cenci theme in *The Marble Faun*) in ways that attempt to defuse its power by turning it from gothic to picturesque. Clifford and Hepzibah are essentially lovers, but Hawthorne devotes such energies to mocking Hepzibah's appearance that one forgets her love for her brother. The sterility that in the gothic would be the fated consequence of sexual transgression is now a petering out of erotic energies into a comic vision of a weird couple. They cling to the house, not as the site of their passions but rather as a tomb of forgotten desires.

Although Faulkner carries the exploration of gender much further than Hawthorne, the text of *House* is frequently occupied with the question. Hawthorne rehearses what I consider to be one of his foundational myths—the decline of an artistic male personality linked to the aristocracy in the face of opposition from a more aggressive male figure, allegedly over the possession of a woman. It is Dimmesdale and Chillingworth, Coverdale and Hollingsworth, Donatello and Kenyon, and of course Clifford and Holgrave, as well as Clifford and Judge Pyncheon. In many of these instances, Hawthorne appears to be of two minds: he has a strong identification with the somewhat feminine male whose privilege is disappearing. In *House*, however, he tries to write in support of the new man, or at least of a new man formed in union with the old. The Judge, who recalls Hawthorne's Uncle Robert Manning, is a scientist and horticulturist, breeding fruit of a "rare variety" (272) in a world that links sex and science. Phoebe and Holgrave, unlike the old Pyncheons, represent a "correct" alignment of genders and the consecration of a new domesticity. Hepzibah is deprived of all sexuality, and Clifford is depicted as androgynous (Lee Person calls him "Hawthorne's most feminine male character" [95]).[6] The Malbone portrait reveals in Clifford "feminine traits, moulded inseparably with those of the other sex!" (60) such that the narrator can ask whether he was not "an early lover of Miss Hepzibah." These render him sterile and thus ensure the doom of the Pyncheons against the forces of the phallic Colonel, whose sexual energy had "worn out three wives," and his later-day relative, the Judge, whose wife "got her death-blow in the honey-moon" (123). Holgrave is imagined as a middle ground of limited masculinity who can be contained in his masculinity by the power of the domestic, his "Black Art" now tempered by Phoebe's "natural magic" (71). Phoebe's comment about the miniature quickly warns against carrying Clifford's softness too far: "it is as sweet as a man's face can be, *or ought to be*" (75, my emphasis). It is hard to be certain whether Hawthorne extended his discussion of Clifford's femininity to the concept of his sexual difference, although there is reason to suggest something of that kind. He is the "sport of boys," "insulted by the filth of the public ways, which they would fling upon him" (247–248), in terms that suggest his violent marginalization and indeed echo the fate of sexual criminals and others exposed in the stocks. There can be no room for the refined in a world where production and reproduction are the central concerns.

Faulkner carries gender and sexual difference much further. Sutpen's two "legitimate" children, Judith and Henry, reverse gender expectations, particularly in the fighting scene. Henry runs away "screaming and vomiting," while his sister looks down calmly from the loft (31, 33). This sexual difference runs throughout the text, in Henry's love for Bon and in Quentin's relationship to Shreve. The feminization of the mulatto is a part of racial stereotyping, of course; it allies the feminine Other to the racial Other. Bon is French, or "Frenchified," which is largely the same as feminized, and is seen "reclining in a flowered, almost feminised gown . . . this man handsome elegant and even catlike" (117). The fear of Judith's marriage to Bon is thus in part the fear of a doubled sexual inversion. Given the stress in the critical debate on the question whether Henry kills Bon because he will be committing incest or because he will be committing miscegenation, it is striking that both arguments assume that Henry wants to save Judith. What if we imagine that he must save Bon for himself, by killing him if necessary? As Mr. Compson puts it, "he loved Bon, who seduced him as surely as he seduced Judith" (118). Or, even more tellingly, "Bon not only loved Judith after his fashion but he loved Henry too and I believe in a deeper sense than merely after his fashion. Perhaps in his fatalism he loved Henry the better of the two, seeing perhaps in the sister merely the shadow, the woman vessel with which to consummate the love whose actual object was the youth" (133). Faulkner's insistence on his racial theme here swerves to acknowledge the bisexuality of incest and to see the possibility of reading a doomed interracial love as homosexuality.

The emphasis on stolen land and bartered bodies joins the two texts of Hawthorne and Faulkner as national narratives and originary myths that locate the gothic as a national repressed, a series of crimes that are not incidental to but rather constitutive of the nation. At the same moment in mid-nineteenth-century America Herman Melville was dealing with similar themes in *Pierre*. Here too the inherited wealth is based on an Indian deed, and this fictionality of property is directly connected to the fiction of paternity. Faulkner's reworking of Hawthorne's material not only makes Hawthorne's own themes clearer by exposing them, but it complicates the question of guilt and, above all, like *Pierre*, renders impossible the happy ending of Hawthorne's romance. If for Hawthorne national guilt can be effaced by a wedding and the provision of a sudden fortune, if the gothic can serve as a farewell to such a past and such desires, for Faulkner it is that wedding itself (whatever form it takes, between races, between classes, between genders) that is damned. For Faulkner there can be no way out of this nightmare of murder and hatred, and a rewritten novel of Hawthorne's serves to stress a will-to-unknowing that is itself criminal.

NOTES

1. Sacvan Bercovitch argues that Hawthorne was undisturbed by "Southern slavery [and] Indian genocide" (236). I would argue that the text experiences these issues differently from its author.

2. Richard Chase argues that "the non-Emersonian tradition of Hawthorne and Melville prepared the way for Faulkner by introducing the strain of dark and sombre drama" (220). I would agree with this statement, while attempting to see that "tradition" in its more concrete darkness.

3. There is an excellent account of many of these issues in Walter Benn Michaels.

4. For the Jim Crow tradition, see Lott (on the black body, see 116).

5. Although Darwin did not publish *On the Origin of Species* until 1859, the ideas were already circulating.

6. I am not sure I can agree with Person's assessment that *House* is "the novel in which [Hawthorne] most thoroughly researched alternative gender identities and roles" (95), since that seems to ignore the multiple sexual possibilities of *The Blithedale Romance* and to underestimate the power of gender conservatism in *House*.

WORKS CITED

Bercovitch, Sacvan. *Rites of Assent*. New York: Routledge, 1993.

Bloom, Harold. *The Anxiety of Influence*. New York: Oxford UP, 1973.

Brodhead, Richard. *Hawthorne, Melville and the Novel*. 1976. Rpt.
    Chicago: U of Chicago P, 1982.

Chase, Richard. *The American Novel and Its Tradition*. Garden City:
    Doubleday, 1957.

Edelman, Lee. "The Part for the (W)hole: Baldwin, Homophobia,
    and the Fantasmatics of 'Race.'" *Homographesis: Essays in Gay
    Literary and Cultural Theory*. New York: Routledge, 1994.

Faulkner, William. *Absalom, Absalom!* New ed. New York: Random House, 1986.

Fiedler, Leslie. *Love and Death in the American Novel.* 1960. Rpt. Cleveland: World, 1962.

Hawthorne, Nathaniel. *The House of the Seven Gables.* Ed. Fredson Bowers, Centenary Ed., vol. 2. Columbus: Ohio State UP, 1965.

Herbert, T. Walter. *Dearest Beloved: The Hawthornes and the Making of the Middle-Class Family.* Berkeley: U of California P, 1993.

Lott, Eric. *Love and Theft: Blackface Minstrelsy and the American Working Class.* New York: Oxford UP, 1993.

Luedtke, Luther S. *Nathaniel Hawthorne and the Romance of the Orient.* Bloomington: Indiana UP, 1989.

Mellow, James R. *Nathaniel Hawthorne in His Times.* Boston: Houghton Mifflin, 1980.

Michaels, Walter Benn. "Romance and Real Estate." *The American Renaissance Reconsidered.* Ed. Michaels and Donald E. Pease. Baltimore: Johns Hopkins UP, 1985.

Person, Leland S. *Aesthetic Headaches: Women and a Masculine Poetics in Poe, Melville, and Hawthorne.* Athens: U of Georgia P, 1988.

Pfister, Joel. *The Production of Personal Life: Class, Gender, and the Psychological in Hawthorne's Fiction.* Stanford: Stanford UP, 1991.

Sundquist, Eric. *Faulkner: The House Divided.* Baltimore: Johns Hopkins UP, 1983.

GEORGE PIGGFORD

Looking into Black Skulls
American Gothic, the Revolutionary Theatre, and Amiri Baraka's *Dutchman*

Amiri Baraka's one-act play *Dutchman* (1964) utilizes gothic conventions—the macabre setting of a haunted subway car "[i]n the flying underbelly" of Manhattan (Baraka, *Dutchman* 3); a quasi-supernatural seductress who is closely related to the mythical Adam's malign, vampiric first wife, Lilith (Sollors 137); and discourses that thematize the "unspeakable" sins of incest and parricide.[1] It has, however, not been read as exemplary of the American gothic tradition.

This seems true for at least three reasons. First, while both Leslie Fiedler's classic examination of American gothic in *Love and Death in the American Novel* (1960) and Baraka's play associate "the Negro problem in the United States . . . [with] the gothic horror of our daily lives" (Fiedler 493), Fiedler's study focuses mainly on the trope of blackness utilized in the writing of *white* Americans. Baraka's text, by contrast, thematizes the trope of whiteness in the black imagination. In Baraka's writing, it is the blacks who are being terrorized, not the whites. Second, Fiedler asserts that only in fiction does American gothic reach "the level of important art" (Fiedler 142), rather than in poetry or drama. Although the plays of Adrienne Kennedy, particularly her *Funnyhouse of a Negro* (1962), have been examined as gothic (Blau 531), readings of the African-American gothic tradition have focused almost exclusively on fiction or, more recently, the "nonfictional" slave narrative.[2] Third, even though Baraka's

Dutchman explores both "the theme of slavery and black revenge," which is, according to Fiedler, the essential sociological
theme of the American tale of terror, and that of incest, which is
its "essential erotic theme" (Fiedler 414), the Black Power political project which informs these themes in Baraka's text has been
criticized for its emphasis on polemics over aesthetics.[3]

Houston Baker has rightly observed that "the radical chic
denizens of bohemia and the casual liberals of the academy"
(Baker 91) have never recognized Baraka's achievement as a
playwright and a poet because his "brilliantly projected conception of black as country—a separate and progressive nation with
values antithetical to those of white America—stands in marked
contrast to the ideas set forth by Baldwin, Wright, Ellison, and
others in the fifties" (Baker 106).[4] That is, according to the
integrationist politics that continue to dominate discussions of
race in the United States, what we might in the 1990s call
the "African-American problem" is indeed seen as the *African-
American's problem* to examine and solve, not the white's. Baraka's
Black Power political agenda, which perceives the United States
as a society at least as black as it is white (Baraka, *Home* 85), a
country built on the gothic horror of slavery and its concomitant
"oppression and destruction" (Baker 106), stands in marked contrast to the general integrationist bent of American racial politics. The call to revolutionary action inscribed into his drama
demands an inversion of both the American social system and its
gothic tradition.

Dutchman amply illustrates the persistence of racial tension in
the United States in the 1960s and represents an emerging militant attitude on the part of American blacks and on the part of
black American playwrights.[5] Baraka himself has claimed that his
play is an early example of the "Revolutionary Theatre," a theater, like Artaud's "theatre of cruelty," that "should force change;
it should be change" (Baraka, *Home* 210).[6] Baraka continues:

> The Revolutionary Theatre must EXPOSE! Show up the insides
> of these humans, look into black skulls. White men will cower
> before this theatre because it hates them. Because they them-
> selves have been trained to hate. The Revolutionary Theatre

must hate them for hating. For presuming with their technology to deny the supremacy of the Spirit. They will all die because of this. (Baraka, *Home* 210–211)

Baraka's strong words point emphatically toward the end of this theater: a revolutionary change in social structures beginning with an examination of the black psyche. This will allow the ghosts of the past, the "white terror," to emerge from black skulls and eventually be dispelled.

The idea that theatrical performance should attempt to force social change was initially articulated by Antonin Artaud in *The Theatre and Its Double*: "our present social state is iniquitous and should be destroyed. If this is a fact for theatre to be concerned with, it is even more a matter for machine guns" (Artaud 42). Theatrical groups such as Julian Beck and Judith Malina's Living Theatre, founded in 1951, attempted to put Artaud's theories into practice. For the directors and performers of the Living Theatre, "[l]ife, revolution and theatre are three words for the same thing: an unconditional NO to the present society" (Beck, qtd. in Shank 9).[7] The black Revolutionary Theatre represents an attempt to racialize the Artaudian "theatre of cruelty" by instigating its audience to act in revolutionary and violent ways to overthrow the dominant white American social order; this order is analogous to the remnant of an aristocratic past typically found in gothic texts that haunts the minds of those attempting to overcome its ordering structures.[8]

For Baraka the theater of which *Dutchman* is an example is centrally political; it will ultimately lead to the (at least) symbolic death of the white race, the murder of the white specter that continues to frighten blacks into submission and silence.[9] It is also, however, a psychological study, though one that exposes the limitations of the psychoanalytic process. As Samuel Hay states it, "[b]lack Revolutionary drama deconstructed both Outer Life *and* Inner Life" (Hay 97). In *Dutchman*, Baraka attempts to psychoanalyze the black male in America, typified by the character Clay. His technique is meant to lay bare the social forces which make black men into neurotic subjects; for blacks the nightmare of racial imbalance needs to be drawn from the unconscious mind and diagnosed.[10] His cure for their neurosis is race revolution and mass murder.

Frantz Fanon, in *Black Skin, White Masks*, extols the power of *language* rather than political activism to solve what he terms the "color problem," suggesting that this problem exists primarily in language itself: "[f]rom all sides dozens and hundreds of pages assail me and try to impose their wills on me. But a single line would be enough. Supply a single answer and the color problem would be stripped of all its importance" (Fanon 10). Fanon implies in this passage that if language is transformed, if the answer to this "problem" is found, then the issue of race will simply disappear, the specter will be exorcised. This assumption is based on Fanon's naive trust in the Freudian psychoanalytic method.[11] Freudian psychoanalysis asserts that one can solve psychological problems through language in a similar way, by making unconscious desires conscious through therapy. The surfacing of a psychological disorder in the conscious mind of the patient through the linguistic give-and-take of psychotherapy should, according to Freud, cure the disorder. He makes this clear in *Dora*: "the practical aim of . . . treatment is to remove all possible symptoms and to replace them by *conscious thoughts*" (Freud 32, my emphasis).

Fanon's approach to the "color problem" reproduces Freud's method within a sociological frame: "I believe that only a psychoanalytical interpretation of the black problem can lay bare the anomalies of affect that are responsible for the structure of the complex" (Fanon 12); by psychoanalyzing the black man as an idea, Fanon hopes to "destroy" the "massive psychoexistential complex" that underlies the juxtaposition of the white and black races "*by analyzing it*" (Fanon 14, my emphasis). Like Freud, Fanon assumes that by making this "psychoexistential complex" conscious, he will eradicate it. *Dutchman* as historical text demonstrates that Fanon's solution was overly optimistic: the problems associated with black and white race relations did not evaporate in the decade between the publication of Fanon's book and the first performance of Baraka's play; indeed, they had multiplied and intensified. Baraka's text explores the gothic themes of incest and parricide by looking "into black skulls" and is in this way similar to a Freudian case study like *Dora*: it provides a thematization of the ways in which race, gender, and sexuality are constructed in American social consciousness.

However, Baraka, unlike Fanon, does not attempt to understand the "color problem" in order to solve it through a psychoanalytic sleight-of-hand; rather, his gothic exposition of the situation of blacks in American culture is geared to an ultimate destruction of that culture: "[t]he Revolutionary Theatre, which is now peopled with victims, will soon begin to be peopled with new kinds of heroes. . . . [T]hese will be new men, new heroes, and their enemies most of you who are reading this" (Baraka, *Home* 214–215). *Dutchman*'s Clay is presented as an example of the "victims" which people the Revolutionary Theatre; he is identifiable as a Faustian antihero rather than a hero. But Baraka's intentions are clear: Clay, characterized primarily by his repressed desires to rape and murder whites, is martyred for the black revolutionary cause; he embodies Baraka's attempt to rid the black psyche of the nightmare of whiteness.

If, as Elizabeth MacAndrew has so famously contended, "[g]othic . . . is a literature of nightmare" (MacAndrew 3), then it is within the "dreamlike" atmosphere of *Dutchman* that the text's antihero, Clay, moves from a state of repression to one of acceptance of his unconscious desires. Indeed, the play encourages its black audience members to do likewise and warns its white viewers that the revolution is coming. Though he eventually expresses his desire to "[m]urder" (Baraka, *Dutchman* 35), Clay refuses to act on this impulse; indeed, it is the white Lula who will murder him. Clay dies at Lula's hands, then, as a self-aware but impotent and castrated subject. Lula functions in *Dutchman* as both Clay's mother and his demonic psychotherapist by bringing Clay's repressed desires to the surface of his consciousness. Through her verbal taunting she eventually peers into Clay's "black skull" and finds his murderous unconscious impulses.

A dutchman, "the theatrical term meaning a strip of cloth used to hid[e] the crack between the seams of flats, or, in a more general sense, a contrivance used to hide a defect of some kind" (Tener 17), connotes something impermanently and fragilely held together, but something that provides the illusion of solidity and permanence. The title *Dutchman* can be understood in this way as a metaphor for "the meretricious façade of civility" (Ralph 58) utilized by Clay both in his dress and in his language to hide his murderous inner desires.[12] It is this façade that Lula relentlessly strips away, as a psychoanalytic therapist might, attempting to access Clay's unconscious by getting behind "whatever surface his unconscious happens to be presenting to his notice at that moment" (Freud 27), by asking him leading questions about his innermost thoughts. Toward the end of scene 1 Lula informs Clay, "You're a murderer, Clay, and you know it," and, anticipating his denial, continues, "You know goddamn well what I mean." The still-repressive Clay uncertainly responds to this accusation with a questioning "I do?" (Baraka, *Dutchman* 21). Lula's pronouncement of Clay's desire to murder whites is based on the assumption that all black men are secretly murderers, and she successfully proves this theory by bringing out the— at least potential—murderer in Clay. This is Clay's innermost "defect," the secret buried in his unconscious mind. In terms of the text's use of gothic conventions, murder is his as yet uncommitted sin, made unspeakable through its repression in Clay's psyche.

Though Lula suggests that Clay is "too serious to be psychoanalyzed" (Baraka, *Dutchman* 28), her comment can only be read as ironic, for she proceeds successfully to psychoanalyze him. As Sherley Anne Williams has correctly observed, "Lula . . . control[s] the situation. *She* picks Clay up. *She* encourages him. And it is she who goads him into revealing things which must have been carefully hidden deep in the most secret places of his heart" (Williams 140). When Lula makes her diagnosis, when she reveals Clay's inner self to him, he resists coming to terms with his own murderous "pumping black heart" (Baraka, *Dutchman* 34):

LULA. . . . Clay. Clay, you got to break out. Don't just sit there dying the way they want you to die. Get up.
CLAY. Oh, sit the fuck down. Sit down, goddamn it.

LULA. Screw yourself, Uncle Tom. Thomas Woolly-head . . .
CLAY. Lula! Lula! Lula . . . you dumb bitch. Why don't you
stop it? (Baraka, *Dutchman* 32)

But she eventually goads him into disclosing his "neurosis":

LULA. You're afraid of white people. And your father was.
Uncle Tom Big Lip!
CLAY. Now shut up and let me talk. Shit, you don't have
any sense, Lula nor feelings either. I could murder you
now. . . . It takes no great effort. . . . Just let me bleed
you, you loud whore. . . . A whole people of neurotics,
struggling to keep from being sane. And the only thing
that would cure the neurosis would be your murder.
Simple as that. I mean if I murdered you, then other
white people would begin to understand me. You
understand? No. . . . Murder. Just murder! Would make
us all sane. (Baraka, *Dutchman* 33–35)

Clay's insanity, according to his newly discovered understanding
of it, is a byproduct of the neurotic, *white* culture which insists
that he hide his inner feelings while it goads him into revealing
them. His neurosis is simply the neurosis endemic to being a
black man living in a nightmare that for him is American culture.
In the above passage, he imagines a utopic space where this neurosis would be eliminated in the act of black revenge for his castration at the hands of whites.

But, even after revealing his inner nature, Clay embraces
the essential repressiveness of his social and cultural situation:
"Ahhh. Shit. But who needs it? I'd rather be a fool. Insane"
(Baraka, *Dutchman* 35). Unlike a Freudian case study and unlike
Fanon's approach to the "color problem," Baraka's text does not
provide a cure to the horrors of the situation of blacks in American society through an understanding of it. Though Fanon's
"single answer" to the "color problem" (Fanon 10) is articulated
by Clay, and that answer is "murder," the problem is not eliminated. For Baraka, a public expression of this answer is a necessary first step, but it is not—as Fanon wrongly assumed—the
revolution itself. Even Freud acknowledges that the efficacy of

psychoanalysis is limited by "the patient's own will and under-standing" (Freud 131), and it is Clay's own desire to remain an "Uncle Tom" that forecloses the possibility of his becoming an actual murderer, at least for the moment.[13]

But, by goading Clay into revealing his unconscious wishes, Lula has produced a self-conscious potential murderer, one who might pose a threat to white society sometime in the future. She has pointed out to Clay his hidden identity: he is a middle-class black, which she identifies with the insulting label "Uncle Tom"; simultaneously, he is a potential revolutionary who wants to murder her. As one Freudian critic explains, "Lula mocks Clay and accuses him of being an Uncle Tom . . . whereas Clay would like to see himself as a black revolutionary. The truth, however, is that he is neither one nor the other, and, hence, feels a real lack of identity" (Phillips 212). This lack can be understood meta-phorically in Freudian terms as evidence of Clay's "castration" by white society, represented ultimately by Lula's murder of Clay with a suspiciously phallic knife. Indeed, Lula indicates clearly to Clay that their entire dialogue is about Clay's status as a man:

> LULA. . . . we'll talk endlessly, endlessly.
> CLAY. About what?
> LULA. About what? About your manhood, what do you think we've been talking about all this time?
> CLAY. Well, I didn't know it was that. That's for sure. Every other thing in the world but that. (Baraka, *Dutchman* 25)

Numerous critics have pointed to Clay's "emasculated life" (Lindberg 141) and have discussed his "castration" at the hands of Lula (Benston 131; Williams 136). Lula's power over Clay is based on what seems to be her uncanny knowledge of him, but when Clay says to her, "Hey, you . . . haven't told me how you know so much about me," Lula responds, "I told you I didn't know anything about *you* . . . you're a well-known type" (Baraka, *Dutchman* 12). *Dutchman* therefore adheres to the pattern of a Freudian case study, in which the neurosis of a particular indi-vidual typifies a general kind of neurosis that can be treated fol-lowing the methods of a particular case.

Lula and Clay are both lovers and mother and son, suggesting that Fiedler's conception of the two themes central to the American gothic, black revenge and incest, are crucial also to Baraka's play. "Clay and Lula are the primordial parents fused in a violent sexual encounter; and in keeping with the fluid identifications of primal scene fantasies, they are also mother and son. Clay's expulsion from the car [after his murder] suggests an image of violent birth" (Weisgram 217). This situation places the two characters in the conventionally gothic position of incestuous seduction. The text raises the issue of incest when Lula tells Clay, "You tried to make it with your sister when you were ten. But I succeeded a few weeks ago" (Baraka, *Dutchman* 9). Not only does this statement suggest "an unconscious incestuous union" (Weisgram 217) between Clay and Lula, but it also places Lula securely in the phallic position in their relationship. After all, Lula is the one who "made it," a phrase used both for Clay's failed attempt and implicitly for Lula's successful attempt to penetrate Clay's sister.

In order to prepare Clay for his death/birth at the end of the text, Lula, playing her part of white phallic mother, even teaches him his proper lines, his proper role, as a mother would instruct her son. But she teaches him the exact words he should use to commence a seduction of her:

LULA. Now you say to me, "Lula, Lula, why don't you go to this party with me tonight?" It's your turn, and let those be your lines.
CLAY. Lula, why don't you go to this party with me tonight, huh?
LULA. Say my name twice before you ask, and no huh's.
CLAY. Lula, Lula, why don't you go to this party with me tonight? (Baraka, *Dutchman* 16)

In this way, Lula teaches Clay to speak in her words, requiring that he merely parrot the lines fed to him by her. This interaction generally parallels what Freud has termed "parental seduction" (qtd. in Kristeva 277); Lula, the mother/lover, attempts to seduce Clay the son/lover, though her seduction will not lead to sexual union but to her murder of Clay. This seduction scene,

with its overtones of miscegenation, suggests what has traditionally been perceived as the horrifying possibility of an incestuous
union between races; Baraka here explores the horror of the sexual aspect of the politics of integration.

According to Baraka, in "American Sexual Reference: Black
Male," "white women become men-things, a weird combination, sucking the male juices to build a navel orange, which is
themselves" (Baraka, *Home* 216). White women are forced to
play this vampiric role because white men have become castrated
and feminine: "[m]ost American white men are trained to be
fags," an identification he associates with powerlessness, femaleness, and therefore castration.[14] He associates the mutilation of
genitals that often accompanied the lynching of black men with
an attempt to remove "the threat of the black man asserting his
manness" (Baraka, *Home* 230), that is, the threat of black men
raping white women, the revenge of black Americans for the
horrifying oppressions of slavery. "America," he asserts, "has always tried to . . . make [the black man] swallow his manhood"
(Baraka, *Home* 230). White women, Baraka claims, are both re-
pulsed by and attracted to black men as sexual identities. The
feelings of black men are mutual: "[f]or the black man, acquisition of a white woman always signified some special power the
black man had managed to obtain in white society" (Baraka,
Home 223).[15] The relationship between black men and white
women can therefore be contextualized in terms of seduction.
Understood in this way, however, the seduction between Lula
and Clay must be in some sense mutual.

One way to make sense of the relationship between Lula and
Clay in *Dutchman* is found in a reading of the text as an internal
conflict. Certainly the "dreamlike" quality of the text noted
above supports a reading of the play as a representation of an
identity crisis experienced within Clay's psyche. At least one
Freudian analysis views Baraka's play as "a play which exemplifies the function of the id, and . . . its so-called 'absurdity'
and 'obscenity' are reflections of its function" (Adams 116).
From this perspective, Lula and Clay become manifestations of
Clay's split self. *Dutchman* raises the possibility that Lula was a
hidden aspect of Clay's own "black skull," an intrinsic part of

Clay's own psyche. Lula is both separate from and a part of Clay, much as white and black America are both distinct and inseparable. Lula can be understood in this text as what bell hooks has discussed—in an inversion of Fiedler's reading of American gothic—as "the representation of whiteness as terrorizing" (hooks 341) in the consciousness of black Americans.[16] Understood in this way, Baraka's play implicitly rejects Fiedler's color-blind metanarrative and suggests that the terror of whiteness must be removed from black skulls before it can be removed from society through political action.

This reading is supported by Julia Kristeva's retheorizing of Freud's notion of parental seduction. According to Kristeva, this seduction happens only in the realm of the imaginary, as a result of an individual's repressed wish *to have been seduced* by his parent: "[w]e thus come to the shaping of this image of the child-parent, the seducing child, a child always already older, born into the world with compound drives, erogenous zones, and even genital desires" (Kristeva 275). This understanding of parental seduction can be associated metaphorically with Baraka's notion of the relationship between white women and black men. Black men want both to murder and to seduce their phallic mothers, the white women who are made "men-things" by American society; for Baraka, as for Fiedler, black men seek both revenge and incestuous union. But for Kristeva this desire exists primarily within an individual psyche: "through the seduction myth, [the child] sees itself as being attached by drive . . . to this object of love" (Kristeva 277)—its phallic mother. This mother is, however, simply an idea generated in the mind of the "child"; she is a "type" rather than a "real" individual.

The dumb show presented before the dialogue begins in *Dutchman* supports the plausibility of this reading:

The man [Clay] looks idly up, until he sees a woman's face staring at him through the window; when it realizes that the man has noticed the face, it begins very premeditatedly to smile. The man smiles too, for a moment, without a trace of self-consciousness. Almost an instinctive though undesirable response. Then a kind of awkwardness or embarrassment

sets in, and the man makes to look away, is further embar-
rassed, so he brings back his eyes to where the face was, but
by now . . . the face would seem to be left behind. (Baraka,
Dutchman 4)

This scene parallels a Lacanian/Kristevan "mirror stage," where
"the Same sees itself altered through the well-known opening
that constitutes it as a representation, sign, and death" (Kristeva
283). In this reading, Lula becomes a "return of the repressed,"
a reenactment of a primal scene in which the subjectivity of Clay
took on identity through the perception of an Other—in this
case his own internalized terror of whiteness—within his own
imagination. Importantly, this entire exchange occurs in the
mise-en-scène of the play, rather than in its relatively naturalistic dialogue.[17]

If *Dutchman* can be understood as an internal conflict, a
dream, it is a dream in which the binaries black and white, male
and female, become contextualized in the individual psyche of
one person.[18] Blackness signifies in this text virtue and naïveté,
whiteness vice and disingenuousness. Maleness signifies castration and femaleness phallic power. The text inverts the significations of the tropes of whiteness and blackness found in most
American gothic.[19] The relationship of these significations to the
themes of incest and parricide, particularly patricide, is made
clear by Clay:

> CLAY. . . . tell this to your father, who's probably the kind of
> man who needs to know at once. So he can plan ahead.
> Tell him not to preach so much rationalism and cold logic
> to these niggers. Let them alone. . . . Don't make the
> mistake, through some irresponsible surge of Christian
> charity, of talking too much about the advantages of
> Western rationalism, or the great intellectual legacy of
> the white man, or maybe they'll begin to listen. And then,
> maybe one day, you'll find they actually do understand
> exactly what you are talking about, all these fantasy
> people. . . . And on that day, as sure as shit, when you
> really believe you can "accept" them into your fold, as
> half-white trustees late of the subject people . . . [t]hey'll

murder you, and have very rational explanations. Very
much like your own. They'll cut your throats, and
drag you to the edge of your cities so the flesh can fall
away from your bones, in sanitary isolation. (Baraka,
Dutchman 36)

Clay's desires are clear: he wants to murder the white father. The
character Clay, himself a castrated, "half-white trustee," here reveals a gothic vision of race revolution and murder, an inversion
of the dominant structure of power. First he will purge the internalized whiteness from his own psyche (the seductive phallic
mother, in Kristeva's terms), then murder the white father who
controls the social structures of racial domination.

Clay's apocalyptic vision also evokes the hellish atmosphere of
Baraka's novel *The System of Dante's Hell*, his exploration of a particularly middle-class black nightmare. While the representation
of a gothic antihero like Clay is a necessary step in the history of
black Revolutionary Theatre, Baraka's attitude toward this neurotic black is expressed in his contemporaneous novel: "I put the
heretics in the deepest part of hell, though Dante had them
spared, on higher ground. It is heresy against one's own sources,
running in terror, from one's deepest responses and insights . . .
that I see as basest evil" (Baraka, *System* 7). *Dutchman*, then, examines the "skull" of a repressed middle-class black in order to
expose the "gothic horror" of his daily life, his personal hell. It
also functions as a warning—both to "heretical" blacks like Clay
who help support the gothic nightmare of black oppression
through inaction and to whites like Fiedler—*that the revolution
is coming*. By exposing the horror of race relations in America
through the gothic case study *Dutchman*, Baraka both diagnoses
the problem in American society—white dominance—and pre-
scribes his cure: race revolution and murder.

NOTES

This essay was published in a different form in *Modern Drama* 40
(1997): 74–85.

   1. The author of *Dutchman* was born Everett LeRoy Jones on October 7, 1934. He published widely under the name LeRoi Jones until
1967, when he rechristened himself Imamu Ameer Baraka, later Imamu

Amiri Baraka, then simply Amiri Baraka. For simplicity, this text will refer to Jones/Baraka as Amiri Baraka, his current name of choice.

Dutchman was originally produced by Theatre 1964 in New York at the Cherry Lane Theatre. It opened on March 24, 1964 (Baraka, *Dutchman* 2). The title refers to the traditional "ghost story" of *The Flying Dutchman*, according to Baraka (Baraka, *Autobiography* 187), but it also suggests the theatrical term "dutchman" (see below).

2. See, for example, Ladell Payne's *Black Novelists and the Southern Literary Tradition* and Kari Winter's important *Subjects of Slavery, Agents of Change: Women and Power in Gothic Novels and Slave Narratives*.

3. Susan Sontag, in her review of *Dutchman* in "Going to the theatre, etc.," argues that the polemics of the play undermine its success as drama. For example, Lula's murder of Clay seems "crude (dramatically), tacked on, willed" (152).

4. But see also Henry Louis Gates, who has argued that black critics of the status quo like Baraka employed "blackness-as-theme to forward one argument or another for the amelioration of the Afro-American's social dilemma. Yet the critical activity altered little, whether that message was integration or whether it was militant separatism. Message was the medium; message reigned supreme; form became a mere convenience or, worse, a contrivance" (31).

5. See Hay (78–99) for a discussion of the transformation of the African American protest drama of W. E. B. DuBois, which viewed theater as an integrationist "political weapon" (80), into the separatist black Revolutionary Theatre of the 1960s, which "no longer represented appeals to share power" but depicted "seizures of power" (96).

6. It is important to emphasize the fact that *Dutchman* is an early, if not the earliest example of the black Revolutionary Theatre. Like James Baldwin's *Blues for Mister Charlie*, which was first performed one month prior to the opening of *Dutchman*, Baraka's play attempts to psychoanalyze the African American male as type (see below), and it asserts the notion that "burning all bridges to white liberals is the first step toward liberation" (Hay 95; see 91–97).

7. See Shank (8–11) for an examination of the reliance of the Open Theatre on Artaud's *Theatre and Its Double*.

8. See Kaufman (192–197).

9. Baraka's *The Slave* dramatizes this revolution in a more direct way than *Dutchman* presents it. Throughout *The Slave*, "explosions . . . continue, sometimes close, sometimes very far away, throughout both acts, and well after the curtain of each act" (Baraka, *Slave* 41), an atmosphere

which makes Baraka's hoped-for race war an immediate "reality" for its audience. For Kaufman, however, *The Slave* "is neither ideologically nor formally a revolutionary play," and one might infer that he does not perceive Baraka's early dramas, including *Dutchman*, as examples of black Revolutionary Theatre since they do not exhibit the "self-conscious emphasis on techniques and values that clearly affirm a course of political action and offer unambiguous moral judgments and self-clarification to their audience" (197) which for him characterizes the black Revolutionary Theatre. Both Hay and Baraka himself argue for a broader definition of this theater.

10. According to Hay, the protest theater convention that "characters personify issues" (Hay 90) was perfected in Loften Mitchell's *A Land beyond the River* (1957), and this convention was adopted by Baraka's Revolutionary Theatre.

11. Fanon was not the only black thinker of this period to apply Freud's psychoanalytic method to the larger sociological field of race and its significations. See, for example, Dominique O. Mannoni, *Prospero and Caliban: The Psychology of Colonisation* (New York: Praeger, 1964).

12. The critic Gerald Early has suggested that the history of Baraka's career has been one of psychological exploration hidden behind various façades, so that Baraka's work "seems no longer to be responding to the world at all but to [his] previous selves"; his entire oeuvre can be understood, according to Early, as "an elaborate form of solipsism" (346).

13. Clay's understanding of the idea of murder is, as Sollors has asserted, an inversion of the attitude of Bigger Thomas in Richard Wright's *Native Son*: "whereas Bigger sees the 'act' of murder (if only by accident) as a perverted form of creativity, as the only 'artistic' endeavor his society leaves open for him, Clay sees art as a neurotic perversion of violence, and violence as the only act which would restore the Black man's sanity" (127).

14. This identification exists at odds with Baraka's more conflicted understanding of homosexuality in his play *The Toilet*, which was running off Broadway at the same time as *Dutchman*. In that text, the mutual homosexual desire between a black student gang leader (Foots) and a white student (Karolis) is treated with complexity and sympathy. After Foots's gang beats up Karolis for sending Foots a "love letter" (though it may have been Foots himself who sent the note), Foots, alone with Karolis, "kneels before the body, weeping and cradling the head in his arms" (Baraka, *The Toilet* 62). In "American Sexual Reference," however, Baraka's simplistic (and often misogynistic and homo-

phobic) discussion of the gender/race system reinscribes the binaristic constructions of male/female, white/black, heterosexual/homosexual. Baraka strives to invert these binaries; he does not challenge the over-arching binaristic system, which privileges one (albeit arbitrary) cate-gory over another. See Edelman for a useful deconstruction of Baraka's "homophobic logic," which "can conclude that 'white racism' equals 'homosexuality' insofar as each of those terms individually can be rep-resented as equal to 'castration'" (55). Edelman points out, in contrast to such logic, that "white racists (literally) *castrate others* while homo-sexuals (figuratively) *castrate themselves*. Though both, in a given cul-tural calculation, may be 'equal' to castration, and therefore 'equal' to each other as well, 'white racism' and 'homosexuality' stand *opposed* to one another when the copular that specifies their status vis-à-vis castra-tion is articulated in the grammatical terms of an active/passive bina-rism" (56, last emphasis mine).

15. Fanon associates this power with the "whitening" of the black man: "[o]ut of the blackest part of my soul . . . surges this desire to be suddenly *white*. I wish to be acknowledged not as *black* but as *white*. Now . . . who but a white woman can do this for me? By loving me she proves that I am worthy of white love. I am loved like a white man" (63).

16. See also Mary Sisney's "The Power and Horror of Whiteness: Wright and Ellison Respond to Poe," which discusses "the horror of whiteness" (Sisney 87) in the fiction of Wright and Ellison.

17. Edward Albee's *Zoo Story* stages a similar naturalistic dialogue which moves through the process of a mutual seduction between two characters (both male), which articulates a pointed social critique, and which ends in murder. As in *Dutchman*, the naturalism of Albee's play is undermined by its sparse and symbolic mise-en-scène. Both plays might for these and other reasons be labeled "absurdist" (see Esslin 266–267).

18. Importantly, Freud found dreams very useful tools for under-standing the unconscious desires of analysands; for him, "the utilization of dreams" (26) is an important psychoanalytic tool.

19. Richard Wright's *Native Son* and Ralph Ellison's *Invisible Man*, exceptions to the dominant tradition of American gothic, thema-tize whiteness and blackness in ways similar to *Dutchman* (see Sis-ney 82–90). Toni Morrison notes: "images of blackness can be evil *and* protective, rebellious *and* forgiving, fearful *and* desirable—all of the self-contradictory features of the self. Whiteness, alone, is mute, meaningless unfathomable, pointless, frozen, veiled, curtained, dreaded, senseless, implacable. Or so our writers seem to say" (Morrison 59).

WORKS CITED

Adams, George R. "Black Militant Drama." *American Imago* 28 (1971): 107–128.

Artaud, Antonin. *The Theatre and Its Double*. Trans. Mary Caroline Richards. New York: Grove, 1958.

Baker, Houston A., Jr. *The Journey Back: Issues in Black Literature and Criticism*. Chicago: U of Chicago P, 1980.

Baraka, Amiri (LeRoi Jones). *The Autobiography of Leroi Jones*. New York: Freundlich, 1984.

———. *Dutchman*. New York: William Morrow, 1964.

———. *Home: Social Essays*. New York: William Morrow, 1966.

———. *The Slave*. New York: William Morrow, 1964.

———. *The System of Dante's Hell*. London: MacGibbon and Kee, 1966.

———. *The Toilet*. New York: Grove, 1963.

Benston, Kimberly W. *Baraka: The Renegade and the Mask*. New Haven: Yale UP, 1976.

Blau, Herbert. "The American Dream in American Gothic: The Plays of Sam Shepard and Adrienne Kennedy." *Modern Drama* 27 (1984): 520–539.

Early, Gerald. "The Case of Leroi Jones/Amiri Baraka." *Salmagundi* 70–71 (1986): 343–352.

Edelman, Lee. "The Part for the (W)hole: Baldwin, Homophobia, and the Fantasmatics of 'Race.'" *Homographesis: Essays in Gay Literary and Cultural Theory*. New York: Routledge, 1994, 42–75.

Esslin, Martin. *The Theatre of the Absurd*. Rev. ed. Garden City, NY: Anchor/Doubleday, 1969.

Fanon, Frantz. *Black Skin, White Masks*. Trans. Charles Lam Markmann. New York: Grove, 1967. Trans. of *Peau Noire, Masques Blancs*. 1952.

Fiedler, Leslie. *Love and Death in the American Novel*. Rev. ed. 1966. New York: Anchor, 1992.

Freud, Sigmund. *Dora: An Analysis of a Case of Hysteria*. Ed. and trans. Philip Rieff. New York: Macmillan, 1963.

Gates, Henry Louis, Jr. *Figures in Black: Words, Signs, and the "Racial" Self*. New York: Oxford UP, 1987.

Hay, Samuel A. *African-American Theatre: A Historical and Critical Analysis*. Cambridge: Cambridge UP, 1994.

hooks, bell. "Representing Whiteness in the Black Imagination." *Cultural Studies*. Ed. Lawrence Grossberg, Cary Nelson, Paula A. Triechler. New York: Routledge, 1992, 338–346.

Kaufman, Michael W. "The Delicate World of Reprobation: A Note on the Black Revolutionary Theatre." *The Theatre of Black Americans*. Ed. Errol Hill. New York: Applause, 1987, 192–209.

Kristeva, Julia. "Place Names." *Desire in Language*. Ed. Léon S. Roudiez. Trans. Thomas Gora, Alice Jardine, and Léon S. Roudiez. New York: Columbia UP, 1980, 271–294. Translation of "Noms de lieu." 1976.

Lindberg, John. "*Dutchman* and *The Slave*: Companions in Revolution." *Imamu Amiri Baraka (Leroi Jones): A Collection of Critical Essays*. Englewood Cliffs, NJ: Prentice-Hall, 1978, 141–147.

MacAndrew, Elizabeth. *The Gothic Tradition in Fiction*. New York: Columbia UP, 1979.

Morrison, Toni. *Playing in the Dark: Whiteness and the Literary Imagination*. Cambridge, MA: Harvard UP, 1990.

Payne, Ladell. *Black Novelists and the Southern Literary Tradition*. Athens: U of Georgia P, 1981.

Phillips, Louis. "LeRoi Jones and Contemporary Black Drama." *The Black American Writer*. Ed. C. W. E. Bigsby. 3 vols. Deland, FL: Everett/Edwards, 1969, 2: 203–217.

Ralph, George. "Jones's *Dutchman*." *Explicator* 43.2 (1985): 58–59.

Shank, Theodore. *American Alternative Theatre*. New York: St. Martin's, 1982.

Sisney, Mary F. "The Power and Horror of Whiteness: Wright and Ellison Respond to Poe." *CLA Journal* 29 (1985): 82–90.

Sollors, Werner. *Amiri Baraka/LeRoi Jones: The Quest for a "Populist Modernism."* New York: Columbia UP, 1978.

Sontag, Susan. "Going to the theatre, etc." 1964. *Against Interpretation*. New York: Anchor/Doubleday, 1990.

Tener, Robert L. "Role Playing as a Dutchman." *Studies in Black Literature* 3.3 (1972): 17–22.

Weisgram, Dianne H. "LeRoi Jones' *Dutchman*: Inter-Racial Ritual of Sexual Violence." *American Imago* 25 (1972): 215–232.

Williams, Sherley Anne. "The Search for Identity in Baraka's *Dutchman*." *Imamu Amiri Baraka (Leroi Jones): A Collection of Critical Essays*. Englewood Cliffs, NJ: Prentice-Hall, 1978, 135–140.

Winter, Kari J. *Subjects of Slavery, Agents of Change: Women and Power in Gothic Novels and Slave Narratives, 1790–1865*. Athens: U of Georgia P, 1992.

PART IV

Gothic Currents in Women's Writing

An Ecstasy of Apprehension
The Gothic Pleasures of Sentimental Fiction

A core of perverse, gothic pleasures lies at the heart of nineteenth-century sentimental fiction. Sentimentality asks its readers to extend themselves generously to another, rewarding them with a sense of their own altruism, with a "thrilling" experience of feeling the other's pain, and with a comforting recognition of their own relatively good fortune. However, because these multiple pleasures derive from the suffering of another, the ideal of selfless devotion to moral solidarity is suspect.[1] Indeed, to the extent that the reader derives pleasure from another's anguish, sympathetic identification has a sadistic quality to it.[2] Susan Warner's 1851 sentimental blockbuster, *The Wide, Wide World*, affords a vivid example of the way sympathy provokes apparently sadistic pleasures. In a scene that occurs about halfway through the novel, the heroine, Ellen Montgomery, is waylaid by Mr. Saunders, a dastardly sales clerk with a grudge against her. He fashions from a sapling "a very good imitation of an ox-whip in size and length, with a fine lash-like point," and begins to threaten Ellen's pony. Warner provocatively observes that Ellen, in a frenzy of sympathy, quivers nervously in "an ecstasy of apprehension" (397).

As the scene plays out, however, Ellen's seemingly sadistic response appears to be an inverted form of masochism. After all, Mr. Saunders tortures Ellen's horse because "[h]is best way of distressing Ellen, he found, was through her horse . . . and he meant to wind up with such a treatment of her pony, real or seeming, as he knew would give great pain to the pony's mistress" (400). He understands that sympathy works as a mechanism for torture because a sympathizer feels what a victim feels. Ellen introjects a mental representation of her pony and experiences its pain along with it: "a smart stroke of the whip upon his haunches made the Brownie spring in a way that brought Ellen's heart into her mouth" (398). Ellen's ecstasy, then, derives from a fantasy of physical pain. Because the abuse is displaced from its intended victim (Ellen) onto a sacrificial substitute (the horse), Ellen is able to delight in a titillating proximity to power rather than suffer genuine agony.

Ellen's masochistic ecstasy in response to another's pain provides a model of the pleasure enjoyed by the reader of sentimental fiction. Like Ellen, the sympathizing reader vicariously experiences a textual victim's pain. The gap between represented pain and real pain enables the reader to transform the imagined pain into pleasure. In order to feel the pleasures of sympathy, there must be a fictional victim whose suffering enables the reader to enjoy sensations of compassion, and to the extent that sentimental fiction stimulates pleasure in response to another's pain, it is sadomasochistic. In this respect, I would like to suggest, sentimental fiction bears a striking resemblance to gothic fiction, which also stimulates pleasure by exploiting the terror of tortured victims. Indeed, I propose that the core of horror in sentimentality is a gothic image. Philip Fisher, drawing on Rousseau, has offered a useful definition of the essential sentimental scene as one in which a man in prison, helpless to act, watches a wild beast tear a baby from the arms of its mother and devour it. (The scene from *The Wide, Wide World* fits this model: the reader helplessly observes a wild patriarchal beast, Mr. Saunders, torment Ellen's baby horse while Ellen maternally suffers vicariously.) Cathy Davidson also focuses on the detachment of the reader from a scene of anguish as a diagnostic feature of sentimentality.[3] The reader of gothic fiction, she claims, experiences terror along with the victim, while the reader of sentimental fiction is helplessly detached from it but forced to watch. These differing perspectives on a central horror account for the differing reader responses: terror for the gothic reader, tears for the sentimental reader.

Recognizing the gothic core of sentimentality is important for a complete understanding of the pleasures and politics of sentimental fiction. Critics have largely ignored the central role of terror in the genre, focusing more typically on its narcissistic or protofeminist gratifications.[4] However, I propose that the pleasures of sentimental sympathy derive from a masochistic identification that gratifies readers with a thrill of fear. To illuminate the perverse pleasures of sentimentality, I turn to critics of the gothic, such as Rosemary Jackson, Terry Heller, and William Patrick Day, who all variously attribute the pleasure of terror to its destabilization of the illusion of coherent identity.[5] It is no coincidence, critics agree, that the gothic arose at the moment when Enlightenment thinkers were idealizing the human being as a coherent, rational self.[6] The gothic represents the underside of this ideal, exposing both the illicit desires and the tactics of terror used to repress them during the construction of hegemonic subjectivities. The core of horror in nineteenth-century sentimentality, I would like to suggest, can also be interpreted as a response to the production of cultural identity in post-Enlightenment society. The masochistic aspects of sentimental sympathy afford transgressive pleasures that arise from a fantasized transcendence of coherent identity. When Mr. Saunders whips the Brownie, Warner writes that Ellen was "beside herself"; her ecstasy of sympathy partly derives from the masochistic pleasures of being other than culture would have her be, of being on the brink of social nonbeing.

Feminist and queer theorists have offered particularly insightful analyses of the gothic as a site that stages the repressive construction of normative gender roles. Gothic implements of torture, they suggest, represent the terror tactics of gender construction, and the genre's characteristically perverse cravings and anxieties represent identifications and desires whose repression is essential for appropriate genders. Michelle Massé, for example, argues that the gothic exposes a widespread "cultural amnesia" obscuring the traumatic destruction of women's independent subjectivity. Gothic horror, she claims, makes visible the terror that is used to force women into positions of subservience and powerlessness. The gothic core of sentimental fiction, I propose, similarly expresses the traumatic destruction of female autonomy, the violent repression of multiple identifications and desires during the construction of "true womanhood." In particular, nineteenth-century sentimentality exposes the culture's cruel ideal of female bodilessness. However, unlike Massé, I see the sadomasochism in sentimentality as a double-edged sword of repression *and* subversion. The "ecstasy of apprehension" that Ellen Montgomery experiences is indeed masochistic, but in that masochistic gesture, Warner is able to imagine the disruption of Ellen's culturally imposed gender identification. The palpability of Ellen's identification with another's pain is transgressive because it makes her body and her passions physically present, undoing the erasure of female corporeality. Certainly, to the extent that Warner trains her female readers to take pleasure in patriarchal violence, her exploitation of the power of horror is repressive; however, to the extent that scenes of horror afford her a trope to imagine the transgression of repressive identity constructs, they subvert patriarchal repression.

According to the legal doctrine of the *femme couverte*, a nineteenth-century woman legally relinquished her identity upon her marriage, so that her identity was "covered" by that of her husband. She remained modestly invisible, screened from the peering eyes of the law. This legal screening of women translated into a culturewide ideal of female invisibility. For example, when the famous clergyman Horace Bushnell refers to the doctrine of *femme couverte* in his 1869 sermon, "Women's Suffrage: The Reform against Nature," he idealizes a woman whose power resides in her nonpresence:

> The man, as in fatherhood, carries the name and flag; the woman, as in motherhood, takes the name on herself and puts it on her children, passing out of sight legally, to be a covert nature included henceforth in her husband. . . . [There is] something sacred, or angelic in such womanhood. The

morally grandest sight we see in this world is a real and ideally true woman. Send her to the polls if you will, give her an
office, set the Hon. before her name, and by that time she is
nobody. (168, 173)

When a woman is public, she "is nobody"; she is an "ideally true
woman" only when she is no-body, "out of sight"; she is "angelic"
only when she is "a covert nature." It is, of course, ironic that the
hidden woman is "the morally grandest sight we see in this
world." In order to perceive the "true woman," a viewer would
intentionally have to not-see her, and so because the body cannot actually be erased, "true womanhood" relies upon an ongoing willful denial of female presence.

As Mary Poovey has written, the nineteenth-century British
"angel in the house" is bodiless: "by the last decades of the eighteenth century, even to refer to the body was considered
'unladylike'" (14).[7] Similar attitudes also characterize American
women's ideals of genteel womanhood. The midcentury diary of
Anna LaRoche Francis, daughter of an eminent Philadelphia
doctor, reiterates that female presence is an affront to genteel
womanhood. The following two entries from her journal afford
an instructive contrast: the first describes men's liberty to be
physically present, and the second describes a girl's attempt to
assume a similar liberty:

Feb 26th 1863—On the 23rd I went to the Democratic
Club. . . . We went in the reserved seats while Papa sat on the
platform. . . . the crowd arose & cheered & screamed . . . after
a second of silence the cheers arose once more—men waved
their hats & hdkfs all those upon the platform arose & helped
to increase the noise—as for Papa I declare that he not only
waved his hat but his cane & hdkfs both & I am not certain
that he did not wave his legs & arms—such was his excitement

May 17th 1863 . . . I had an amusing letter from Penn [a
female friend] who says she stood on the door step as the
Democrats were passing & cried "Bravo democrats"—it was
immediately responded to by cheers which caused her en-
raged family to seize her by the back & draw her in.

Anna is "amused" not by Penn's physical presence, which must be permitted, but by Penn's transgression of the implied taboo against conceding that physical presence. A woman was to negotiate the contradiction between her own embodiment and the ideal of bodilessness through a self-effacing form of presence, acting *as though* she lacked a body. The ideal of bodiless women had striking longevity in the nineteenth century (indeed, it still afflicts women today). An 1898 conduct book proposed that a true woman who wanted to appear in public should be "wrapped in a mantle of proper reserve . . . seeing and hearing nothing that she ought not to see and hear . . . always unobtrusive, never . . . to attract the attention of the passers-by."[8] Social codes enabled women to "wrap" themselves in modesty, to deny the signs of their persistently tangible bodies, and to ignore vulgar, corporeal phenomena. Subtle cues urging viewers to agree tacitly to a woman's bodilessness served as markers of class distinction.

Erasure of the female body is not merely repression; it is abjection. As Judith Butler writes, abjection is a social process that constructs dominant subjectivities through the active repudiation of desires and modes of identification that are deemed socially unacceptable. It is a process of identity construction that uses repression. Butler writes, "[T]he subject is constituted through the force of exclusion and abjection, one which produces a constitutive outside to the subject, an abjected outside, which is, after all, 'inside' the subject as its own founding repudiation" (3). For example, heterosexual identities are constructed through the abjection of same-sex erotic attractions: repudiated homosexual desires, theoretically "outside," are internalized as the necessary foundation of a heterosexual self. I would like to suggest that the female body itself serves as this abjected outside for the nineteenth-century "true woman"; the body remains "inside" her as a repudiated component of the self that is necessary to distinguish the "true woman" from other women. The "true woman" does not forget about her body; rather, she engages in an ongoing repudiation of it in order to constitute her socially accepted identity. In doing so, she not only avoids being thought unladylike or even disgusting, but she constitutes her self.[9]

Abjection of the female body is one of the most prominently featured mechanisms of the construction of female subjectivity in nineteenth-century gothic and sentimental fiction. As Cathy Davidson claims, sentimental novels illustrate that for "the quintessential *feme covert* . . . female being, by her own definition and her culture's definition, is nothingness" (148). They represent the true woman as "a cipher in search of an integer, an empty sign seeking for another's excess of significance to provide her own meaning" (148). In order to be a *femme couverte*, in other words, the body had to be actively suppressed.

The Wide, Wide World portrays the construction of a lady, featuring a series of trials designed to eradicate all traces of Ellen Montgomery's presence. In the course of her education, Ellen achieves an advanced degree of bodilessness, an ability to *be*, invisibly. Her beloved adoptive brother John Humphreys admiringly tells her, "Step as you please, and do not shut the doors carefully. I see you and hear you; but without any disturbance" (461). Ellen is justifiably proud of her ability to be present in such a way that her body makes no disturbance. She has learned the social cues necessary for noncorporeal corporeality, as the last line of the book indicates: "[s]he went back to spend her life with the friends and guardians she best loved, and to be to them . . . 'the light of the eyes'" (569). The successfully acculturated woman shares the paradoxical properties of light: she is visible but insubstantial. She exists "to them"; her existence is contingent upon others whose presence she can illuminate.

The Wide, Wide World is a fascinating study in the subtle ways women repudiated their bodies in order to produce the desired "nullity at the core" of their existence (Davidson 148). A scene near the end of the novel exemplifies how a woman can use bodily cues to affirm—paradoxically—her physical absence, and how that self-absention is constitutive of her identity. Ellen has been separated from the Humphreys, exiled to a life of shallow hedonism in the Edinburgh mansion of her Scottish relatives. She longs for John's Christian severity, which would help her vanquish her will and liberate her from her intransigent desires. John comes to visit Ellen, but before addressing her, he spies on her in order to see how her good character has been faring during her period of freedom. John finds Ellen among a group of people singing around a piano:

> Ellen's eyes were bent on the floor. The expression on her face touched and pleased him greatly; it was precisely what he wished to see. Without having the least shadow of sorrow upon it, there was in all its lines that singular mixture of gravity and sweetness that is never seen but where religion and discipline have done their work well. Ellen at the moment had escaped from the company and the noisy sounds of the performer at her side; and while her eye was curiously tracing out the pattern of the carpet her mind was resting itself in one of the verses she had been reading that same evening. (559)

Although Ellen is physically present, her bodily signs speak only of her absence. She neutralizes her body with tasks that keep it under restraint: with her "eyes . . . bent on the floor," "curiously tracing out the pattern of the carpet," she prevents herself from seeing anything that might urge her to join the company. Like the lady who "wraps herself in modesty," Ellen is "seeing and hearing nothing that she ought not to," despite her unquenchable curiosity. Her expression of "gravity," bespeaking an otherworldly orientation, stands in mute, unmistakable separation from the "noisy sounds of the performer" who appears particularly worldly by contrast. The narrator seems to search for Ellen's presence but finds that presence continuously deferred: we begin with a view of Ellen from the outside, but we realize that she is not there; our view then shifts to looking at Ellen from the inside, but she is not there either. Rather, she is "*in* one of the verses," dissolved into a spiritual body, effectively disembodied. Ellen had wondered how she would "keep [her]self right," as she put it, without John's ongoing disciplinary presence. We see here that abjection of the body is a key process in maintaining her "right" self; denying her physical presence enables her continuously to consolidate her coherent identity.

This scene can be read as a sentimental variation on the classic gothic scene of a woman imprisoned in a castle. Ellen *looks* free; we see no chains or implements of torture, as we would in a gothic scene. But the chains are there, implicit in the expression on Ellen's face: "there was in all its lines that singular mixture of gravity and sweetness that is never seen but where religion and discipline have done their work well." As Foucault observes in *Discipline and Punish*, whereas premodern methods of social control rely upon visible punishments (burning at the stake, flogging, drawing and quartering), modern power works through internalized control based upon religion and discipline. Such modes of internal oppression arise in a world resembling Jeremy Bentham's model panopticon, in which

> [h]e who is subjected to a field of visibility, and who knows it, assumes responsibility for the constraints of power; he makes them play spontaneously upon himself; he inscribes in himself the power relations in which he simultaneously plays both roles; he becomes the principle of his own subjection. By this very fact, the external power may throw off its physical weight. (Foucault 202–203)

Enlightenment ideals of social control, hygiene, and discipline produced the gothic, whose dungeons, whips, chains, incarcerations, and physical abuse hark back to the lurid forms of repression characteristic of earlier modes of discipline. The gothic exposes the violent repression that is the invisible underside of Enlightenment rationality and orderliness. Sentimentality, by contrast, evokes the kinder, gentler panopticon. In creating a scene in which Ellen's self-erasure is "precisely what he wished to see," Warner first subjects Ellen to "a field of visibility" and then rewards her good behavior with a surprise visit from the warden, a dearly longed-for reward for the ongoing, painful renunciations. And yet, as Foucault points out, modern social structures—prisons, boarding schools, corporations—contain traces of the violence they simultaneously inflict and erase.

In exposing the self-incarceration that is part of female being, Warner expresses both her repressed anger and fear and her sexual desire. For paradoxically, in her world, female invisibility is alluring, as though, as Poovey claims, the elaborate efforts to repudiate the body only draw attention more emphatically to its hidden delights. Ellen's desire is to be "precisely what [John] wished to see," and her success in being it is rewarded with romantic and erotic gratification: four pages later, John suggests that he would like to marry her ("I think you belong to me more than to any body"). John's declaration of possessive desire confirms that in the spying scene, he gazes upon Ellen with more than brotherly or pastoral interest. Detailing the minutiae of abjection enables Warner to express the sexual desire and the persistence of female embodiment that she overtly repudiates.

It is true that expressing and stimulating desire are not necessarily transgressive phenomena, as Ann Cvetkovich has shown.[10] Indeed, John's desire sets in motion what Foucault calls "perpetual spirals of power and pleasure" (44–45). Again and again, it stimulates in Ellen a profoundly physical passion that serves as a justification for his lovingly severe disciplinary intervention. In this scene, for instance, Ellen collapses in "an agony of joy," weeping "with all the vehement passion of her childhood, quivering from head to foot with convulsive sobs," and her inappropriate physical stimulation justifies physical restraint: "[John] possessed himself of one of her hands; and when in her excitement the hand struggled to get away again, it was not permitted. Ellen understood that very well and immediately checked herself. Better than words, the calm firm grasp of his hand quieted her. . . . [H]is hand quickly imprisoned hers again" (560). By imagining "Ellen" as being split from her unruly body, Warner imagines for her heroine a momentary escape from the prison of identity; however, that escape prods Ellen to redouble her commitment to her self through the physical "imprisonment" John conveniently imposes. It leads her to desire his physical restraint, exemplifying Foucault's hypothesis that resistance serves power by offering a site where subjects crave the intensification of power.

While the physical affect featured in sentimental scenes of agony, imprisonment, convulsions, and escape does eroticize the power that constrains it, that eroticization at least partly exceeds the mechanisms that attempt to contain it. The reader who witnesses the gothic horror in this scene can masochistically experience in fantasy the perverse pleasures of Ellen's exhibitionism and agonizing self-abnegation, and this stimulation of the

reader's passion undermines the novel's own ideal of bodilessness. Warner was well aware that reading could stimulate
a subversive corporeal passion. At the opening of the novel,
Dr. Green associates Mrs. Montgomery's fatal illness with novel
reading, chiding Ellen, "[S]he looks to me as if she had been too
much excited. I've a notion she has been taking half a bottle of
wine, or reading some furious kind of a novel or something of
that sort" (19). And at the end of the novel, when Ellen asks John
how she can keep herself right without him, he commands,
"Read no novels" (564). Thus, Warner acknowledges the danger
textual affect poses to true womanhood. She escaped the evident
contradiction in these lines by claiming that she herself wrote
"stories," not "novels," but the novel is notorious for its stimulation of passion, belying its author's protestations to the contrary.
Simultaneously provoking the reader's experience of affect and a
guilty recognition of her own desire for that passion, *The Wide,
Wide World* actually intensifies the reader's passion and her sense
of the limitations of true womanhood.

The capacity of sentimental affect to subvert prohibitions on
passion recurs throughout sentimental fiction. Readers' fantasized identifications with the thrilling horror scenes that com-
pose the core of sentimental sympathy frequently exceed, at
least partly, the mechanisms intended to contain them. Consider
Maria Cummins's *The Lamplighter*, whose violent opening is
supposed to advocate the abjection of female passion. Cummins
portrays a savage boardinghouse keeper who is obliged to raise
an orphan, Gerty, whom she beats mercilessly. One day, she intensifies her abuse by taking it out on Gerty's "darling kitten":

> Nan . . . firmly pushed [Gerty] back with one hand, while with
> the other she threw the kitten half across the room. Gerty
> heard a sudden splash and a piercing cry. Nan had flung the
> poor creature into a large vessel of steaming-hot water, which
> stood ready for some household purpose. The little animal
> struggled and writhed for an instant, then died in torture. (11)

Gerty explodes in a violent outburst of anger, which Cummins
vigorously denounces; Gerty must tolerate even extravagant cruelty without anger, and her passion calls for severe disciplinary

interventions. Cummins presents this torture as the culmination of a series of cruelties inflicted upon Gerty, with the kitten acting as stand-in for Gerty, and so the moral suggests that Gerty must even acquiesce to her own torture. However, the impression of cruelty exceeds the moral intended to contain it. Nan's injustice is so palpable that the scene stands more as an indictment of the prevailing norms of identity than it does of Gerty's passion.[11] The "thrill" of horror the reader experiences in vicariously feeling Nan's cruel torture represents a transgressive flirtation with extreme, irrational states of being, again directing an implicit critique toward the bland states sanctioned by prevailing norms of femininity.

In exposing the physical violence that is part of Gerty's socialization, Cummins's textual abjection evades the process it is intended to reinforce. Julia Kristeva has analyzed the possibility for transcendence in textual representations of abjection. In *Powers of Horror*, Kristeva observes that transgressive fantasies— such as gothic fictions—enable readers to experience vicariously the dismantling of their own identity. Horror offers the possibility of encountering the terrifying components of the repressed unconscious, a process that shatters the illusion of coherent subjectivity, enabling readers to imagine an ecstatic merging with the totality of existence. Lacan refers to this ecstatic merging as an "eternal and irreducible human desire . . . an eternal desire for the nonrelationship of zero, where identity is meaningless."[12] The pleasures of the reader's masochistic identification with Gerty's kitten resemble an ecstatic *jouissance*, a transcendence of conventional, coherent identity, where the idea of being on the brink of nonbeing is a fantasy of being free of hegemonic identity.

In drawing on the affective power of tortured pets, Cummins was most likely copying a technique perfected by her predecessor, Susan Warner. In *The Wide, Wide World*, Warner consistently depicts abused horses as substitutes for women, stimulating in both reader and character a passionate outpouring of sympathy that simultaneously indicts and condones patriarchal violence. The third page of *The Wide, Wide World* establishes a book-long identification of Ellen with a horse. When the little girl has a violent outburst of passion upon learning that her mother will be abandoning her, the narrator chides her, reminding the reader that Ellen's "passions were by nature very strong, and by education very imperfectly controlled; and time, 'that rider that breaks youth,' had not as yet tried his hand upon her" (11). John later reiterates the time-honored connection between breaking women and breaking horses when he commands, "[Y]ou must not talk when you are riding unless you can contrive to manage two things at once; and no more lose command of your horse than you would of yourself" (463).

The violence that is consistently inflicted upon horses during the course of this book, then, can be read as coded representations of the violence done to women during the course of their acculturation. However, it also represents the ecstatic subversion of coherent norms of identity. This double-edgedness of textual abjection is evident in a scene in which Ellen has been given a new pony and her friend Sophia advises her to whip it immediately:

> "I don't want to whip him, I am sure; and I should be afraid to besides."
>
> "Hasn't John taught you that lesson yet?" said the young lady;—"he is perfect in it himself. Do you remember, Alice, the chastening he gave that fine black horse of ours we called the 'Black Prince'?—a beautiful creature he was,—more than a year ago?—My conscience! he frightened me to death."
>
> "I remember," said Alice; "I remember I could not look on."
>
> "What did he do that for?" said Ellen.
>
> "What's the matter, Ellen Montgomery?" said Miss Sophia, laughing,—"where did you get that long face? Are you thinking of John or the horse? . . . I advise you, Ellen, not to trust your pony to Mr. John; he will have no mercy on him." (377)

John's horsewhipping exposes the violence implicit in the abjection of the female body. As Sophia recognizes, Ellen identifies with the "Black Prince," a "beautiful creature," fearfully meditating upon the necessity of disciplinary violence. By naming the

proud horse "Black Prince," Warner draws an implicit comparison between Ellen's body and Satan, suggesting that the female
body is a reservoir of sinfulness within female nature.[13] By making the body sinful, Warner posits the "breaking" of female passion as a crucial and desirable component of becoming a Christian. And so, Warner has Alice justify John's violence:

> "It was a clear case of obstinacy. The horse was resolved to
> have his own way and not do what his rider required of him;
> it was necessary that either the horse or the man should give
> up; and as John has no fancy for giving up, he carried his
> point,—partly by management, partly, I confess, by a judi-
> cious use of the whip and spur; but there was no such furious
> flagellation as Sophia seems to mean, and which a good horse-
> man would scarce be guilty of."

Alice contradicts herself by disparaging Sophia's accusation of a
"furious flagellation" despite having admitted that the beating
was too brutal for her to watch. This rupture in Alice's speech exposes the contradiction between what she cannot bear to watch
and what is supposed to be her true desire. Because Alice's identity has been constructed through an ongoing submission, based
upon the premise that violence is God's will, she must make
sense of that violence. She therefore attempts to resolve her contradiction by locating the violence within the codified discursive
field of law: "judicious use of the whip and spur." Doing so enables her to advocate the erasure of her body at the same time
that she erases her own body's revulsion to that disembodiment.

While Alice implicitly rationalizes the use of violence in the
construction of female identity, in this scene she also imagines
the deconstruction of that identity. As Elaine Scarry demonstrates, pain destroys the constructed universe, restricting a victim's world to the confines of the body. *The Body in Pain* focuses
on the misery inherent in such a deconstruction, the agonizing
collapse of the mental and imaginative extensions of the self
in the world. However, Scarry's argument about "unmaking"
also suggests how fantasies of pain might also produce pleasure.
When the constructed world is conceived as a prison of social
identity, then "unmaking" can be a form of unshackling. This

horsewhipping scene offers the girls the vicarious pleasures of a
beating fantasy: fantasized pain shatters the ideological construct
of "true womanhood," confining the girls to the extent of their
own bodies. The prison of the body, however, is paradoxically
liberating when the "making" of a woman's identity hinges upon
the abjection of her body, for pain restores the physical presence
of the abjected body.

It is not coincidental that John is both the novel's erotic hero
and a famous horsewhipper. Indeed, it is precisely his prowess as
a beater that constitutes him as an erotic hero who can both whip
up and curb women's passion. The girls' debate over the lawful-
ness of John's violence and the repeated subsequent references to
his repressed violence betray a fascination with the fantasy of
subjection to his power. This is not surprising, as women are
trained to view violence as a form of love in this novel. A few
pages earlier, John had encouraged Ellen to affirm "Oh, how *love
I thy law!*" to God, and to God's substitute, himself (352, emphasis in original). John later comments, "My dear Ellen . . . let
sorrow but bring us closer to him. . . . if *we* are made to suffer,
we know and we love the hand that has done it,—do not we
Ellie?" (443, emphasis in original). Again, though John does say
"we," he is the novel's principal inflicter of pain in the name of
love and Ellen (and his horse) its recipient. As the "judicious"
and powerful law-giver, John represents what Lacan calls "the
symbolic father," his flagellations symbolizing his lawful possession of the phallus. Within Warner's patriarchal world, his phallic power is desirable, particularly for a young girl who has been
emptied of self and who seeks someone worthy of her being and
powerful enough to sustain it. The language that Ellen uses to
express her love for John not surprisingly intermixes erotic desire with filial respect for his disciplinary capabilities. She ap-
preciates in John "a higher style of kindness that entered into all
her innermost feelings and wants; and his was a higher style of
authority too, that reached where [others'] could never attain"
(538–539). John penetrates Ellen, not only advancing her education but gratifying her "innermost feelings."

Thus, the horsewhipping scenes in *The Wide, Wide World*
serve as models of sentimental subversion through displaced

gothic horror. The portrayal of a righteous conqueror whose erotic passion is barely sublimated enables Warner to articulate and stimulate physical desire. Displacing the beating onto a horse enables Ellen to sympathize with her pony in an imaginative extension of herself that makes present her body and her passionate desires. Moreover, the beating fantasy unmakes Ellen's identity by imaginatively reducing her to a merely physical existence, and within the regime she inhabits, that unmaking represents a liberation from the prison of a bodiless identity. The scene with which I began, in which the dastardly sales clerk is tormenting Ellen, can be seen as a particularly vivid expression of the desire for the ecstatic unmaking of identity that pulses throughout the book. Ellen not only understands that Mr. Saunders's cruelty to her pony is a displaced form of cruelty to her, but she covertly relishes his threatened violence, which tantalizes her with the sadomasochistic *jouissance* of transgressing identity boundaries. Like John, who sarcastically calls Mr. Saunders "brother," the bully provokes in Ellen a terror that is thrilling because the liminal vulnerability he makes her feel affords an experience of the full extent of her body and its abiding, irrepressible passions.

NOTES

1. My understanding of the sadomasochistic qualities of sympathy is influenced by Bersani.

2. While the terms "sadism" and "masochism" therefore originally had an explicitly sexual connotation, I am using the terms more loosely, as Webster's dictionary invites. Masochism: "a tendency to take pleasure in physical or mental suffering inflicted on one by oneself or by another in the practice of extreme self-denial or self-punishment: a taste for suffering." Sadism: "the satisfaction of outwardly directed destructive impulses as a source of libidinal gratification."

3. Davidson writes, "[t]he reader vicariously accompanies the [Gothic] heroine throughout her various trials. This relationship between reader and text marks another departure from the sentimental form. . . . The reader is sidelined by the conventionally sentimental, is cast as a voyeuristic observer of the protagonist's private affairs. . . . By contrast, the Gothic reader and the Gothic protagonist all along occupy much the same position" (223).

4. Ann Douglas reads sentimental fiction as a politically conservative genre training women to accept consumerism and narcissism as
consolation prizes for their abdication of political and economic power.
Jane Tompkins, by contrast, argues that sentimentality constructs an alternate sphere for women that rivals the male-dominated marketplace.
According to Laura Wexler, this debate over sentimentality effectively
turns on the question of whether or not sentimentality fosters masochistic identities for its readers. If it does, the argument goes, then the
works are agents of female oppression; if it does not, then the works
can be agents of female empowerment. For Wexler, the question of
whether the genre works for or against women obscures the more important stakes for nonwhite women. She reveals the negative effects of
sentimental models of femininity on Native American women, and
Franny Nudelman makes a similar argument regarding slave women. I
want to propose that we can escape the binaristic cul-de-sac over sentimental politics by bringing pressure to bear on the masochistic elements themselves. One of the results of sentimental masochism is the
recuperation of the female body, and while such a recuperation may
seem insignificant today, it represented an important mode of empowerment, given the way women's bodies were understood in mid-
nineteenth-century ideologies.

5. Jackson and Heller both focus explicitly on the implications of
Lacanian analysis for criticism of the gothic. Drawing on Lacan's claim
that identity is an illusion acquired through gazing at a mirror, they argue that the fear stimulated by the gothic provides the reader a thrilling
escape from the fiction of coherent selfhood. William Patrick Day argues that in the gothic, the self is defined through conflict, as a giver or
receiver of pain in a sadomasochistic dynamic, and he claims that gothic
subversion plays this game of domination and subordination, wielding
power in turning the tools of power against itself rather than overtly
challenging power.

6. Fiedler's *Love and Death in the American Novel* makes the original
case for the intrinsic relationship between the gothic and American culture. Gross presents a clear outline of the broad historical argument
with regard to postrevolutionary American culture.

7. Poovey observes that in 1782, Hester Thrale shocked her female
companions by reading aloud a passage from the *Spectator*; as she reports, "even the Maid who was dressing my Hair, burst out laughing at
the Idea of *a Lady* saying her Stomach ach'd, or that something stuck
between her Teeth" (14).

8. *Etiquette for Americans by a Woman of Fashion* (Chicago: Herbert S.

Stone, 1898) 74–79, 85. Quoted in the Norton critical edition of *The Awakening*, ed. Margo Culley (New York: Norton, 1994).

9. The epithet "disgusting" appears in Sprague: "[b]eware also of an ostentatious manner. By this I mean that kind of manner which savors too much of display; which indicates a disposition to make yourself too conspicuous . . . I had rather you should excite, by your bashfulness, a feeling of compassion, than by your excessive confidence a feeling of disgust" (83).

10. As Ann Cvetkovich argues, the repressive hypothesis disproves the argument that sensation is intrinsically subversive. The production of affect in Victorian sensation fiction, she points out, is not a rebellious act but rather part of the operation of power, in that the reader's excessive affect justifies disciplinary intervention.

11. D. A. Miller's analysis of Victorian sensation fiction depicts a process of stimulation and recontainment similar to the one Cvetkovich describes. However, he also suggests that the exposure of the barbarous abuse inflicted by the dominant culture enables this popular genre to exceed the mechanisms intended to contain it.

12. Jacques Lacan, *The Language of the Self*, 191, qtd. in Jackson 77.

13. The phrase "black prince" also serves as a racial marker, reinforcing predominant stereotypes equating blackness with sinfulness. As Wexler notes, valorization of whiteness in sentimentality fostered repressive identity values for nonwhite women. The reference can also be seen as an example of Toni Morrison's argument in *Playing in the Dark* that an Africanist presence in American literature serves as the crucial Other that gives meaning to such cherished national ideals as "freedom," "civilized," and "beautiful." In this instance, blackness serves as the necessarily repudiated Other, enabling Ellen's "true womanhood" to take on positive meaning by contrast.

WORKS CITED

Anonymous. *Etiquette for Americans by a Woman of Fashion*. Chicago: Herbert S. Stone, 1898. Quoted in *The Awakening* (Norton critical edition). Ed. Margo Culley. New York: Norton, 1994.

Bersani, Leo. "Representation and Its Discontents." *Allegory and Representation*. Ed. Stephen Greenblatt. Baltimore, MD: Johns Hopkins UP, 1981.

Bushnell, Horace. *Selected Writings on Language, Religion, and American Culture*. Ed. David L. Smith, Chico, CA: Scholars P, 1984.

Butler, Judith. *Bodies that Matter*. New York: Routledge, 1993.

Castle, Terry. *The Female Thermometer: Eighteenth Century Culture and the Invention of the Uncanny*. New York: Oxford, 1995.

Chancer, Lynn. *Sadomasochism in Everyday Life: The Dynamics of Power and Powerlessness*. New Brunswick, NJ: Rutgers UP, 1992.

Cott, Nancy. "Passionlessness: An Interpretation of Victorian Sexual Ideology, 1790–1850." *Signs* 4.2 (1978): 219–236.

Cummins, Maria. *The Lamplighter*. 1854. New Brunswick, NJ: Rutgers UP, 1988.

Cvetkovich, Ann. *Mixed Feelings: Feminism, Mall Culture, and Victorian Sensationalism*. New Brunswick, NJ: Rutgers, 1992.

Davidson, Cathy. *Revolution and the World: The Rise of the Novel in America*. New York: Oxford, 1986.

Day, William Patrick. *In the Circles of Fear and Desire: A Study of Gothic Fantasy*. Chicago: U of Chicago P, 1985.

DeLamotte, Eugenia C. *Perils of the Night: A Feminist Study of Nineteenth-Century Gothic*. New York: Oxford, 1990.

Douglas, Ann. *The Feminization of American Culture*. New York: Anchor, 1977.

Fiedler, Leslie. *Love and Death in the American Novel*. New York: Criterion, 1960.

Fisher, Philip. *Hard Facts: Form and Setting in American Fiction*. New York: Oxford, 1985.

Foucault, Michel. *Discipline and Punish*. 1975. Trans. Alan Sheridan. New York: Vintage, 1979.

Francis, Anna Mercer LaRoche. "Journal—Note Book: 1856–1879." Columbia University Special Collection.

Heller, Terry. *The Delights of Terror: An Aesthetics of the Tale of Terror*. Urbana: U of Illinois P, 1987.

Hendler, Glenn. "Louisa May Alcott and the Limits of Sympathy." *American Literary History* 3.4 (1991): 685–706.

Jackson, Rosemary. *Fantasy: The Literature of Subversion*. London: Methuen, 1981.

Kristeva, Julia. *Powers of Horror: An Essay on Abjection*. New York: Columbia UP, 1982.

Massé, Michelle A. *In the Name of Love: Women, Masochism, and the Gothic*. Ithaca: Cornell UP, 1992.

Miller, D. A. *The Novel and the Police*. Berkeley: U of California P, 1987.

Morrison, Toni. *Playing in the Dark: Whiteness and the Literary Imagination*. New York: Vintage, 1992.

Nudelman, Franny. "Harriet Jacobs and the Sentimental Politics of Female Suffering." *ELH* 59 (1992): 939–964.

Poovey, Mary. *The Proper Lady and the Woman Writer: Ideology as Style in the Works of Mary Wollstonecraft, Mary Shelley and Jane Austen.* Chicago: U of Chicago P, 1984.

Rossington, Michael. "The Wanton Muse: Politics and Gender in Gothic Theory after 1760." *Beyond Romanticism: New Approaches to Texts and Contexts, 1780–1832.* Ed. Stephen Copley and John Whale. New York: Routledge, 1992.

Scarry, Elaine. *The Body in Pain: The Making and Unmaking of the World.* New York: Oxford, 1985.

Sedgwick, Eve Kosovsky. *Between Men: English Literature and Male Homosocial Desire.* New York: Columbia UP, 1985.

Sprague, William B. *Letters on Practical Subjects to a Daughter.* New York: Haven, 1831.

Tompkins, Jane. *Sensational Designs: The Cultural Work of American Fiction 1790-1860.* New York: Oxford, 1985.

Warner, Susan. *The Wide, Wide World.* New York: Feminist P, 1987.

Weinberg, Thomas, and G. W. Levi Kamel, eds. *S and M: Studies in Sadomasochism.* New York: Prometheus, 1983.

Wexler, Laura. "Tender Violence: Literary Eavesdropping, Domestic Fiction, and Educational Reform." *The Culture of Sentiment: Race, Gender and Sentimentality in Nineteenth-Century America.* Ed. Shirley Samuels. New York: Oxford UP, 1992.

Winter, Kari J. *Subjects of Slavery, Agents of Change: Women and Power in Gothic Novels and Slave Narratives, 1790–1885.* Athens: U of Georgia P, 1992.

Wolstenhome, Susan. *Gothic (Re)visions: Writing Women as Readers.* Albany: SUNY P, 1993.

MARY CHAPMAN

The Masochistic Pleasures
of the Gothic
Paternal Incest in Alcott's "A Marble Woman"

Women are encouraged to commit incest as a way of life. . . .
As opposed to marrying our fathers, we marry men like our fathers . . .
men who are older than us, have more money than us, more
power than us, are taller than us . . . our fathers.
PHYLLIS CHESLER, "Rape and Psychotherapy"

Locating the emergence of the gothic in the period of the American and French Revolutions, many scholars have remarked on the ways in which the gothic asserts equality in the face of domination, most noticeably in its attention to marginalized or dominated groups such as women, colonials, and homosexuals.[1] Gothic fiction has been described as "fundamental[ly] subversiv[e]," as "a movement toward freedom and away from the control of discipline," as "a liberated and liberating alternative to the conventional novel," and as a mode that allows the "shattering of sexual [and] social roles."[2] Contradictory to this gothic desire for subversion, however, is the desire for domination: according to theorists of the gothic, protagonists and readers of gothic texts both crave "the delights of terror" (Heller 1) and the "pain [that] gives rise to delight" (Burke 147), which Brendan Hennessy has claimed are "as much part of human nature as the need to laugh" (7). This pleasure in being dominated, whether by supernatural or earthly powers, complicates the subversive potential of the gothic.

This tension, rendered politically as a tension between subversion and domination, is rendered erotically as a tension between a woman's desire for romantic equality and her longing for masochistic subordination to another, especially in the subgenre known as "female gothic." Claims for the subversiveness of female gothic have been common among feminist critics like Kate Ellis, who argues that the female gothic asserts the "validity of female rebellion against an aristocratic father" (57). Casting off paternal authority, most often by marrying someone other than the father's choice, is symptomatic of women's desire for subversion in the gothic novel. However, like the gothic reader who craves the "delights of terror," the gothic heroine often also locates pleasure precisely in the unwanted, the "terror-inflected Richardsonian courtship," and the painful initiation into patriarchal culture (Massé 11, 1). The subversiveness of the female gothic, then, is often compromised by the heroine's masochistic desire for a lover who dominates her, whether this man is the woman's father or a lover who merges with this figure.

In many ways, the struggle between a young woman's desire for autonomy and her desire for her tyrannical father, as represented in the paternal incest tale, is paradigmatic of the tension between the desires for subversion and domination I have outlined as symptomatic of the gothic. Incest, both sibling and paternal, has been a stock theme of American gothic literature from the fiction of the early republic to contemporary fiction.[3] Leslie Fiedler claims the "secret sin" of the gothic is the "incest of brother and sister-daughter bred out of an original incest of mother-son" (129); Louis Gross similarly claims incest in American gothic fiction is "primarily brother-sister pairings" (53). Although there are far fewer scenes of paternal incest, American gothic texts are often structured by titillating plots which threaten it, such as the standard plot of the early American novel in which the "lascivious career of an older man is halted when he seduces a poor young woman who proves to be his cast off daughter" (Dalke 189), or they gesture toward this taboo without being able to represent it openly. For example, Bill Christophersen reads Brockden Brown's *Ormond* (1799) as a veiled "fable of incest" (57), and in slave narratives, a form influenced by the gothic, the most common abuse recounted is women's rape by their masters/fathers. That readers experience pleasure reading about paternal incest and that gothic heroines often desire the father while simultaneously fearing him are two linked manifestations of the masochism of the gothic: just as the reader's desire for the freedom of the protagonist with whom she identifies is compromised by her love of terror, the female protagonist's own emergent autonomy is threatened by her erotic ties to her father.

This essay will explore the masochistic pleasures of the gothic tale of paternal incest and, by extension, the masochistic pleasures of the gothic by taking Louisa May Alcott's "A Marble Woman" (1865) as a case study. "A Marble Woman" explores the oppressive relationship that develops between Cecilia ("Cecil") Bazil Stein, a young artist, and her guardian, a reclusive sculptor named Bazil Yorke, who, the narrative hints, may be Cecil's father. The plot depicts Cecil's maturation from adolescent to woman as a masochistic attempt to live up to "promises" her guardian extracts: to be content with no friends other than him, to ask no questions, to entertain no suitors—in short, to abandon the life of the sentiments. Cecil is able to comply with these terms only by abusing herself, most noticeably through her nearly fatal opium addiction.

It is tempting to read the story's ending—Yorke's confession of romantic love for his ward after the death of her recently identified biological father—as subversive because Cecil's masochistic behavior defeats Yorke's vow to ban all passion from his life before her addiction can kill her: Cecil's sentiment conquers Yorke's reason, love defeats law, female outsmarts male, student teaches teacher. Their marriage appears to replace the abusive relationship structured in terms of a father's control of his daughter. Ultimately, however, the tale's subversiveness of the closure is complicated by the fact that the closure desired by the gothic tale of subversion—marriage to the daughter's chosen suitor—condones the possibility of father-daughter incest raised earlier or, at the very least, condones the economy of domination that perpetuates the dominated's desire for the dominator. While the female gothic often removes the threat of paternal incest through the daughter's marriage to her chosen partner, "A Marble Woman" turns in upon itself, so that the closure maps incest onto marriage. Its ending reinscribes a problematic economy that links erotic pleasure and domination.

The female gothic is haunted by its inability to reconcile the daughter's desire for erotic freedom with the ways in which culture structures her desire as always already a desire for the father, in the same way that the gothic is also haunted by its own problematic tension between subversive and repressive strategies. Alcott's "A Marble Woman" raises key questions about the politics of the gothic form, its plots and pleasures, which I will attempt to answer here. How does one account for the masochistic structure of gothic pleasure, especially in the female gothic? Is masochism a "trend in the life of the human instincts" and "an expression of feminine nature," as Freud asserted in 1924 in "The Economic Problem of Masochism" (257)? Is masochism a contract which, when followed to the letter, can criticize the law, as Gilles Deleuze argues in *Coldness and Cruelty*? Similarly, is masochism a subversive strategy, as Michelle Massé claims in *In the Name of Love: Women, Masochism and the Gothic*? Although each of these scholars interprets masochism differently, each invites us to read the tensions implicit in the gothic form— between equality and subordination, between pleasure and pain—as either inevitable because natural or desirable because contractual and/or subversive, rather than inquire about the ways in which these tensions are historically and culturally determined.

I will argue that paternal incest and the erotics of domination it represents are not natural, contractual, or subversive but rather grounded in a family structure particularly prominent in nineteenth-century Western culture, characterized in part by the ideology of separate spheres which renders the home a site of patriarchal lawlessness and structures female erotic desire as determined by the father-daughter relationship. The gothic mode's mixture of fear and desire offers writers such as Alcott a means of expressing a transgressive desire for love of the father while at the same time articulating their revulsion from the gendering structures that socialize women to feel this desire.

INCEST, MASOCHISM, AND THE IDEOLOGY
OF SEPARATE SPHERES

Scholarship on masochism has invited a variety of readings of the painful pleasures of domination that may be applied to the gothic. According to Freud's "The Economic Problem of Masochism," for example, the masochist desires to be "forced to obey unconditionally," to be "treated like a little helpless, dependent child," and to "be beaten by the father" or some other "loved person" (258, 261, 262). Although the masochist is not always female, according to Freud, the passive posture is "feminine," and "[t]he wish to be beaten by the father . . . is closely connected with the other wish, to have some passive (feminine) sexual relations with him, and is only a regressive distortion of the latter" (266). In his earlier "Three Essays on Theories of Sexuality" (1905), Freud addresses female masochism more specifically, describing it as a natural aspect of female sexual development. According to this model, when the pre-Oedipal girl recognizes that neither she nor her mother possesses the Phallus, she abandons her mother as libidinal object and seeks the father's recognition and approval. Often this involves changing from an active, "masculine" child to a passive "feminine" adolescent; this coincides with a turning inward of the natural drives, renouncing the will to know, to see, and to master. At this time, the female child recognizes that she must give up her autonomy in order to be guaranteed the love of the father. The daughter who desperately wants to be recognized by the father will therefore not resist the terms of affection he offers.

Whereas Freud reads a girl's masochistic response as natural and passive, Deleuze in *Coldness and Cruelty* ascribes agency to the masochist:

> The masochist appears to be held by real chains, but in fact he is bound by his word alone. . . . In the structure of masochism in general, the contract represents the ideal form of the love relationship and its necessary precondition. A contract is

drawn up between the subject and the torturess. . . . The
masochistic contract implies not only the necessity of the victim's consent, but his ability to persuade, and his pedagogical
and judicial efforts to train his torturer. (75, 88)

Where Freud structures masochism as a girl's passive response,
Deleuze reads it as a contract engaged in by a male masochist
and a female torturer (a contract which he regards as an inversion of the nineteenth-century marriage) which, when followed
to the letter, can subvert the law: "[t]he masochist's apparent
obedience conceals a criticism and a provocation. He simply attacks the law on another flank" (88).

Similarly, recent feminist scholarship on the gothic has attempted to ascribe female masochism with agency, reading it as
a deliberate strategy of subverting patriarchal authority. For example, in *In the Circles of Fear and Desire*, William Patrick Day
reads the gothic heroine's masquerade of passivity and acceptance as a "style of resistance and self-assertion" (20). In *In the
Name of Love*, Massé reads female masochism in gothic texts as a
deliberate strategy of subversion. Subversion, unlike aggression,
Massé writes,

> seeks to undermine domination from within. Its mutinies are
> quiet: no warning salvos mark the opening of its well-behaved
> rebellion . . . [S]ubversion, with its gentle, seemingly non-
> resistant blankness, gradually erodes domination. . . .
>
> Subversion, then, with its letter-perfect miming of what
> ideology demands, has a secret knowingness. It takes the tools
> of oppression and renders them impotent. (250)

While each of these scholars reads the masochistic relation to
domination in slightly different ways—as a natural instinct (and
therefore passive), as an actively negotiated contract between
equals, and as a strategy of subversion—all invite us to see similarities between the masochistic strategy and the power imbalance implicit in father-daughter incest. Freud's explanation of
adolescent femininity effectively naturalizes father-daughter incest, seeing the daughter's desire for the father as transhistorical
rather than a propensity encouraged by a particular social or fa-

milial structure. Deleuze's model of masochism, which is completely unaware of how gender might complicate it, presumes that any unequal relationship (including father-daughter incest) is the choice of both participants rather than the result of the players' unequal access to power. Perhaps the most glaring deficiency of Deleuze's figure of masochism as a contract is its failure to take into account the ways in which the rights of women to engage in contracts were limited, if not nonexistent, even when Masoch was writing fictions depicting masochistic relationships in the 1870s. Massé's feminist interpretation of gothic masochism reads a daughter's passive acceptance of the law of the Father, her "letter-perfect miming of what ideology demands," as finally subversive without taking into account the ways in which the daughter can be disciplined by her own masquerade of compliance.

Rather than explain father-daughter incest and the larger issue of female masochism as transhistorical inevitabilities, contracts, or subversive strategies, I would like to explore both as phenomena located within the historically determined structures of the gothic family. As Elizabeth MacAndrew notes, from the earliest gothic novel, *The Castle of Otranto* (1764), "the problem of evil is already presented as a psychological problem created in the ambience of the family" (12). Whether the "ambience of the family" central to the gothic refers to the "sins of the fathers" revisiting their children (the problem of finding a rightful heir, hereditary madness, or incest), the recurrence of threats and injuries related to the nuclear family suggests that this emerging unit is structurally problematic. Significantly, the rise of the gothic novel, a central theme of which is father-daughter incest, coincided with two significant developments which changed the way in which the family functioned: the introduction of the ideology of the separate spheres (and the related cult of domesticity), which characterized the home as the site of maternal affect and a place of safety, and the emergence of a new parental ideal, inspired by the theories of John Locke, which encouraged relationships of affection and equality rather than tyranny and subjugation between parents and their children.

According to historians, the structure of the American family changed significantly in the mid– to late eighteenth century.[4] As Anne Dalke explains,

> For the bourgeois American family of the late eighteenth century . . . the authority of the English patriarch had given way to the Lockean ideal of the "natural family" in which the mutual rights and obligations of mother and children were balanced against those of the father. . . . The formal equality of the bourgeois family meant both that the father could not, or at least should not, stand against the independent action of his children. (191)

The repression of the tyrannical model of controlling children (and colonies) was not without its consequences. In *Fathers and Children: Andrew Jackson and the Subjugation of the American Indian*, for example, historian Michael Rogin argues that "the paternal authority repressed out of liberal politics [in the late eighteenth century] returned in Indian paternalism [in the early nineteenth century]" (10). Evidence of paternal abuse of daughters in the gothic novel suggests that the paternal authority repressed by newly egalitarian relationships between fathers and sons (and imperial nations and their former colonies) returns in the subordination of daughters, who even as adults are metaphorically and literally treated as children. The gothic form simply exposes the shortcomings of this new egalitarian family structure.

Similarly, the gothic exposes the shortcomings of the ideology of separate spheres. The domestic enclosure the gothic novel depicts (haunted house or villa) is the inversion of the notion of home celebrated by separate spheres ideology: a place of imprisonment, torture, and threatened rape or death for its female heroines. The fiction that separate spheres ideology promotes— that the home is safe and overseen by benign maternal figures— in turn veils the operation of the paternal law (perhaps, more accurately, paternal lawlessness) within the private sphere. In the privacy of the home, the father as head of the family is free to exert his power without limitations. The characteristic absence of protective mothers from gothic fiction (they are usually dead, invalid, or otherwise absent) bespeaks female powerlessness to control the domestic sphere that is actually regulated by male power. By designating the home the site of affect, separate spheres ideology also risks turning eroticism in on itself, making incest (psychological if not physical) the inevitable result. If the unmarried daughter is not permitted to circulate outside the home, she can have only one male-female relationship at a time: with her father while she lives under his roof, with her husband when she marries. This husband is preferably a paternally sanctioned suitor whom the father chooses precisely for his resemblance to himself. The daughter's romantic relationship is, in fact, modeled on her relationship with her father, making a daughter's attachment to the father or father figure inevitable. Within this familial economy, if the daughter is socialized to view the father as her first erotic choice, the female adult will always be treated as a daughter and child.

If marriage requires the daughter's departure from her family home, after she has been raised to know and desire nothing beyond its walls, then desiring the father provides one means of satisfying the daughter's desire to remain at home. As Lynda Zwinger puts it, attempts by nineteenth-century bourgeois women novelists to entertain sustained father-daughter relationships reflect their desires to imagine "a daughter never banished from home" (133). The daughter's fantasies are structured by the cultural impossibility of simultaneously remaining in her childhood home and being sexually satisfied.

THE FATHER-LOVER IN "A MARBLE WOMAN"

The ways in which the late-eighteenth-century and early-nineteenth-century family structure determines the daughter's incestuous desires for her father are apparent in Alcott's "A Marble Woman; or the Mysterious Model" (1865), a serially published tale whose closure sanctions the marriage of an orphan to her abusive surrogate father. Like much feminine gothic, in which female sexuality is initially expressed as curiosity about real parentage (Ellis 69), "A Marble Woman" has two interwoven plots: an orphan's quest for romantic love and for her real father. In the course of the story Cecil develops relationships with three men, each of whom is cast as possible lover: Alf, a "rosy bright-eyed boy about her own age" (134) who lives next door to Cecil, and the two men who are former lovers of Cecil's deceased mother: Germain, the sensual man with the "strange uncanny face" (138) whose attentions to Cecil are initially read as romantic until he is later revealed to be her biological father, and Bazil Yorke, the repressed sculptor who is Cecil's surrogate father (and hinted to be her long-lost father) at the beginning of the story and her lover/husband at the end. Cecil's relationships with these men signal the problematic tension between the drive for equality and the drive for domination in the gothic text; her decision to marry her surrogate father rather than the boy next door continues to uphold an erotic economy based on domination rather than equality, on figural incest rather than exogamy.

The story begins with Cecil's arrival at Yorke's forbidding mansion with a letter from her deceased mother instructing Yorke to serve as her guardian. Although she is only eleven, in many ways Cecil resembles the young bride of the "marital gothic" form as she arrives at the home of her guardian with only letter and luggage in hand. The bride's fear of abandonment as she moves away from her family to her new home and adopts a new identity and name is mapped on to the child's fear of her new guardian, who is supposed to replace her deceased mother.

In the first scene, Cecil forms a friendship with eleven-year-old Alf while she waits in the garden to meet her guardian. Like Cecil, Alf is gregarious and "full of . . . pleasant audacity" (134). When he presents her with a rose and proposes to be her sweetheart, the reader guesses that he is the gothic hero by offering a romantic alternative to the tyrannical Yorke. From the start, Alcott voices her approval of the boy next door through a series of contrasts with Yorke. Whereas Alf is social and warm, Yorke is reclusive and remote; whereas Alf's garden is a "blooming plot" full of roses, Yorke's is "dismal" (134), sterile, and neglected; whereas Yorke attempts to raise Cecil to be "done with love" (151), Alf introduces Cecil to poetry and romance; whereas Yorke competes with Cecil as an artist, Alf cherishes her sculptures; and whereas Alf is exactly Cecil's age, Yorke is old enough to be her father. Of all three possible lovers, Alf presents the greatest opportunity for a relationship of equality. In the binary of the two father figures, Germain and Yorke, Alf creates a third term, the possibility of escaping a repetition of Cecil's mother's romantic life: her choice between the artistically inspiring but emotionally remote Yorke and the seductive, sensual Germain. Yet Cecil rejects the boy next door, as Jo rejects Laurie in *Little Women*, for an older, more severe, emotionally stunted individual not unlike the absent-minded Professor, suggesting that the gothic heroine cannot experience erotic desire and equality simultaneously.

Cecil's comfortable romantic interest in Alf is quickly replaced by her fascination with the two other men, both of whom raise in her complex emotions combining fear and desire. For example, on her first evening at Yorke's, when Cecil sees Germain, the man with the "strange, uncanny face," she experiences a "thrill of alarm" and feels "fascinated by fear" (138). Throughout the story, although she also feels fear, Cecil remains attracted to this strange, familiar gentleman by a "tender tie" (227) she does not understand but which is associated with his sensuality, which Alcott represents through her emphasis on Germain's affectionate and expressive hands, which give Cecil the caresses she longs for from her guardian.[5]

In contrast to Alf's offer of love and companionship and Germain's sensual affection, York forces Cecil to promise herself exclusively to her guardian. "Will you stay and work with me, Cecil, and be content with no friend but myself, no playmate but old Judas [the dog]? Can you see and hear things and yet not ask questions or tell tales?" (142), he demands on her arrival. Yorke makes his acceptance of the guardian role conditional on the orphan's acceptance of his terms: "[n]othing which goes on in my house is to be talked about outside of it . . . So remember if you forget your promise, you march at once" (142). A few years later, he asks the adolescent Cecil, "Can you be content year after year with study, solitude, steady progress, and in time fame for yourself, but never any knowledge of love as Al[f] paints it? . . . Will you have faith in me, and believe that what I do is done for the best?" (150, 152). At this point, Cecil's masochistic acceptance of the law of the Father begins. She promises her guardian that she will be "a marble woman like your Psyche, with no heart to love you, only grace and beauty to please your eye and bring you honor" (151). Yorke's tyrannical regulation of Cecil is extended when, on her eighteenth birthday, Yorke convinces Cecil to accept a sexless marriage in order to silence gossip about the improprieties of a single man living with his beautiful ward. "To the world," he suggests to her, "we can be husband and wife, [but] here guardian and ward as we have been for six pleasant years" (172).

Extreme as these edicts sound, Yorke's requests of his ward are only the limit case of the ideology of the separate spheres, which limited the daughter's exposure outside the home, regulated the daughter's sexuality by making her suitors dependent on paternal sanction, and permitted, by its privacy, paternal lawlessness. Yorke's insistence that great art (his own and Cecil's) can only be achieved in reclusion merely veils his incestuous desire to monopolize his ward's attentions. While Cecil agrees to his terms, it is important to note that these "promises" cannot be read as "contracts" between equals, as Deleuze might argue, but rather as laws imposed on an orphaned, vulnerable child by the higher authority of a surrogate parent.

Yorke's rules protect him from all affect but most especially the risk of sexual feelings toward his female ward; insisting that Cecilia be called Cecil, for example, Yorke genders Cecil male and thereby offsets the risk of his attraction to her. We can read his regulation of her drives for knowledge, sexual knowledge especially, as motivated by his desire not to allow her sexual activity with anyone, because he cannot allow it with himself. As Irigaray has argued, "it is neither simply true, nor indeed false, to claim that the little girl fantasizes being seduced by her father, since it is equally valid to assume that the father seduces the daughter but that because he refuses to recognize and live out his desire, he lays down a law that prohibits him from doing so" (38). Yorke furthers this by preventing Cecil's access to possible suitors, even Germain, who Yorke knows is Cecil's father. Claiming Germain is "another lover . . . and a strange one" (163), Yorke demands that Cecil promise "never [to] listen to him, never meet him, or countenance his mad pursuit of [her]" (163).

In response to these demands, Cecil slowly cuts off her outside friendships until Alf eventually "replace[s] [Cecil's] image with a more gracious one" (236) and Germain dies; at the end of the story, Cecil marries her reclusive guardian in earnest.

The shift in Cecil's romantic interest from Alf and Germain to Yorke coincides with a shift in emphasis from her drive for equality to her drive for domination and the masochistic behavior typical of this shift. When she first arrives at Yorke's house, she is the inquisitive, independent eleven-year-old "Miss Stein." Raised by a single mother, she does not acknowledge the social limitations of her femininity; she asks questions, commands servants, and shamelessly declares that she aspires to be a sculptor. Five years later, however, Cecil's independence and active ambition have vanished, traded in for her masochistic attempts to gain Yorke's love and recognition. Entitled "The Broken Cupid," the second chapter of the story charts this change by describing Cecil in the language of sculpture—marble, cold, motionless— rather than ascribing her with the active passionate descriptors of the artist:

> Five years later, a new statue stood in the studio; we might have said two new statues, though one was a living creature . . .
> The human figure was Cecil, changed from a rosy child into a slender, deep-eyed girl. Colorless, like a plant deprived of sunshine, strangely unyouthful in the quiet grace of her motions, the sweet seriousness of her expression, but as beautiful as [Bazil's sculpture of] Psyche and almost as cold. (144)

This shift from activity to passivity, from artist to objet d'art, is accompanied by Cecil's destruction of her sculptures, her passive tolerance of Yorke's regulations, her use of opium to "tame [her]self to the quiet, lonely life" (191) Yorke wishes her to lead, and her growing love for the man who motivates this masochistic behavior.

The most problematic of these is Cecil's development of a romantic attachment to her surrogate father. The threat of incest is the unspoken theme of "A Marble Woman," overdetermined by the multiple father figures in the text and Cecil's lack of knowledge about her biological father's identity. The attraction

Cecil feels for Yorke in the first chapter of the story, "an attraction she did not understand" (141), is first explained by textual suggestions that Yorke may be her father. When Cecil says she is almost twelve years old, for example, Yorke muses, "Twelve years, twelve long years since I saw her [Cecil's mother] last, and gave up the world" (138). And although their relationship is cast as a father-daughter bond, it is also, from the start, erotically shaded by the gothic repetition that sets Cecil up to stand in for her dead mother. "She didn't tell me [how she was unkind to you]," Cecil says to Yorke on her arrival, "but I wish you would, so that I may be careful not to do it while I am here" (141). As the reader learns later, Cecil's mother's "unkind" action involves leaving the remote Bazil for the sensual Germain, a transgression for which Cecil must atone.

The narrative possibility of incest is doubled in the figure of Germain, who is similar to Yorke in age, height, dress, and coloring. Germain's presence in the text, rather than removing the incestuous tone of Cecil's relationship with her guardian, enhances it. The unwanted physical embraces of this mysterious man who calls Cecil "my darling," and "wrap[s] [her] in a cloak so closely that [she] [can] not speak, though [she is] kissed more than once" (149), therefore, serve to enact the physical violation Yorke's abusive rules can only gesture toward—his regulation of Cecil's sexuality through the series of contracts he exacts from her. Split into two (a psychic trope of denial), Germain and Yorke are halves of one unrepresentable person—the father-lover—divided safely into surrogate father and mysterious lover, roles they reverse to allow the story's problematic closure. The attentions of both these men are made more sinister to the reader by the fact that Cecil responds to both with a mixture of pleasure and fear. Just as she is drawn to Yorke by "an uncontrollable longing" (141–142), she responds to Germain with "the excitement of novelty and a lingering touch of fear," "like a fascinated bird" (139, 158).[6]

Where the paternal incest theme is often explored in the gothic as a function of what Dalke describes as the "wide-ranging sexual activity of the father" (197), what threatens Cecil here is precisely the lack of physical affection from her surrogate father. Although Germain's physical embraces are unwanted, Cecil is so starved for affection from her repressed surrogate father that she is thrilled by his attention. Unlike many gothic heroines, Alcott's protagonist is "aware of her own sexual longings" (Massé 10–11). However, this challenge to gothic conventions means that in order to free Cecil from the emotional repression Yorke's regulations represent, the story's closure must unite her with the man who begins the story as her surrogate father. Where many gothic works address the Oedipal girl's efforts to grow out of an incestuous attachment to a father figure by shifting to a more suitable partner, here the threat of incest continues until the final pages of the story, when Germain's sudden confession that he is Cecil's father miraculously (and unconvincingly) removes the incest taboo separating Yorke and his ward. Their marriage, however, is problematized by the fact that it can never be one of equals: Yorke's career comes first; Cecil destroys her artistic works, like many of Alcott's heroines. Cecil's victory over Yorke's repressive contract, then, continues to uphold an erotic economy based on incest rather than exogamy, domination rather than equality. In fact, equality seems to preclude erotic desire, as Cecil intuits when she defines her egalitarien relationship with Alf as friendship rather than love.

How should one read Cecil's loss of the drive toward equality and her masochistic acceptance of domination, her rejection of Alf and subsequent marriage to her surrogate father? It would be simple to naturalize Cecil's shift from a desire for equality to an acceptance of domination by applying Freud's model of adolescent femininity; to perceive her subordination as something she agrees to, as Deleuze might suggest; or to read "Cecil's painstaking obedience to the letter of Yorke's law," as Michelle Massé does, as an active response, the "conscious tactic" through which "Cecil causes her guardian-husband to regret his Pygmalion role" (252). But the economy that structures this text is much more complex than these readings allow.

Massé, for example, fails to note that Cecil's "obe[dience] to the letter," fulfillment of Yorke's desire for a "marble woman" until he recognizes the error of his ways, is described in the classic language of the sadomasochistic relationship which suggests a circularity of positions of subordination and domination rather than a disruption of this erotic power dynamic:

> [Yorke] wondered if she remembered the time when his will was law, and it was herself who obeyed with a weakness he had not yet learned. Now this was changed, and he called himself a fool for losing his old power, yet gaining no new hold upon her. She ruled him, but seemed not to know it, and keeping her smiles for others, showed her darkest side to him, being as lovely and thorny as any brier rose. (202)

The dynamic of "A Marble Woman" is perhaps better explained by an analysis of the ways the nuclear family structures and then regulates the daughter's desires. Like many gothic texts, Alcott's story depicts the home as a frightening realm where desire is, as Foucault claimed, both repressed and determined by the law. The separate spheres ideology effectively entitles Yorke, as Cecil's guardian, to stipulate the terms under which he will agree to accept her as his child and (later) his wife. As a result of these conditions, Cecil becomes increasingly reduced to silence and passivity as she becomes increasingly subjected to her surrogate father's law. Cecil's marriage in earnest to Yorke is finally permitted when Germain identifies himself as her real father. This removes the incest while his death permits Yorke to take Cecil's father's place. To presume that Cecil's marriage frees her is to assume that her desire is free from rather than shaped by patriarchal structures of affect. It also denies that the closure of this text is, as Zwinger suggests, "a formal convention invented precisely to cover up the unsightly, asymmetrical body of heterosexuality's fictions" (140), which the marital gothic responds to when it depicts the horror returning "in the new home of the couple, conjured up by renewed denial of the heroine's identity and autonomy" (Massé 20).

Significantly, much of the convoluted plot of "A Marble Woman" is made possible by the fact that the semiotic of the separate spheres contains no vocabulary to distinguish between the embraces of a father and the caresses of a lover. And, paradoxically, it is this very illegibility that motivates the reader's and the protagonist's desire throughout "A Marble Woman," where the threat and excitement of incest are enhanced by the ways in which Germain's paternal attentions can be misread as romantic and Yorke's erotic interest in Cecil can mask itself as paternal.

Grounding the prevalence of father-daughter incest plots in gothic texts and the problematic pleasures of the gothic in the structure of the family provides us with a cultural rather than natural explanation for the tension between the drive for equality and the drive for domination both enacted by and represented by the gothic text, suggesting that these desires are similarly culturally and historically determined rather than natural. Contrary to Lovecraft, who argued that horror "restores some primordial or instinctual human intuition about the world" through a feeling of cosmic fear, perhaps more appropriately considered awe (qtd. in Carroll 163), I propose to read the drive for domination as emerging out of the particular familial structure that characterizes the gothic. While it has perhaps been universal to feel "cosmic awe" for supernatural beings and religious figures greater than oneself, the desire to be dominated by another human being seems particularly unique to the gothic text.

The subversion of this erotic economy must begin not by "obeying the letter of the law," masochistically accepting the suffering dealt the victim by the torturer, as Massé and Deleuze imply, but rather by reimagining a family structure that does not necessitate a daughter's rejection of the mother that coincides with her quest for the father's recognition. The incestuous relationship between Cecil and her guardian in Alcott's story, regardless of Cecil's apparent victory over her torturer, marks a desperate circularity that reinscribes the ideology of the separate spheres on the face of the family.

NOTES

1. See especially Gross.

2. See Graham (xiii), Sadleir (7), Haggerty (3), Gross (1).

3. Incest or the threat of it appears in William Hill Brown's *The Power of Sympathy*; Susanna Rowson's *Mentoria* and *The Trials of the Hu-*

man Heart; Charles Brockden Brown's *Wieland* and *Ormond*; Richard Hildreth's *The Slave; or, Memoirs of Archy Moore*; Melville's *Pierre*; Hawthorne's "Alice Doane's Appeal"; Susan Warner's *The Wide, Wide World*; Poe's "The Fall of the House of Usher"; Elizabeth Maddox Roberts's *My Heart and My Flesh*; Faulkner's *The Sound and the Fury* and *Absalom, Absalom!*; V. C. Andrews's *Flowers in the Attic*; Tennessee Williams's *The Glass Menagerie*; Shirley Jackson's *Hangsaman* and *Come Along with Me*; Russell Banks's *Rule of the Bone*; Sam Shepard's *Buried Child*; Toni Morrison's *The Bluest Eye*; Anne Rice's *The Witching Hour, Lahser*, and *Vampire Lestat*; and Stephen King's *Dolores Claiborne*. For an inflammatory discussion of American writers' sustained interest in incest, see Roiphe.

4. See Rogin, Fliegelman, and Dalke.

5. Whereas Yorke's hands are associated with repression, attention to inanimate objects such as sculpture, and his desire to "mold" Cecil to pay her mother's debt, Germain's hands are associated with passion, sensuality, and affection: "[s]o sure was she that a hand had touched her . . . that she looked over the balustrade. . . . a man was going slowly down, wrapped in a cloak, with a shadowy hat drawn low over his brows. A slender hand shone white against the dark cloak" (139).

6. Cecil's risk of incest is perhaps best reflected by her name which combines the names of her mother, her mother's childhood sweetheart, and her mother's husband, implying that Cecil is at once her mother and herself and hence both daughter and lover to both Yorke and Germain.

WORKS CITED

Alcott, Louisa May. *Plots and Counterplots: More Unknown Thrillers of Louisa May Alcott*. Ed. Madeleine Stern. New York: Morrow and Company, 1976.

Burke, Edmund. "On the Sublime and the Beautiful." *The Works of Edmund Burke*. Vol. 1. London: George Bell, 1906.

Carroll, Noel. *The Philosophy of Horror; or, Paradoxes of the Heart*. New York: Routledge, 1990.

Chesler, Phyllis. "Rape and Psychotherapy." *Rape: The 1st Sourcebook for Women*. Ed. Noreen Connel and Cassandra Wilson. New York: New American Library, 1974.

Christophersen, Bill. *The Apparition in the Glass: Charles Brockden Brown's American Gothic*. Athens and London: U of Georgia P, 1993.

Dalke, Anne. "Original Vice: The Political Implications of Incest in the Early American Novel." *Early American Literature* 23.2 (1988): 188–201.

Day, William Patrick. *In the Circles of Fear and Desire: A Study of Gothic Fantasy*. Chicago: U of Chicago P, 1995.

Deleuze, Gilles. *Masochism: Coldness and Cruelty*. 1967. New York: Zone Books, 1991.

Ellis, Kate Ferguson. *The Contested Castle: Gothic Novels and the Subversion of Domestic Ideology*. U of Illinois P, 1989.

Fiedler, Leslie. *Love and Death in the American Novel*. New York: Anchor Books, 1992.

Freud, Sigmund. *Three Essays on the Theory of Sexuality*. 1905. Ed. and trans. James Strachey. London: Hogarth, 1962.

Graham, Kenneth W., ed. *Gothic Fictions: Prohibition / Transgression*. New York: AMS P, 1989.

Gross, Louis. *Redefining American Gothic: From* Wieland *to* Day of the Dead. UMI Research P, 1989.

Haggerty, George E. *Gothic Fiction / Gothic Form*. University Park: Pennsylvania State UP, 1989.

Heller, Terry. *The Delights of Terror: An Aesthetics of the Tale of Terror*. Chicago: U of Illinois P, 1987.

Hennessy, Brendan. *The Gothic Novel*. Burnt Mill, UK: Longman House, 1978.

Irigaray, Luce. *The Speculum of the Other Woman*. Ithaca: Cornell UP, 1985.

MacAndrew, Elizabeth. *The Gothic Tradition in Fiction*. New York: Columbia UP, 1979.

Massé, Michelle. *In the Name of Love: Women, Masochism, and the Gothic*. Ithaca: Cornell UP, 1992.

Rogin, Michael. *Fathers and Children: Andrew Jackson and the Subjugation of the American Indian*. New York: Knopf, 1975.

Roiphe, Katie. "Making the Incest Scene." *Harper's Magazine* (November 1995): 65–71.

Sadleir, Michael. *The Northanger Novels. A Footnote to Jane Austen*. English Association, pamphlet no. 68. Oxford: Oxford UP, 1927.

Zwinger, Lynda. *Daughters, Fathers and the Novel: The Sentimental Romance of Heterosexuality*. Madison: U of Wisconsin P, 1992.

If a Building Is a Sentence, So Is a Body
Kathy Acker and the Postcolonial Gothic

Gothic narratives have long been theorized according to familiar topoi: dungeons, trapdoors, passages, cellars, convents, decaying houses, and crypts, all of these inhabited by monks, nuns, aristocrats, banditti, and vulnerable heroines. These topoi function within traditional gothicism as coded spaces which, according to Foucault, articulated the fear that haunted the latter half of the eighteenth century in both France and England, namely, the Enlightenment's overdetermined refusal to tolerate "areas of darkness" in a political and moral order founded upon notions of transparency and the "full visibility of things, men and truths" (Foucault 153–154). The exportation of the gothic novel to America, it seems, remains true to Enlightenment values, as Leslie Fiedler's remarks suggest. American fiction, "from Charles Brockden Brown to William Faulkner or Eudora Welty, Paul Bowles or John Hawkes is a gothic fiction, sadistic and melodramatic—a literature of darkness and the grotesque in a land of light and affirmation" (Fiedler 28–29). Keeping in mind that light is *the* philosophic metaphor, it is not difficult to understand how the binary opposition light/darkness found its way into the gothic novel to represent what Fiedler calls "the dark vision of the American" and "the hidden blackness of the human soul and society" (27). As Foucault's and Fiedler's remarks suggest, photological metaphors have not only dominated philosophical discourses but have also determined literary tropes and critical responses to those tropes. If photological metaphors have been instrumental not only in spinning out the ethos of Othering in the linking of woman to matter, nature, and evil but also in justifying the brutal exploitation of non-European cultures by Western colonial and imperial forces, then how is one to speculate on a *postcolonial* gothic literature without becoming ensnared in these same epistemological and ontological binary oppositions and replicating what might be merely an economy of the same? Specifically, what distinguishes a postcolonial gothic text from, say, any other? Is postcolonialism both a reading and a writing practice? If American gothic fiction is traditionally racialized, what tropes might be characteristic of such a text? How are issues of race, not to mention class, sex, and gender, which I think cannot be separated, addressed in what would be called postcolonial gothicism? Finally, is such a genre possible?

One might argue that a new strain of gothicism *is* being produced within a postcolonial America, one which opens full throttle into colonialism's and imperialism's *horror*, namely, all that has been excluded as "meaningless," "senseless," and "aberrant." But so far this doesn't seem any different from gothic novels as they are described by Fiedler and Foucault. The *new* species of gothicism, however, seems to be paradoxical, setting up a double bind, since it causes not only "gender trouble" (to use Judith Butler's term) but also race trouble and class trouble, which might also be called "gothic trouble" because it violently ruptures the ethos of Othering implicit in gothic fiction. By problematizing these issues in terms of the so-called body, this new strain of gothicism destabilizes notions of identity not only by reflecting on how, as Butler asserts, "'the body' is itself shaped by political forces with strategic interests in keeping that body bounded and constituted by the markers of sex" (*Gender Trouble* 129) but also by implying an analogy between those "forces" in the politics of violence in the gothic and colonial/imperialist practices.

This hybrid species of gothicism, to which I am alluding, retains the familiar topoi: dark and gloomy surroundings, ruined buildings, sexual violence. But there the similarity ends. Peopled by orphans, nomads, judges, and intertextual specters of Freud and Schreber, Kathy Acker's phantasmagoric *Empire of the Senseless* posits an alien ontology, one that seems an anathema to gothic production—that of the cyborg, an indeterminate species whose "replication [according to Donna Harraway] is uncoupled from organic reproduction" (150). The cyborg's province thus falls out of the realm of the dualisms which in Western traditions have, according to Donna Harraway, "been systemic to the logics and practices of domination of women, people of colour, nature, workers, animals—in short, domination of all constituted as others" (177). As an indeterminate species, the cyborg launches an interrogation of the boundaries of what counts as human and thus into the discursive practices, including gothicism, that determine those boundaries. This essay, then, seeks to explore the terms of what I will provisionally call "cybergothic," a mutant form, a hybrid born of traditional gothicism, science fiction, and cyberpunk, in fact, a genre that represents a generational rupture in gothic narrative because it imagines what Donna Harraway refers to in another context as "a monstrous world without gender" (181). This world is monstrous, she argues, because "[t]he cyborg skips the step of original unity, of identification with nature in the Western sense" and thus "does not dream of community on the model of the organic family, this time without the oedipal project" (151). In fact, it is *because* the figure of the cyborg deranges naturalist systems of classification that issues of "evil," "horror," and abjection necessarily become differently centered.

While this essay seeks to develop some of the theoretical framework of postcolonial gothic, it will do so by making reference to Kathy Acker's experimental work, *Empire of the Senseless*, a profoundly dystopic novel in which Acker presents Abhor, a terrorist and writer who is female, "part robot, and part black" (we are not told *which* parts, an issue to which I will later return), a product of the military-industrial complex who journeys with her partner, Thivai, a would-be pirate and cyborg, through the phantasmagoria of postrevolutionary, disease-ridden Paris, Algeria, New York, and Washington, D.C. Rather than perform a detailed exegesis of Acker's work, I would prefer to discuss the way that Acker's *Empire* functions as a test site for the *generation* of theories of postcolonial gothic narrative since it takes the meaning or the "sense" of "empire" in new directions. By deploying a compositional attitude that not only resists the dualisms that function at the heart of empire building, Acker's novel takes issue with the "senselessness" of empire building, showing how, to use Goya's terms, it is "the dream of reason that breeds monsters." This essay then theorizes the cyborg, and particularly Acker's Abhor, as a candidate to herald the emergence of postcolonial gothic writing in America, since these "odd boundary creatures," to again use Donna Harraway's terminology, serve as the West's "worst nightmare," not only because they efface the distinction between humans and machines, thus rupturing the dream of organic wholeness and original unity, but also because the boundary confusion generated by the so-called female cyborg bursts apart the Nature/Woman conjunction that naturalizes traditional narratives, including those of the gothic.

Abhor: the etymology of her name suggests what is at stake. From the Latin *abhorrére*, a verb meaning "to shrink back in dread, to be far from, to be inconsistent with; to regard with horror, extreme repugnance or disgust; to hate utterly, loathe, abominate"—in a word, "horror," "the quality or condition of exciting repugnance or dread; a thing or person which excites these feelings." The presence of horror, however, signals desire, and where there is desire there is taboo, terror, and fascination. According to Georges Bataille, "repugnance and horror are the mainsprings of desire [which] is only aroused as long as its object causes a chasm no less deep than death to yawn within, and that this desire originates in its opposite, horror" (59). Similarly, says Bataille, "[t]aboo and transgression reflect two contradictory urges. The taboo would forbid the transgression but the fascination compels it" (68). Although it is not made explicit, what Bataille's remarks draw our attention to are the dynamics of eroticism as they are determined by the social or, more precisely, *familial* relations that are legitimized in the Name-of-the-Father. Indeed, Leslie Fiedler argues that the sense of guilt and anxiety produced by the basic gothic story is one of innocence and guilt in the face of incest, albeit a particular one: "incest of brother and sister-daughter bred out of an original incest of mother and son—the breach of the primal taboo and *the offence against the father*!" (132, my emphasis). Fiedler also remarks that, "[i]n more general terms, the guilt which underlies the gothic and motivates its plots is the guilt of the revolutionary haunted by the (paternal) past which he has been striving to destroy: and the fear that possesses the gothic and motivates its tone is the fear that in destroying the old ego-ideals of Church and State, the West has opened a way for the inruption of darkness: for insanity and the disintegration of the self" (132).

Fiedler's assertions are telling here, I think, because they direct our attention to the way that psycho/socio/sexual relations appear to be modeled upon the family, legitimized by the (word of the) father, who in this family romance is the only one who remains guilt-free. Thus, it would seem that "taboo," "horror," "transgression," and "guilt" are all grounded in terms of the family. Perhaps, then, what is so *monstrous* about Abhor is that she has no truck with the family romance. Neither does her partner, Thivai, whose mother told him when he was eight years old that his "real father wasn't Alpha-Centaurian, but robotic" (Acker 155). Like Abhor, Thivai angers the man who calls himself "Daddy" when he says to him: "I'm not human. Whatever HU-MAN is, it's not human. We live in New York City between people who own most of the money in this world and people who own so little they're not human" (Acker 155). As Donna Harraway points out, "[t]he main trouble with cyborgs is that they are the illegitimate offspring of militarism and patriarchal capitalism, not to mention state socialism. But illegitimate offspring are often exceedingly unfaithful to their origins. *Their fathers, after all, are inessential*" (151, my emphasis). What Harraway's remarks draw our attention to is not the way that capitalism has been modeled on the family but rather the way that the so-called family is produced in the service of social regulation and control of sexuality by capitalism and militarism (we can now hear colonialism/imperialism), a complex historical system that produces the naturalized term "family" as part of a strategy to conceal and, hence, to perpetuate power relations. According to Deleuze and Guattari,

> Oedipus depends upon [a] nationalistic, religious racist senti-
> ment and not the reverse: it is not the father who is projected
> onto the boss, but the boss who is applied to the father, either
> in order to tell us "you will not surpass your father," or "you
> will surpass him to find our forefathers." Lacan [they say] has
> demonstrated in a profound way the link between Oedipus
> and segregation [by means of integration into a group]. (104)

When Abhor says, "I would like the whole apparatus—family and memory—to go to hell," we hear a cyborg invective, an indictment of the family as it functions not as an organic unity but as a modern ideological state apparatus in the service of capitalism. Abhor's indictment of the family is "monstrous" and, perhaps, "abhorrent" because it leaps the horizon of "truth" and stampedes through the "oedipalized territories" of Family, Church, School, Nation, and Party, those linguistically coded strongholds of "identity." As a writer, Abhor reflects upon those codes:

> Ten years ago [she says], it seemed possible to destroy lan-
> guage through language: to destroy language which normal-
> izes and controls by cutting that language. Nonsense would
> attack the empire-making (empirical) empire of language, the
> prisons of meaning.
>
> But this nonsense, since it depended on sense, simply
> pointed back to the normalizing institutions.
>
> What is the language of the "unconscious"? (If this ideal
> unconscious or freedom doesn't exist: pretend it does, use
> fiction, for the sake of survival, all of our survival.) Its primary
> language must be taboo, all that is forbidden. Thus, an attack
> on the institutions of prison via language would demand the
> use of a language or languages that aren't acceptable, which
> are forbidden. Language, on one level, constitutes a set of
> codes and social and historical agreements. Nonsense doesn't

per se break down the codes; speaking precisely that which the codes *forbid* breaks the codes. (Acker 134, my emphasis)

Abhor's exhortation to speak "precisely that which the codes forbid" finds resonance in Donna Harraway's argument that "the most terrible and perhaps the most promising monsters in cyborg worlds are embodied in non-oedipal narratives with a different logic of repression" (150). If we take Thomas Laqueur's assertion that "systems of knowledge determine what can be thought within them" and couple that remark with Kristeva's take on "abjection"—"[i]t is not lack of cleanliness or health that causes abjection but what disturbs identity, system, order" (4)— we can make inferences that are differently centered regarding the concepts of "horror" and "evil." Donna Harraway's assertion concerning "cyborg writing" suggests what is at stake: "[c]yborg writing is about the power to survive, not on the basis of original innocence, but on the basis of seizing the tools to mark the world that marked them as other" (175), a remark which leads not only in the direction of the body but also to issues of "sex," "gender," and "race."

In *Empire of the Senseless*, the figure of Dr. Schreber, who is Abhor's "boss," appears as a hybrid character comprised of Dr. Freud and Freud's psychoanalytic record of Judge Sterner, who, as a child, is taught what Deleuze and Guattari call "resignation to Oedipus." It is in this familial realm that most gothic fictions, concerned with desire, castration, guilt, and the uncanny, are rooted. Abhor recounts the (case) "history" of Schreber's childhood, a narrative of restraint and torture which, as signifying practices, mark out the domain of social hegemony known as "the body." Thus "Schreberized," the body of the child emerges as the site of the enactment and reproduction of social regulation and control (as taboo) under the auspices of the family, who wields the instruments and teaches that "resignation to Oedipus" I mentioned earlier. Cultural intelligibility thus demands what Deleuze and Guattari refer to as the "assumption of one's sex" according to the colonizing inscription of empire's power on the body (59). Schreber's case history appears, there-

fore, not as a marginal cultural manifestation but as the clearest
site of normative construction of the so-called body through
which, to use Deleuze and Guattari's terms, "the imperialism
of Oedipus is founded" (60). According to Abhor, Schreber's
"mother bathed him only in ice-water according to her husband's
instructions"; his father "made various toys for his son including
a shoulder-band [in the form of] a figure eight of metal and
leather whose two loops, after curving round the boy's front, met
in the middle of the back; [a]nother toy, a 'straight-hold,' an iron
cross-bar fastened to the table, by pressing against the child's
collarbones and shoulders, prevented both bad posture and any
movement" (Acker 45).

In this system, the "Word made flesh" is the "individual
subject" who emerges as "the effect and the object of power"
which inscribes or "writes" the "political anatomy of the body"
(Foucault 189). That a "power of writing" functions as an "essential part in the mechanisms of discipline" (Foucault 189)
becomes clear in light of the fact that, according to Abhor,
Dr./Judge Schreber, "who had such beliefs dominating his consciousness," went on to invent the "head crusher," an apparatus
which "resembled the metal egg-cap the doctor's father used to
ensure his son always maintained his proper posture" (Acker 46).
Schreber thus figuratively and literally reproduces the "horror"
of the "apparatus" which produced him.

If Kurtz's last words, "[t]he horror, the horror," can be heard
to echo here, it seems to me to be no coincidence, since *Empire
of the Senseless* takes up the question of imperialism and colonialism where Conrad's *Heart of Darkness* leaves off. A chapter entitled "Let the Algerians Take over Paris" resonates with Kurtz's
mandate to "[e]xterminate the brutes" when Abhor recalls how
the atrocities once perpetrated by the French in North Africa
were continued in Paris by the Parisian and French govern-
ments, who, she says, "desired simply to exterminate the Algerian trash, the terrorists, the gypsies" (Acker 75). If the obsessive
Colonel Kurtz can be understood as the quintessential imperialist, his dying utterance resonates with profound implications for
the collapse of what Marlow glowingly refers to as the "idea at

the back of [the conquest of the earth]; not a sentimental pretence [he says] but an idea; and an unselfish belief in the idea— something you can set up, and bow down before, and offer a sacrifice to" (Conrad 32). While the representation of Kurtz points, in one way, to the *horror* of imperialism when defrocked of its idealisms, his dying utterance also reverberates with the will to power's *dread* of losing that power. But where Conrad's *Heart of Darkness* gestures toward the collapse of colonialism in the fallen figure of Kurtz, Acker's *Empire* opens full throttle into imperialism's "horror"—Abhor, female, part robot, part black, signaling the collapse of distinctions and the failure of exclusionary practices which maintain those distinctions. Abhor, Kurtz's *wrong* word made flesh—and machine. Part robot, part black. Which parts? Private parts? For the most part? Playing a part? Parts of speech? Abhor, then, a monstrous writing machine, disobedient in the face of syntactical requirements that guarantee cultural intelligibility. Says Donna Harraway, "[w]riting has a special significance for all colonized groups. Writing has been crucial to the Western myth of the distinction between oral and written cultures, primitive and civilized mentalities, and more recently to the erosion of that distinction in 'postmodernist' theories attacking the phallogocentrism of the West, with its worship of the monotheistic, phallic, authoritative work, the unique and perfect name" (175). It is not difficult to imagine in what profound *dread* authoritative discourse holds that which threatens to "contaminate" its semantic purity. What was once on the tip of Kurtz's tongue returns to tell the Other side of the story.

Speaking from a postrebellion, disease-ridden Paris, Abhor chronicles the uprising of the Algerians headed by the voodoo practitioner, Mackandal, whose arm had been crushed in a cane mill shaft in Africa, where he had labored as a child under "white Parisian owners." While Abhor examines the conditions of poverty and oppression which fueled the Algerian uprising, her story makes explicit the ways that all colonizers inscribe their power and exercise their sovereignty upon the incredulous flesh of their "subjects." Abhor recalls that the Caribbean English slave owners of the nineteenth century had injected a chemical similar to formic acid, taken from two members of the stinging nettle family, into the already broken skins of the recalcitrant slaves. Ants crawl ceaselessly under the top layer of skin. And forced the unwilling servants to eat Jamaican "dumbcane" whose leaves, as if they were actually tiny slivers of glass, irritating the larynx and causing local swelling, made breathing difficult and speaking impossible. (Acker 74)

Abhor also tells the story of Toussaint L'Ouverture, who, she says, used "voodoo to defeat Western hegemony" but not before

[the] masters, white, had poured burning wax on parts of other bodies, arms and hands and shoulders, emptied boiling cane sugar over heads of their slaves, burned others alive, roasted some on slow fires, filled some other bodies with gunpowder and blown them up by a match, buried others in sand or dirt up to the necks then smeared the heads in honey so that huge flies would devour them, placed some next to nests of red ants and wasps, made others drink their own piss eat their own shit and lick off the saliva of other slaves. The minds of whoever survived lived in and were pain. (Acker 65)

Here, writing on the body: the inscription of power, pure power, the application of which in past colonial practice is not dissimilar to that process of "Schreberization" and which Abhor links to global capitalism.

According to Abhor, the code of nineteenth-century bourgeois realism translates into "*God* equals *capitalism*" (Acker 45–56), an equation that directs our attention to the way that the energy flow which drives the desiring machine of capitalism works. Say Deleuze and Guattari, "if *what* we term libido is the connective 'labor' of desiring-production is *not* God it is [however] divine, when it attracts to itself the entire process of production and serves as its miraculate enchanted service, inscribing it in each and every one of its disjunctions. Hence the strange relationship that Shreber has with God" (13). And hence the relationship between empire building and the divine, since Schreber's divine, say Deleuze and Guattari, is "inseparable from the disjunctions he employs to divide himself up into *parts*: earlier empires, later empires; later empires of a superior God, and those of an inferior God" (13). Recalling those problem "parts" of Abhor's discussed earlier, Schreber's body becomes (a) "colonized (subject)," his body the recording site/sight of the central myths of origin of Western culture which are retold in gothic fiction from Walpole to Stephen King.

So, where do we go from here? In this essay I have speculated on the emergence of the gothic in a postcolonial America and have suggested that the politics of violence in the gothic has found a new incarnation in the cyberfiction of a modern military/industrial society that cleaves to the politics of domination, however subtly deployed in a global economy. *Empire of the Senseless* does not claim that imperialist practices went down with the figure of Kurtz. On the contrary, Acker's novel moves into territory previously uncharted by gothic fiction, namely, global culture, which, as Fredric Jameson asserts, is "the internal and superstructural expression of a whole new wave of American military and economic domination throughout the world: in this sense, as throughout class history, the underside of culture is blood, torture, death, and terror" (5), elements that as I see them are also integral to gothic narratives. Although Jameson claims that the gothic is a "boring and exhausted paradigm" in which "a sheltered woman of some kind is terrorized and victimized by an 'evil' male," he does agree that the genre has resonance in a modern culture "when the individual 'victim'—male or female—is substituted for the collectivity itself, the U.S. public, [for example,] which now lives out the anxieties of its economic privileges and its sheltered 'exceptionalism' in a pseudo-political version of the gothic—under the threats of stereotypical madmen and 'terrorists' (mostly Arabs or Iranians for some reason)" (289). Although Jameson is referring to film production, his remarks are relevant here since they suggest that although *colonialism* is officially dead, a new form of imperialism slips in to generate a new form of the Other, whose task, "to mirror the Self the One who is not dominated," remains the same as the old one. The reappearance of these old familiar dualisms in Jameson's critical position suggests to me that Acker's text is a cyborgian one itself since it performs a difficult maneuver which might be characteristic of gothicism's emergence in postcolonial America. Because it is a gothic text that undoes itself, Acker's *Empire* configures the "space" of "*neither/nor*" that, according to Judith Butler (in her discussion of the insufficiency of notions evoking the "word's materiality"), "enables the logic of either-or, which takes idealism and materialism as its two poles" (*Bodies* 254). It is, therefore, the evocation of an *impossible space* that interests me, one in which *Empire*, like the cyborg, is an indeterminate species that nonetheless acknowledges its gothic ancestry by becoming the "worst nightmare" of both colonialism/imperialism and gothicism since, in linking the power politics of traditional gothicism with these practices, it mends the breach, or the perceived dualism, between them, suturing both "reason" and "monstrosity" in what might be a decidedly anxious coupling.

WORKS CITED

Acker, Kathy. *Empire of the Senseless*. New York: Grove, Weidenfeld, 1988.

Bataille, Georges. *Eroticism: Death and Sensuality*. Trans. Mary Dalwood. San Francisco: City Lights Books, 1986.

Butler, Judith. *Bodies that Matter: On the Discursive Limits of "Sex."* New York: Routledge, 1993.

———. *Gender Trouble: Feminism and the Subversion of Identity*. New York: Routledge, 1990.

Conrad, Joseph. *Heart of Darkness*. New York: Penguin Books, 1983.

Deleuze, Gilles, and Félix Guattari. *Anti-Oedipus: Capitalism and Schizophrenia*. Trans. Robert Hurley, Mark Seem, and Helen R. Lane. Minneapolis: U of Minnesota P, 1983.

Fiedler, Leslie A. *Love and Death in the American Novel*. Rev. ed. New York: Stein and Day, 1966.

Foucault, Michel. "The Eye of Power," *Power/Knowledge: Selected Interviews and Other Writings 1972–1977*. Ed. Colin Gordon. Trans. Colin Gordon, Leo Marshall, John Mepham, and Kate Soper. New York: Pantheon Books, 1980.

Harraway, Donna. "A Cyborg Manifesto," *Simians, Cyborgs and Women: The Reinvention of Nature*. New York: Routledge, 1991.

Jameson, Fredric. *Postmodernism, or, The Cultural Logic of Late Capitalism*. Durham: Duke UP, 1992.

Kristeva, Julia. *Powers of Horror: An Essay in Abjection*. Trans. Léon S. Roudiez. New York: Columbia UP, 1982.

Laqueur, Thomas. *Making Sex: Body and Gender from the Greeks to Freud*. Cambridge, MA: Harvard UP, 1980.

PART V

The Gothic Postmodern

NICOLA NIXON

Making Monsters, or
Serializing Killers

For all that it had the veneer of currency, with its special effects and dalliance with the quasi-scientific "paranormal" and "parapsychological," Tobe Hooper's *Poltergeist* seemed, in 1982, to be merely a residual demon-possession film, a latecomer to the already rather shopworn seventies occult movie. Lagging behind *The Exorcist* (1973), *The Omen* (1976), *The Sentinel* (1977), *The Amityville Horror* (1979), and *The Shining* (1980), *Poltergeist* nevertheless had all the ingredients: a nice family, a haunted house, a possessed child, and, most important, the ever-menacing danger of unholy spirits and the "Beast" lurking just beyond the reality of the bucolic suburbia of Cuesta Verde. And yet *Poltergeist* also presented something else, something other than a drafty window or bricked-in basement as the liminal space between the demonic and domestic world: it posited a television set as the interstice and conduit between specular reality and what gets portentously referred to throughout the film as the "other side." Experiencing the most profound effects of this liminal space is a little female viewer, Carol Anne Freeling, who is sucked into the interstice through her apparently one-sided interaction with "TV people." That the "TV people" are merely pleasant illusions, produced to occlude the horror of the Beast from Carol Anne, is made clear by the time Hooper shifts the cinematic emphasis from the white noise and snow-filled holding pattern of the perpetually on television to the bedrooms upstairs, in which the scene of Carol Anne's metaphoric rebirth into American suburbia is enacted. As with *The Amityville Horror*, the Beast is eventually thwarted, and the now-reunited Freeling family abandon their home, drive to a Holiday Inn, and, as a parting shot, proceed to stick the hotel television set out in the hall— presumably to stave off any further unwitting submission to its dangerous enticement.[1]

If *Poltergeist* was effectively among the last gasps of the popular seventies genre of occult or Satanic-possession films, its early eighties take on that genre equally registered, as did David Cronenberg's *Videodrome* (also of 1982), the emergence of what would become one of the more gnawed-over and politically fraught debates in eighties and nineties America: the problematic relationship between fictional illusion, or "TV people," and its youthful American consumers. And if, in terms of those debates at any rate, the Satanic Beast was dropped out of the triangulated relation of real viewer, fictional screen, and otherworldly gothic demon, this lacuna suggests as much about a shift away from the popular seventies articulation of horror as it does about a realignment of the locus of monstrosity. What seems to disappear in the removal of the Beast is horror's representation within arcane religious tropes and a thematics of the "other side."

Now, to a point, the situating of the monstrous and its horror within the parameters of religious extremes made perfect sense in the seventies, when the supposed prevalence of strange "brainwashing" cults and their charismatic leaders prompted alarmist anticult propaganda. With the trials of Charles Manson and the Manson "family" in 1970, with Mansonite Lynette "Squeaky" Fromme's failed shooting of President Gerald Ford and her trial in 1975, with the Jonestown massacre in 1978, and with the repeated hysterical efforts to have Reverend Sun Myung Moon deported and his Unification Church disbanded in the late seventies, it is scarcely surprising that the decade's horror films should at least tangentially reflect real fears of an emergent evangelical menace. Given their focus on the mysterious "possession" of middle-class American family members, who speak with the voice and words of the symbolically recognizable but always elided, faceless, otherworldly Beast of the apocalypse, films like

The Exorcist and *The Amityville Horror* accentuate the helplessness of vulnerable youth in the face of a far greater occult power.
In the post-Watergate early eighties, however, when television
had proven itself useful for the simultaneous propagation of
comforting fictions and exposure of the shocking truth behind
them, when Cronenberg's Father O'Blivion had heralded the
emergence of the more benign but equally avaricious televange-
list Jimmy Baker, the construct of horror and its representation
had changed.

By the time Reverend Moon had been dispatched to a Con-
necticut prison on a vaguely trumped-up charge of tax evasion in
1984, the cinema's metaphysical gothic Beast, whose presence
was merely suggested representationally with gusts of frigid
wind, swarms of flies, low gutteral growls, and the tip of a lash-
ing tail, had given way to a more visceral, because more "real,"
form of the monstrous. The American serial killer, who left human detritus in his wake from New York and Texas to Washington, D.C., and Milwaukee, had come to occupy the symbolic
space of montrosity in the public imagination. Indeed, nothing
could have quite illustrated the dissolution or reification of the
myth of demonic possession as clearly as Son of Sam's failed insanity defense in 1978 and its aftermath in 1979. While he was
killing, David Berkowitz wrote to the *New York Daily News* that
he was driven to kill by the "Duke of Death," the "Wicked King
Wicker," and the "22 Disciples of Hell" (*Serial* 171); he wrote
taunting letters to New York police captain Joseph Borrelli that
he signed "Mr Monster" (Klausner 142). At his trial Berkowitz
described "demonic inner choirs," hellish noises under his floor-
boards, and compulsions from the depths of hell; his defense attorney offered samples of the doodles and graffiti from the walls
of his house: "I am possessed" and "demons torment me" (*Serial*
182). Declared insane and delusional (although not "possessed")
by a panel of three psychiatrists, Berkowitz was nevertheless
reevaluated, determined fit to stand trial, and convicted as a sane
murderer. Eight months later, much to the surprise of the prison
psychologists and much to the satisfaction of both New York
district attorneys, Berkowitz recanted: in February of 1979 he

held a press conference at Attica, at which he assured reporters that the demons were fabrications "invented by me in my own mind to condone what I was doing" (*Serial* 182).

This dispelling of illusory or obfuscatory fictions and disclosure of the "facts" of Berkowitz's true guilt speak not only of the inadequacy, at the end of the seventies, of the literal "devil-made-me-do-it" defense but equally of the confident separation of the fictional and the real, in which the latter can produce the affect, if not exactly the content, that was once exclusively in the sphere of the former. And the seemingly pragmatic rejection of the gothic *other* side as the locus of horror brings forth a symptomatic overvaluation of *this* side's true serial killers. That America thought it had horrifyingly "real" monsters instead of fictional demons is unquestionably reflected in the emergence and stunning efflorescence of eighties "true-crime" books like Ann Rule's *The Stranger beside Me* (1980), Terry Sullivan's *Killer Clown: The John Wayne Gacy Murders* (1983), Stephen Michaud and Hugh Aynesworth's *The Only Living Witness* (1983) and *Ted Bundy: Conversations with a Killer* (1989), Lawrence Klausner's *Son of Sam* (1981), and scores of other books about the so-called superstar killers, who, according to Elliott Leyton, had made "lifelong *celebrity career[s]*" (2) out of their multiple murders.

Gallows jokes aside about the acute brevity of the "*lifelong*" celebrity careers of, say, the late Ted Bundy, Jeffrey Dahmer, or John Wayne Gacy, much of that celebrity emerged out of the frisson of fear offered by the "real" rather than by the merely fictional gothic Beast. But that seemingly confident divide between the fictional gothic and the "real" is not, I would argue, unproblematic. Nor is it a divide that can simply accommodate a Berkowitz-like claim to be first a monster and then a liar, as if the monstrous were eminently dispatchable to the pages of a novel (the "other side" of truth) while the real were pristinely articulable within the pages of true crime, purporting to present its unmediated horror. The dust jackets, for example, invite us to read "The Shocking True Story of American's Most Notorious Serial Killer" (Henry Lee Lucas), "The Shocking True-Crime Story of America's Most Twisted Serial Sex Killer" (Jeffrey Dahmer), "The Shocking True Story of the Man Convicted of More Murders than Any Other Person in United States History!" (Gacy) and enjoin us to peruse the accompanying "8 Pages of Chilling [or "Gripping" or "Dramatic" or "Shocking"] Photos." Contrary to their billing, the photographs are neither "shocking" nor "gripping," consisting almost exclusively of high-school yearbook photos of the victims, mug shots or courtroom pictures of the killers, and, occasionally, grainy, indistinct polaroids of investigators at one of the crime scenes. Conventional and scarcely "chilling," they confer above all the air of bland verisimilitude.

For all their hyperbolic claims to shock with "truth," true-crime books, and indeed the entire discourse around serial killers, nevertheless register an ongoing difficulty: how, in the true-crime story, to marshal "fact" into "story" and seemingly banal people into satisfying characters; how, in other words, to generate comprehension and explicability out of a real that, unlike fiction, potentially defies satisfying organization and mimetic representation. The "facts" about serial killers—at least those that form the real base of true-crime books—are little more than catalogs of the killers' effects on their victims, whose corpses testify silently to pre- or postmortem torture, mutilation, dismemberment, sexual assault, cannibalism, necrophilia, exposure, paraphelia. Typically such catalogs are lightly larded with thumbnail sketches of the young, innocent victims' lives and last-known movements, embellished slightly with speculation about the killers' modus operandi, and explicit about the totemic body parts or pieces of clothing and jewelry that the killer removed from the victim. And, as if to offer some vague sociological or psychological justification for the killers' actions, true-crime writers hark back to cryptic biographical facts about the killers' childhoods and early, premurderous, years.

Like forensic reports, however, such catalogs of facts in the true crime story are grossly lacking in "story" potential, confounding, as they do, any organizational principles that would offer familiar readerly comprehensibility. Indeed, given the randomness, repetition, and seeming motivelessness of the killings, the crimes themselves pose a stony resistance to even the loosest picaresque narrative models.[2] When, for example, Joyce Carol

Oates criticizes Nick Broomfield's *Aileen Wuornos: The Selling of a Serial Killer* (1994) as "one of those hand-held-camera documentaries that make of their own limitations and rebuffs a theme of the narrative, and which can only be viewed by VCR, with one's thumb firmly on the fast-forward button" (55), she simply fails to register the on going narrative problem with the true-crime story. She fails, in other words, to acknowledge that the "theme of the narrative" must be constructed as that of documentary filmmaking, just as the theme of Edgar Allan Poe's "The Mystery of Marie Rogêt" had to be that of Auguste Dupin's detection, because the "factual" material cannot itself sustain the burden of the narrative.

If the killers' actions, in their abject plotlessness, are intrinsically bereft of any narrative potential to proffer comprehensibility, the killers' characters do not compensate. In *The Journalist and the Murderer* (1990) Janet Malcolm attempts to appraise Joe McGinniss's obvious difficulties with his subject in *Fatal Vision* (1983), his true-crime bestseller about convicted murderer Dr. Jeffrey MacDonald. Reading over the trial transcripts and listening to tape recordings, Malcolm is surprised to find that MacDonald's language is "dead, flat, soft, clichéd," that the "plain words" have an "awful puerility" (67). The "bland dullness" of MacDonald on tape strikes her as "unusual . . . because of its contrast to the excitingly dire character of the crime for which he stood convicted: a murderer shouldn't sound like an accountant" (70). The *New Yorker's* Alec Wilkinson makes an almost identical observation about Gacy: that his voice "rarely change[d] pitch" as he went "over the same ground again and again," and sometimes Gacy's "company was so dreary that I would take off my watch, so I couldn't see how slowly the time was passing"—"[w]hat personality he may once have had collapsed long ago and has been replaced by a catalogue of gestures and attitudes" (59). Ted Bundy's biographers or interviewers, Stephen Michaud and Hugh Aynesworth, had to spell each other off when they were interviewing Bundy, perceiving him as simultaneously "empty" and grandiose; they finally gave up altogether and published barely edited transcripts in *Ted Bundy: Conversations with a Killer*, concluding the book with a veiled apology for their lack of perseverance or fortitude. And Anne Schwartz, in her book on Jeffrey Dahmer, *The Man Who Could Not Kill Enough* (1992), comments that the intellectually "dull normal" Dahmer had no apparent craziness or charm: "[t]here was just nothing to him" (180).

The real MacDonalds or Gacys, the real Bundys or Dahmers, unlike the charismatic gothic killers of, say, Thomas Harris's recent fiction, are deeply dull and blandly ordinary.[3] They are so ordinary, in fact, that Malcolm suggests that McGinniss, having "found out too late . . . that the subject of his book was not up to scratch—not suitable for a work of nonfiction, not a member of the wonderful race of auto-fictionalizers . . . on whom the New Journalism and the 'nonfiction novel' depend for their lives," had to find a "solution to his literary problem of making Mac-Donald into a believable murderer" (71–72, 75). This "literary" problem of having to create believability or explicability virtually ex nihilo, emerges from the kind of assumption Malcolm makes so explicit—that crimes with "excitingly dire" characters are supposed to have equally "excitingly dire" killers as their agents. Ironically, of course, it is precisely their ordinariness, their characteristic of "sounding like accountants" and being employed in low-profile "unexciting" jobs like construction/contracting, mail sorting, vat mixing at a chocolate factory that makes their crimes seem all the more shocking. And yet, Malcolm is focusing on the pragmatics of journalistic representation, which demand that startlingly grisly effects necessitate the "literary production" of monstrous causes. While FBI special agents may assert bluntly, "We're not interested in causes, and we're not interested in cures. We're interested in identification, apprehension, incarceration and prosecution" (Oates 53), the "just-the-facts-ma'am" attitude produces only data banks at Quantico, not answers to public bewilderment, not the consolation of vague explanation, and certainly not a story whose explicit project is to communicate the horror of the real.

It is, I would argue, precisely in the space of this representational vacuum, in the space of absent causes—both the killers' absent characters and the plot-producing motives for their actions—that the "real" becomes inadequate and the "literary solutions" become crucial to the creation of the true-crime story. If the ongoing assumption is that the killer is not what he seems, that he is "excitingly dire" behind the mere illusion of ordinariness, it shouldn't surprise us that writers about serial killers turn to a rearticulation of the nineteenth-century gothic as both a paradigm and a constellation of metaphors. The gothic is, after all, traditionally the genre best equipped for the representation of a collective fear in the seemingly incomprehensible or occultly ineffable, just as it proffers a full complement of metaphors for the monstrously knowledgeable and the virtuously innocent and ignorant. Poe's tortured Roderick Usher, Melville's monomaniacal but lucid Ahab, Henry James's ultraproper governess and permanently youthful Grace Brissenden, Stoker's urbane Count Dracula, and Stevenson's driven Dr. Jekyll all conceal the possibility of horror and madness beneath their beauty, charm, or charisma, all offer the potential for an uncanny supernatural or monstrous transcendence of the ordinary, and all occupy the upper position in the hierarchy of victimizer and victim. As "literary solutions," in other words, gothic figures flesh out with fiction what is otherwise unavailable in the real and, in turn, make "story" possible—although true crime generally fails to acknowledge the debt.

Even the most cursory glance at most of the self-consciously "nonfiction" work on serial killers, from psychologists' and anthropologists' textbooks to true-crime books and journalists' interviews, reveals the degree to which gothic metaphors and the attendant rhetoric of monstrosity pertain almost exclusively. In *The Only Living Witness*, for example, Michaud and Aynesworth describe the real Ted Bundy as containing a malignant "entity," a "slithering hunchback": "[o]nly by means of his astounding capacity to compartmentalize had [he] been able to keep the hunchback from raging through the mask [of sanity] and destroying him. When at last it did, *Ted* became the hunchback" (6, 13). In his psychobiological treatise *Serial Killers*, psychologist Joel Norris details one of what he determines to be the seven phases of serial murder: the "aura" phase, the point at which superficially "normal-looking individuals" are "translated into a different kind of creature. Whatever is human in [them] recedes for a while, and [they] enter into a shadowy existence, a death in life" (24); later he describes Henry Lee Lucas as living his "years in a kind of phantom world," as "belong[ing] to the walking dead" (125, 126). In *Hunting Humans* anthropologist Elliott Leyton enjoins us, at one point, not to consider John Kemper III a "deranged Frankenstein monster" with a mind filled with "fantasies of demons and spirit forces" but at another to wonder why Henry Lee Lucas spent decades "exorcising [his mother's] ghost by killing 'her' over and over again" (36, 4).

Even the killers themselves feel compelled to respond to and dispute the all-pervasive constructions of them as gothic monsters. Bundy, for example, announced flatly to the *New York Times*, "I am not a monster" (Rule 446). And more recently Gacy fumed to Wilkinson that his alleged victims were all presented at his trial as "Boy Scouts and altar boys, and I was the monster. . . . Jesus, I didn't even want to run into myself the way they described me" (69). Granted, Gacy's figural monstrosity was accentuated rather profoundly at his trial when Sam Amirante, his attorney, attempted to bolster Gacy's insanity defense by reading aloud passages of Stevenson's *The Strange Case of Dr. Jekyll and Mr. Hyde*. He then urged the jury members to view Gacy not as a mere human killer but as the "personification of this novel written in 1886" (Sullivan and Maiken 365).

What is peculiar about Amirante's construction of Gacy as a "personification" of a novel, apart from his apparent difficulty with the trope of "personification," is the way in which his inadvertent reversal of the human and the rhetorical figure actually reflects a similar confusion in the representation of serial killers. According to Amirante, Stevenson's novel is the human ground or template and Gacy the rhetorical figure of imitation. An analogue not of a human being or even a fictional character but of a book, Gacy is connotatively an inhuman reflection of a fully humanized fiction. When the gothic—or the "literary solution," the Jekyll/Hyde response to the banality and ordinariness of the killers—prevails, in other words, "real" killers become, as Norris suggests, only "translations" of fictional creatures. This metaphoric "translation," in true crime, of the real serial killer into a figural gothic monster—a "demon," "Frankenstein monster," "vampire," "incubus," "zombie," "malevolent entity," "slithering hunchback," "Mr. Hyde," "different kind of creature"—displays the extent to which fiction ultimately provides the bedrock for all attempts to represent the "real" serial killers.

More than merely providing monster prototypes, however, the paradigmatic gothic presents a number of other satisfying components that the real cannot. Not only does it situate collective fear within the familiar gothic construct of feminine victimization, in which "an entire community . . . [can be] frozen with terror" (Norris, *Serial Killers* 14), "all of Milwaukee [can feel] victimized by [a] Dahmer" (Schwartz 176), and "entire cities are traumatized when everyone becomes a victim" (Norris, *Serial Killers* 74), but it equally absolves the rest of humanity of monstrousness by positing an extreme of the human that seems to exist only in fiction. Above all, perhaps, gothic paradigms allow for the creation of a compelling narrative and, consequently, the generation of character and plot out of "bland ordinariness" and incomprehensible randomness. Indeed, the most readable true-crime stories are organized around the formal principles of the nineteenth-century gothic monster novel, which, as Christopher Craft points out, inscribes a "tripartite cycle of [the monster's] admission-entertainment-expulsion" (217).

Typically, the true-crime story introduces a stalwart police detective, the soon-to-be final victims, and the slick killer. The victims are disarmed by the killer's smooth charm; the detective is equally duped. Eventually, the detective retrieves facts that link the killer to the crimes, then unearths some grisly evidence that exposes his monstrousness. Tracking, then capturing the killer, the detective finally participates in a lavishly detailed courtroom drama that concludes with the monster's terminal expulsion via the electric chair, lethal injection, or prison fatality. Alternately, true crime deploys a first-person narrative by a "friend" of the killer. Ann Rule's *The Stranger beside Me*, for example, charts her involvement with the seductive Ted Bundy, her initial whispered confidences, gradual awareness of a subtle "dark side," her realization that her "friend" is a monster, and final rejection of him, complete with bewildered head shaking and theatrical shudders. The formal movement of both versions of true crime is roughly the same, presenting the intersection of the monstrously inhuman outsider who, once absorbed temporarily within the symbolic "ordinary," precipitates the dichotomy of victimizer and victim, and it allows for the articulation of an uncanny fear that is structurally resolved at the end of the narrative. But the "friend"-centered model emphasizes confessions of self-deception, and the detective-centered model aggrandizes the profession and its legal might. The introduction and celebration of the heroic counterpredator—the canny FBI agents, the state troopers, or the metropolitan police, who, like Van Helsing and Victor Frankenstein, can stalk the monster—not only offer the means to plot organization but equally offer tidy orderliness to an otherwise unnarratable chaos.

The heroic counterstalker is as much a fantastic construct as the gothic monster in that, for all their resources, the police or FBI can boast the capture of probably less than 1 percent of serial killers, and even then they succeed only by sheer blind luck and not exhaustive police work. On some level the fictionality of the counterstalkers is tacitly acknowledged: when the FBI's team from the Behavioral Science Unit at Quantico arrived in upstate New York to investigate a quadruple homicide, for instance, they were hailed in local newspaper headlines as the "A Team" (Wilson and Seaman 134). But on another level, the enthusiasm with which the apparent success of this almost-fictional counterstalker is met and celebrated by readers suggests the profundity of the public desire to believe implicitly in the gothic narrative and not in the "facts" of the "real." We need only look to a number of extremely popular novels—Thomas Harris's *Red Dragon* (1981) and *The Silence of the Lambs* (1988), Patricia Cornwell's *Postmortem* (1990) and *All that Remains* (1992), Julie Smith's *Tourist Trap* (1986)—to see how consolatory such constructions are in their positing of the capture of monsters like Francis Dolarhyde, Roy McCorkle, and Jame Gumb.

If fictional consolation is thus approved wholeheartedly, the controversial unpopularity of such works as Bret Easton Ellis's *American Psycho* (1991) and John McNaughton's quasi-documentary *Henry: Portrait of a Serial Killer* is telling: the former was condemned by American feminists as promoting violence against women, and the latter, which was completed in 1986, had its release held up until 1990 because it couldn't get a rating. Neither work offers even a particle of consolation. Based loosely on the life of Henry Lee Lucas, *Henry* is bleakly naturalistic and grimly plotless, beginning innocuously and trailing off with a final dumped corpse and a last glimpse of disappearing taillights. The fictional *American Psycho* practically offers a critique of true crime's dependence on fiction, and, like *Henry*, it eschews familiar formal plot structures. Ellis's emphasis on the dull, yuppy, consumer-mad routine of Patrick Bateman's superficial life—on the endless round of restaurant dinners, afterwork drinks, aerobic workouts, health spa facials, and shopping sprees at Bloomingdale's—accentuates the absence of a recognizable chronology. And his insistence on Bateman's blandly generic good looks and banal conversation, which prompt people to confuse him regularly with someone else, equally highlights the emptiness of Bateman's character, an emptiness he attempts to fill by borrowing from the similarly blank characters of Ted Bundy, John Gacy, Ed Gein, Dennis Nilsen, et al. The vociferous objections to *Henry* and *American Psycho*, both of which are, ironically, probably more mimetic than true-crime books because they re-fuse gothic figurations and thematize the unfitness of their characters to be "up to scratch," suggest a decided public preference for lack of mimetic fidelity in favor of the more hopeful, distinctly less real fictions of monstrous villains and valiant apprehenders, of excitingly dire criminals and heroic gumshoes.

Now, much as gothic paradigms and the rhetoric of monstrosity do allow for a schematic organization of narrative, much as they therefore create explicability out of the confounding actions and characters of serial killers, their presence is problematically double-edged. Once the serial killer is fashioned into a "personification" or "translated" into a monster, that narratorially satisfying formation nevertheless implicitly invites censorious scrutiny, for once the killer is explicable and representable as fiction, he necessarily moves into an overdetermined arena of incendiary controversy. As long as the serial killer is "real," in other words, he stands outside the burning eighties and nineties debates about fictions and consumers, about represented violence and real violence, about "TV people" and little girls. But because the serial killer cannot, as I have suggested, be articulated as anything but a literary figure (and surely the very "serial" sobriquet invites connotative links between repeat murderers and magazine installments or soap operas),[4] there is simply no mimetic "other side" available. When David Berkowitz claims to be a demonically inspired monster, he is apparently offering fictions; when he confesses to having manufactured fictions to "condone" what he was doing, he is supposedly offering reality; and when he is represented in nonfiction, he is a monster who tried to claim fictional monstrosity to "condone" his monstrous acts. The convoluted logic here points to the slippage between what the killer can say about himself and what can be said about him, between the lesser authority of the acts and the greater authority of their textual representation, between, as Malcolm would have it, the murderer who kills and the journalist who makes monsters.

If the fictions have such ascendancy over the actions themselves (and, given the tenor of the American censorship lobby's decrying of the evil influence of all fictions, at any rate, they are considerably more dangerous than murders because they precede them), then killers like Bundy and Gacy are, understandably, quick to insist that they are not monsters. Clearly, it is far better to be in the camp of the damaged consumers of illusion than it is to be in the camp of the damaging illusions themselves. On the night before his execution in Florida in January 1989, Bundy agreed to be interviewed by the Reverend James Dobson, an evangelist and antipornography crusader. Stressing a causal relationship between real and represented violence, Bundy attempted to exclude himself from the otherworldly demonic: "[t]hose of us who are, or who have been, so much influenced by violence in the media, in particular pornographic violence, are not some kind of inherent monsters. . . . We are your sons and we are your husbands and we grew up in regular families. And pornography can reach out and snatch a kid out of any house to-

day. It snatched me out of my home twenty, thirty years ago. . . .
[T]here is no protection against the kinds of influences that are
loose in society" (Michaud and Aynesworth, *The Only* 353).

While Bundy's biographers, Michaud and Aynesworth, con-
temptuously pooh-poohed "Ted's twist on the devil-made-me-
do-it defense" (353) in their 1989 afterword to *The Only Living
Witness*, screenwriters Rebecca Haggerty and Richard O'Regan
took Bundy's claims far more seriously six years later. In their
1995 Arts and Entertainment television biography, "Ted Bundy:
The Mind of a Killer," they try to unearth what made him into
a killer. First Bundy's attorney, Polly Nelson, remarks on his
early reading of detective novels and magazines; then narrator
Jack Perkins gives a voice-over commentary while the camera
shows photographic stills of the lurid covers of *True Detective*,
the "magazines that drove his [Bundy's] fantasies" with their focus on "angry men, frightened women" ("Ted"). The shift here
from a human agent to magazines that "drive" fantasies and
pornography that "reaches" out and "snatches" kids from their
homes, in which the viewer or reader is not only entirely passive
and victimized but wholly lacking in responsibility for his subsequent actions, is symptomatic of a shift in perceptions about the
influence of fiction. In effect, Bundy's assessment of pornography is, at least metaphorically, the 1989 version of *Poltergeist*,
with a synonymy of victimhood between young Ted and Carol
Anne, except in the later version there is no demon or Beast on
the other side of the illusory TV people. Instead, there is only an
absence of human agency—just violent films, detective magazines, TV, pornography, or Hollywood as monoliths that reach
out and snatch good sons out of regular American families in
Anyhouse, U.S.A.

The fact that the 1986 Meese Commission on Pornography
and the Surgeon General's Conference on Pornography, for all
they were desperate to do so, could find no significant correla-
tion between those who watched pornography and those who
committed violent rapes has no bearing on the ongoing American certainty that there must be a causal relationship between
viewed and performed violence.[5] Witness, for example, the mid-

eighties trials of Ozzie Osbourne in California and Judas Priest
in Nevada and the trials of Mark Chapman and John Hinckley,
in which both heavy-metal music and violent films were argued,
albeit unsuccessfully, to be held accountable for their impact on
youthful American consumers. Witness Catherine MacKinnon's
Only Words (1993), in which she insists that pornography should
be designated as an "act" that is therefore actionable in court.
Such arguments for a direct causality between viewing and doing offer a sort of Twinkie defense for the attribution of fictional
violence to the motives for real actions.

Certainly such a defense has plenty of support from the
American proponents of censorship. The National Coalition on
Television Violence used the occasion of Jeffrey Dahmer's trial
in 1991 to issue a statement that "TV violence, slasher-type
movies, and pornography" were "contributing factors in the
Dahmer case" (Schwartz 157). They argued that films like *Nightmare on Elm Street* were really "how-tos for budding killers"
because "young people see murderous movie characters like
Freddy Krueger . . . as heroes" (Schwartz 157). The coalition's
implication, as sociologist Professor James Fox pointed out
to Schwartz, is that "Jeffery Dahmers are created by the media" (Schwartz 157). And prosecuting counsel made much of
Dahmer's possession of copies of *The Exorcist II* and gay porn
like *Cocktales* and *Rock Hard*, just as journalists made hay with
Bundy's reading of *True Detective*, Gacy's viewing of "stag" films,
Canadian Paul Bernardo's reading of *American Psycho*. Dr. Park
Dietz, who served as the state's expert witness on Dahmer's
sanity and convinced the jury that Dahmer was sane, encap-
sulated the common arguments about fiction's "influence" for
the *New Yorker*: "when I get to the bottom of each problem I
look at, I keep finding television, Hollywood, the media, an un-
regulated industry standing behind the First Amendment, and
gaining power despite their harmfulness, because they—unlike everyone else—needn't be accountable or compensate their
victims" (Johnson 50). Surely Oliver Stone takes a similar stand
in *Natural Born Killers* (1994), which has been viewed almost exclusively as a scathing indictment not of killers but of comics,

television, the media—the influences that are, at least according to Bundy, "loose in society" and against which we have "no protection."

Interviewed after the release of *Natural Born Killers*, Stone observed that Mickey and Mallory (Woody Harrelson and Juliet Lewis) are at once "the children of television" and "the rotten fruit of [the twentieth] century" (Denerstein 3). Made from TV and not, like *Poltergeist*'s Carol Anne, recovered from TV's dangerous enticements, Mickey and Mallory are conceived, like Bundy the vampire, Gacy the Mr. Hyde, Dahmer the demon seed, as fiction's monstrous progeny. What we have, then, is fiction as simultaneously monolithic producer and symptomatic product, as simultaneously monstrous cause and monstrous effect. Within this construction of fiction's mirroring or looping back on itself, in which agency resides in the screen itself and a virtual absence of authorship, there is no possibility of mimetic representation. Real killers, vaunted as more horrific than fictional monsters precisely because they "exist" outside the pages or frames of gothic fiction, simply occupy the nether world of the unrepresentable real, in the same way, ironically, that the Beast in *Poltergeist* and the other demon-possession films necessarily occupies the "other side" of the representational screen.

As fictions, however, as "literary problems," "personifications" of novels, or loosed "influences," serial killers are, at least in terms of articulated cultural fears, far more frightening. Their transformation or translation into gothic demons may well be necessary for their representation in true crime and elsewhere, but the alarmist rhetoric about them as influential fictions "made by the media" emphasizes eighties and nineties America's fascination not with serial killers or mass murderers as such, not with "real" violence and real victims, but with the screen that represents them. As J. Hoberman observes in "Serial Chic," the "fetishistic slaughter of successive innocents has become subsumed in the spectacle of American entertainment" (40). But Hoberman's idea that the slaughter is fetishized obscures the fetishization of the spectacle itself, the representation that produces all the affect of actual killing, with the added twist that it can supposedly produce more killers. Nowhere is this fascination with the culpability and progenitive capacity of spectacle more pronounced than in *Natural Born Killers*, a specular meta-commentary on the American fictions that make monsters. Stone intercuts television sit-coms of Mickey and Mallory with comic strip animation of them as superheroes and throws in clips from *Geraldo*-like talk shows and snippets of video surveillance footage for good measure, all in an effort to explore the external, media ingredients that combine to create the "natural born killer." And to ensure that we don't miss the point, Stone offers a scene of transcendent obviousness—when Mickey and Mallory find themselves confronted by a cartoonishly wise Indian shaman. Naturally, he is able to see the "truth" about them: the words "demon" projected on Mallory's chest and "too much TV" on Mickey's.

While this equation of monster and media, this absolute synonymy of demon and TV, should not surprise us, particularly given the pervasive demonization of the media as being simultaneously too graphic and not truthful, what is interesting about Stone's configuration is that the serial killers are quite literally the screen on which the message is communicated. With the conflation of gothic demon and TV screen, the real is effaced altogether, serving only to present a reflective surface for projected illusions. For all that the serial killer, invested with the architecture of gothic horror, is supposed to be the very icon of real contemporary monstrosity, then, he is not, for, as merely a fictional projection, his villainy can be traced back to the cathode emissions that produced him. As a blank incomprehensibility, the serial killer thus serves as a convenient vessel for the articulation of what American society finds truly monstrous in the late twentieth century—the "TV people," or the authorless but authority-filled killer screen that drives fantasies, reaches out and snatches kids from their homes, and transforms them into demons. And as such a representational cypher, the real American serial killer is, finally, identical to his fictional monster counterpart: a textual figure that can simultaneously expose and occlude what is culturally too horrible to be viewed directly.

NOTES

1. Carol Clover argues that *Poltergeist* presents a common thematic: "[o]ver and over, and in a remarkable variety of ways, modern horror plays out the same adversarial scenario. Film after film presents us with stories in which audiences are assaulted by cameras, invaded by video signals or film images, attacked from screens" (199).

2. Mark Seltzer finds that the killers' repetitious actions are machinelike, that "serial killing is inseparable from the problem of the body in machine culture" (127). But much of his argument in "Serial Killers (I)" and "Serial Killers (II)" focuses on popular accounts of the killers' acts as symptomatic of specific issues emergent in technology-driven culture. Seltzer's focus, in other words, is less on the actual narratives about serial killers—or narratorial problems with their production—than on certain ideologically fraught misconceptions about the killers.

3. Harris's Hannibal Lecter in *Red Dragon* and particularly in *The Silence of the Lambs* has come to represent the quintessential serial killer: attractive, charismatic, intelligent, cunning, individualistic. Perhaps the most fictional serial killer in terms of character and therefore eminently representable, Lecter is nevertheless entirely motiveless in his killings and therefore resists explication in the same manner that the actual killers do. Ironically, convicted serial killer Dennis Nilsen decried Lecter's fictionality, telling his biographer, Brian Masters, that Lecter was a "fraudulent fiction. He is shown as a potent figure, which is pure myth" (quoted in Wilson 310–311).

4. Stephen Michaud wrote in the *New York Times* in October 1986 that Robert Ressler (of the FBI's Behavioral Science Unit) "started using the term [serial killer] because such an offender's behavior is so distinctly episodic, like the movie house serials he enjoyed as a boy" (quoted in Wilson 110).

5. In 1992 Republican senators McConnell of Kentucky, Grassley of Iowa, and Thurmond of South Carolina tried to get the Pornography Victim's Compensation Bill through the Senate's Judiciary Committee; Bill 1521 would have forced publishers and distributers of pornography to compensate their victims. John Irving lambasted the bill, commenting on the "censorial times" and attacking the "moral reprehensibility" of shifting the "responsibility for any sexual crime onto a third party" (24).

WORKS CITED

Clover, Carol J. *Men, Women and Chainsaws: Gender in the Modern Horror Film*. Princeton, NJ: Princeton UP, 1992.

Craft, Christopher. "'Kiss Me with Those Red Lips': Gender and Inversion in Bram Stoker's *Dracula*." *Speaking of Gender*. Ed. Elaine Showalter. New York: Routledge, 1989, 216–242.

Denerstein, Robert. "My Demons Are Still There." *Globe and Mail* (Toronto, Ontario), August 26, 1994, C3.

Dvorchak, Robert, and Lisa Holewa. *Milwaukee Massacre: Jeffrey Dahmer and the Milwaukee Murders*. New York: Dell Publishing, 1991.

Ellis, Bret Easton. *American Psycho*. New York: Vintage, 1991.

Hoberman, J. "Serial Chic." *Premiere* (August 1994): 39–40.

Irving, John. "Pornography and the New Puritans." *New York Times Book Review*, March 29, 1992, 1, 24–25, 27.

Johnson, Joyce. "Witness for the Prosecution." *New Yorker*, May 16, 1994, 42–51.

Klausner, Lawrence. *Son of Sam: Based on the Authorized Transcription of the Tapes, Official Documents and Diaries of David Berkowitz*. New York: McGraw-Hill, 1981.

Leyton, Elliott. *Hunting Humans: The Rise of the Modern Multiple Murderer*. Toronto: McLelland and Stewart, 1986.

Malcolm, Janet. *The Journalist and the Murderer*. New York: Vintage, 1990.

Michaud, Stephen, and Hugh Aynesworth. *The Only Living Witness*. New York: Signet, 1989.

———. *Ted Bundy: Conversations with a Killer*. New York: New American Library, 1989.

Norris, Joel. *Henry Lee Lucas: The Shocking True Story of America's Most Notorious Serial Killer*. New York: Zebra Books, 1991.

———. *Serial Killers*. New York: Anchor Doubleday, 1988.

Oates, Joyce Carol. "'I Had No Other Thrill or Happiness.'" *New York Review of Books*, March 24, 1994, 52–59.

Rule, Ann. *The Stranger beside Me*. New York: Signet, 1989.

Schwartz, Anne. *The Man Who Could Not Kill Enough: The Secret Murders of Milwaukee's Jeffrey Dahmer*. New York: Birch Lane Press, 1992.

Seltzer, Mark. "Serial Killers (II): The Pathological Public Sphere." *Critical Inquiry* 22 (Autumn 1995): 122–149.

Serial Killers: Profiles of Today's Most Terrifying Criminals. New York: Time-Life Books, 1992.

Sullivan, Terry, and Peter Maiken. *Killer Clown: The John Wayne Gacy Murders*. New York: Pinnacle Books, 1983.

"Ted Bundy: The Mind of a Killer." Narrated by Jack Perkins. Produced, directed, and written by Rebecca Haggerty and Richard O'Regan. *Biography: Inside the Criminal Mind*. Claypoint Productions, in assoc. with A & E Network. September 1995.

Wilkinson, Alec. "Conversations with a Killer." *New Yorker*, April 18, 1994, 58–76.

Wilson, Colin, and Donald Seaman. *The Serial Killers: A Study in the Psychology of Violence*. London: Virgin Publishing, 1990.

KIM IAN MICHASIW

Some Stations of Suburban Gothic

CERTAIN AXIOMS

1. Whatever else, gothic is a mode of fantasy that facilitates the molding of anxiety. It is cognate, then, with desire as a mode of fantasy facilitating libido.

2. As desire is a symptomatic manner of binding the free play of the drive, hence of defending the human subject against the consequences of such free play, gothic is symptomatic binding of free anxiety, hence a defense against the consequences of focusless, drifting dread.

3. As desired objects are *un*representative representations of all those objects to which the drive might affix itself, so the feared or phobic objects of gothic are saving placements (rather than *dis*placements, strictly speaking) of anxiety where that anxiety may be mastered, though it need not be.

4. The object of desire is not the whence of desiring; neither is the gothic object the whence of fear.

5. To speak of objects is misleading. Better to speak of scenes, stage set, in or on which anxiety takes place. (This is, after all, the genius of the game of CLUE: never Colonel Mustard alone; rather, gas-masked Mustard in the solarium with a chainsaw.)

6. Gothic, then, defines a scene, terrain, geography, for something terrible. The indeterminacy of the act is psychically essential as it maintains, within limits, the formlessness of the root anxiety. Not: the cannibal monster *is* in the nursery snacking on the soft skulls of the infant twins. Rather: the cannibal monster *may be* in the nursery, or he may be somewhere else, or she may

be in the nursery disguised as one of the twins. Or: there may be
no cannibal at all, though this would be a fine place for one.

7. As with all displacements, there is a relation between the
gothic scene and the other scene it masks. Because anxiety exceeds determinate cause, the analyst must locate these relations
along extended categorical axes. Thus both the grand epistemological *cri* of the eighteenth-century gothic heroine and the Romantic gothic hero's great revelatory moment of false ontology
indicate differing categories in which anxiety has been framed
(Michasiw 209–216). Such categories are, however, characteristically and dissimulatively represented by more concrete fears.
Will my (surrogate) father rape/kill me? Will some omnipotent
being discover and punish me for my crimes? Will something
that looks almost exactly human extract my brain stem, cloak me
in polyester, and chain me to the gas barbecue?

LOCALES, STATIONS, TERMINI

If, then, gothic somethings-to-be-scared-of are secondary formations designed to obscure, through naturalizing, the primary
defensive function of place, it is important for us not to be dis-
tracted by trappings. It is important also to recognize that as one
of the prime functions of the culture industry is to organize desire in symptomatic, accommodating manners, so too is a primary function of the culture industry to provide appropriate
screens on which anxieties may assume appropriate forms. It is
an intimation of failed appropriateness, I think, that underlies
Fredric Jameson's indictment of gothic as "that boring and exhausted paradigm . . . [in which] a sheltered woman of some kind
is terrorized and victimized by an 'evil' male" (289). Recognizing the exhaustion of the paradigm thus stylized registers the inadequacy, the datedness, of the narrative frame to "real" anxieties. The dialectic of shelter and privilege that Jameson sees
inscribed in gothic is no longer apt or, if apt, is so only literally.
If the early gothic heroine gets herself to the Castle of Udolpho
in order to work through the complexly enmeshed fears of and
desires for physical freedom, the late-twentieth-century dweller
in a gated community only fears random mobility. The essential
contributory element of desire is absent, leaving the residual

figure of the auburn-haired endangered Regency female on the supermarket-novel cover, emptily nostalgic.

Jameson mistakes the trappings for the form, but his misprision is useful in illustrating the trajectory of the embalmed scene. The usefulness of the imagined monastery, for instance, as screen on which to give form to anxieties recedes as the scenarios possible on that screen become more and more obviously escapist displacements. The axes of contiguity and resemblance, however distorted, are replaced by conventions of arbitrary metaphor: at this point both psychical and ideological usefulness are at an end, and the observer wanders about this set of trappings like a visitor to a theme-park exhibition of anxieties defunct.

There is, however, something rather disingenuous about Jameson's dismissal of gothic, a point to which I'll return below. For the moment, though, I want to suggest how mass-cultural frames for the play of anxiety operate. To do this I wish to translate to the field of fantasy a pair of terms employed by John Fiske to describe nodal points of "consciousness, position in the social space, and physical place" (34): station and locale. In Fiske's words

> a locale always involves continuities between interior and exterior, between consciousness, bodies, places and times. A locale is a bottom-up product of localizing power and as such it is always in a contestatory relationship with imperializing power. . . . A station is the opposite, but equivalent, of a locale. A station is both a physical place where the social order is imposed upon an individual and the social positioning (stationing) of that individual in the system of social relations. (12)

This opposition is not lost on those who have social power who attempt "to stop people producing their own locales by providing them with *stations*" (12). My suggestion, then, is that this opposition, though ideally adapted to spatial and geographical relations, is no less appropriate when discussing the cultural provision of fantasy and of fear. Consumers are offered prefab patterns of desire; so too they are given things, and places, to be scared of. These patterns, should they be accepted, station the subject as effectively as any physical constraints. This suggestion is obviously unoriginal: recognizing the power of imposed fears to station elements of the populace is essential to any process of scapegoating, of demonizing, of giving dogs bad names to hang them by. The notion of station, however, suggests the possibility of less determinately objectified fears: not of those notorious for poisoning wells but of the fragility of the water supply itself; not of someone arriving to boil the bunny and bleed in the bathtub, or of the nanny running off with the child, or even—though this is closer—of the Satanists who run the local day-care center but anxiety about . . .

The chain of representations begun here is easily enough continued, especially if one recognizes that the trajectory leads back, gradually, toward the subject's implication in the scene but does not in fact arrive there. An exemplary peeling back of the layers might be useful as witness to the function of the station. Taking, exemplarily, the series of predatory women portrayed in a sequence of Hollywood films through the late 1980s and early to mid-1990s, from *Fatal Attraction* to *Disclosure*, we can see how such representations serve as screens for a variety of fears. Such films are made by men and addressed to a "crossover" audience of men and women (a "crossover" as well between teenage and adult audiences). The films depend, on the manifest level, on men's fear of being unable to keep their trousers on and on women's fears of being collateral damage in the inevitable phallic explosion. Such fears depend in their turn on anxieties concerning the failure of fit between prevailing subject positions and the duties of the monogamous bourgeois family. That the baggy, sagging Michael Douglas becomes the object of predatory female lust and that the straight-from-the-fifties, desexualized Anne Archer is the endangered mother/wife are sufficient indices of the mixture of melancholy self-pity and more melancholy self-congratulation engaged here. The classic American film hero just says no—unless he is given the far better option of sending the desiring female off to jail as well. Noir heroes embrace their fall to temptation with a fatalistic glee. Michael Douglas, at most, howls "No" with his trousers down round his knees. The fear of male weakness, however, depends on a deeper fear of female strength. Boys can't help it, so women have to—but what if they don't? This, of course, is the antifeminist text of such films accounted by Susan Faludi and others. The non-procreating, successful woman is, of course, a predator who only wants what the procreative successful-through-her-mate woman has. That the desires of the two female figures are essentially identical, and identical to the norms of heterosexist womanhood, marks out a space for darker masculinist fears. This trajectory leads, I'd suggest, to its parodic apogee in the advertising tag-line for 1995's exemplary predatory *and* maternal female: the She-Who-Could-Lay-a-Thousand-Eggs of *Species*.

What is important to recognize here, though, is the possibility that the transparent antifeminism of such films, their rejection of both the need for employment equity or sexual harassment codes (women are more powerful than men anyway) and a nongendered workplace (women's real desires are for children and monogamous pairing), is less what is screened than an essential component of the screen itself. The obvious unacceptability of *Fatal Attraction*'s manifest ideology, at least to a significant segment of its viewership, is an earmark of the faux oppositionality of the gothic station. *They*, those oppressive spokesfolk for supposedly hegemonic liberal doxa, are telling us that women don't use sex as a weapon, as a tool in their unrelenting, indomitable pursuit of babies and suburban homes, but *this* film dares speak the truth. (In a precisely parallel way, the anti-Catholicism of early English gothics was a "daring" response from the prevailing ideology to those progressive apologists for the Catholic Church who would have allowed Catholics the vote and would have succored refugee priests and nuns arriving from revolutionary France.) And it is this formation—where the ingrained reactionary response is recoded as newly revealed, if embattled, truth—that enables the station to function most effectively to bind free-floating anxiety. A kind of dual recognition takes place in the viewer. First, that's not what *I'm* afraid of, given my circumstances, but I can see why other people would be afraid. Second, even though I'm not really afraid of that, that's the sort of thing that could only happen in this kind of world, so "that" can stand, as representative, for what makes me anxious. The combination of nostalgia (played upon an insistent comtemporaneity, whether of decor, accessories, attributes) and violation (anyone can be the victim, even the bunny) bonds with a disingenuous oppositionality to make the station serve even for those who cannot name their fears.

That the ideological station is defined by its malleability and by its veneer of resistance to a projected orthodoxy may explain the troubling sentimentality inhering in Fiske's "locales," in his image of homeless men cheering as the executives explode in *Die Hard*. Locales, like de Certeau's tactics, Baudrillard's fatality, and Hebdige's impossible objects,[1] offer the possibility of bottom-up alternative takes on mass cultural artifacts and strategies. Yet even without resorting to the tired mantra of "subversive *and* complicit," it is often difficult to discern many utopian locales amid mass culture. Slasher films perhaps, or a certain positioning of the viewer of the slasher film? "Go O. J.!" T-shirts? Private systems of fear cocooning within the latex gloves of riot cops, the selective omissions of baggage handlers, the refusal of the middle class to believe that violent crime is on the wane?

Maybe—but on the logic sketched above the success of the gothic scene depends precisely on its openness to customization, the apparent ease with which the objects of fear may be tailored to individual phobia. In this malleability, though, the gothic scene maintains its occluded extension to the end of the line, the terminus, the terminal forms of power. Thus fears of plagues various or assaults of many kinds may *appear* to contravene the top-down stationing of anxiety, may well defy the express orders of those in power, but in fact confirm the contingent grasp of persons in power on the places they hold. As early gothic heroines discovered on their way to necessary enlightenment, those who appear to rule by tyranny have but temporary authority pilfered from greater, truly unopposable powers, and gothic victory involves the destruction of one level of power through submission to a greater.

TWO STATIONS

After this overextended preface, let me introduce three different ways in which cultural critics have located in the contemporary

American suburb a place with which to be afraid. These need, however, to be distinguished as a group from two other formations, from one of which they, in part, derive and to the other of which, perhaps, they lead. The first manifests itself in the laments of intellectuals in the 1950s at the uniformity of suburban development and the mass conformity it supposedly nourished. Twenty years ago, Herbert J. Gans summarized this viewpoint: "[s]uburbia was intellectually debilitating, culturally oppressive, and politically dangerous, breeding bland mass men without respect for the arts of democracy" (xvi). Gans, as participant-observer, researched his ground-breaking study of suburban life by purchasing a house and living in it for two years in Levittown, New Jersey. After those years he concluded that, whatever might be wrong with the life enforced upon its inhabitants by the structure of suburban development, the assertion that "the suburbs were breeding a new set of Americans, as mass produced as the houses they lived in . . . bored and lonely, alienated, atomized, and depersonalized" (xv), was myth making and *only* that.

But the myth has proved to have greater staying power, at least among the intellectual and artistic classes, than has Gans's attempt to explode it. The underpinnings of this persistence are admirably caught by Lois Craig:

> In retrospect, the anti-suburban literature and imagery, the intellectual and visual neglect [of the suburbs since the 1950s] add up to something more than a curiosity. Rather they suggest a profound class resistance grounded in cultural and aesthetic considerations. . . . Members of the cultured class . . . "[r]ecoil from the commonplace, as the first line of defense in the battle for spiritual dignity and self-identity," denigrating the materialism and technology that are important to the upward mobility of poor people. (29–30; embedded quotation Graña 129–130)

For those who regard the postwar suburb, and especially for those who regard it from the pseudo-aristocratic position of the displaced European intellectual,[2] the suburb was the domain of a lower-middle-class kitsch: it would eat away at all cultural exertion, would find all the painting and poetry it required on Hallmark cards and all its music on the Perry Como show. The suburb marks the debasement of revolution where the only victory in the class struggle would be won on the only ground about which the ruling orders did not care.

This sort of anxiety finds gothic frames in tales—told both at the drive-in and at the height of social theory—of cloning, podding, one dimensionality, mass uniformity that have distinctly traceable genealogical relations to more recent suburban gothics. (Philip Kaufman's 1978 remake of *Invasion of the Body Snatchers* is index enough of this.)[3] But truly high-cultural anxieties are harder to locate in the 1990s and harder still to confess. Hence certain shifts, of which more in a moment. There is, however, a second emergent gothic frame deserving of mention in passing, a frame suggested by Brett Easton Ellis's fiction and by such films as *The River's Edge* and, more campily, in a variety of suburban teenage vampire films from *The Lost Boys* to *Buffy the Vampire Slayer*. This variation takes note of Gans's demonstration that those who bought homes in 1950s suburbs remain substantially the same people they were when they lived elsewhere. Thus the danger cannot arrive from postwar, "first generation" suburbanites or even from their children, who remain tied somehow to a life and to values outside the suburb. No, the danger will come with the third generation, those growing up in either what are now called the old suburbs—now seen as in decay—or the newest and furthest flung of the developments (which tend, for reasons of land prices, to occupy the top and the bottom end of the price scale). Such children, utterly removed both from the rural and the urban, ignorant equally of nature and civilization, appear perfect candidates for the label "a new set of Americans . . . bored and lonely, alienated, atomized, and depersonalized" that elitist social critics saw in their parents or grandparents.

That this frame has not yet fully been gothicized is evident in critical writing about Generation X, about grunge, about urban primitives. From the slacker aesthetic, through the neotribal rites of tattooing, piercing, and branding, to responses to Kurt Cobain's suicide, the attributes attached critically to a generation

of "kids from the suburbs" have been remarkably free of demon-
izings. Frightening teenagers still tend to come from the inner
city. There have been blips: a plague of "swarmings" a few sum-
mers back, the attempts to imagine ranks of affectless TV zom-
bies, occasional outbursts of casual looting. In general, though,
the economically and socially displaced daughters and sons of
the late seventies and eighties suburbs have yet to appear as
consistently threatening presences. However, "yet" is the crucial word.

THREE MORE

The first is connected with the class anxieties noted above but
differs importantly. Consider the following from Arthur Kroker:

> Most of all, it is the lawns which are sinister. Fuji green and
> expansive, they are a visual relief to the freeway and its ac-
> companying tunnel vision. Even ahead of the golden arches,
> they are welcoming as the approach of a new urban sign-
> value. The frenzy sites of a decaying Christian culture where
> reclining lawn chairs, people in the sun, barbecues and
> summer-time swimming pools can give off the pleasant odors
> of an imploding Calvinist culture, playing psychologically at
> the edge of the parasite and the predator. (Kroker, Kroker,
> and Cook 211–212)

Whatever else the reader is to make of this passage, the separation between the observing subject and its supposed object is
clear enough. For Kroker the inhabitants here are the "real-life"
descendants of *Invasion of the Body Snatchers*'s pod people, each
"equipped . . . with a Harlequin life programmed to Scott Peck's
The Road Less Travelled. Each person in his or her own way 'born
again,' the better to imitate the Way . . . a way of life that grows
on you, feeds from you, parasites you." The suburbanite as the
colonial subject, as the host to a slowly devouring thing, as
fullest embodiment of "postmodern 'rural idiocy' (Marx), or as
Blake has it, 'vegetable consciousness'" (Kroker, Kroker, and
Cook 213).

Kroker argues that his response is keyed to the artificiality
and boredom of suburban life, that his revulsion arises from the

routinization of nature and the compartmentalizing shrink-wrap applied to being and consciousness. There is something else, though. What is unspeakable about the suburbanite is its secret devotion to some criminal obscenity the academic tourist knows not how to name. Kroker's suburbanites, tied umbilically to the television, the mall, the lawn, differ from the lonely, atomized suburbanites of the 1950s because they enjoy. And it is in this that they are both dangerous and frightening. When confronted with the suburban, the critic senses another sort of danger, even when the inhabitants are rhetorically consigned wholesale to vegetable metaphor. Suburban pod folk may be alien, but they are not alien enough. The protective, differentiating cover of acquired high culture and critical stance has grown very thin and worn. Memories of Horkheimer may do nothing to stop the something that might seep from the unnaturally vigorous turf and make us one of them or, worse, the something that might ooze from us and fuse us with the lawn.

In this, Kroker comes across the transferential being proposed by Mladen Dolar: the subject presumed to enjoy. This subject derives from the "supposed existence, in the other, of an insupportable, limitless, horrifying *jouissance*. . . . [T]his subject does not have to exist effectively: to produce his effects, it is enough to presume that he exists" (Žižek, *Sublime* 187–188; Dolar 37). These effects are disgust, envy, and a fear of metamorphosis. Like Harker observing Dracula in his coffin, Kroker observes in the suburbanite access to enjoyments he has denied himself so effectively that they are unnamable. Yet the lure of such unknown pleasures, the possibility of becoming ecstatically enslaved and transformed by them, is exactly vampiric. Hence the charge not that they are undead but that they are unreal. They are the simulacra dwelling "where living means real, imitation life" (Kroker, Kroker, and Cook 213).

But where, one might ask, is this real imitation life taking place? Would we have any more luck in locating Kroker's suburb on a map than we would with Radcliffe's Udolpho, or is his perverse paradise something of an obscure homage to Wallace Stevens, a description without place? This is not an incidental question, especially if the fantasy simulation has replaced en-

tirely that material reality for which it supposedly stands. Is this
another instance of what Joel Garreau laments as "the intellectual absence" from discussions of the material conditions of what
were once called the suburbs "of so many people I had always
viewed as the guardians of our built environment" (232). What
has Kroker's hallucinatory vision to do with demonstrable conditions in what practicing urbanologists call "multinucleated
metropolitan regions" or, more popularly, "centerless cities,"
"edge cities," or "technoburbs"?[4] Maybe such prodigal acts of
naming are beside the point. Perhaps Kroker is reacting to the
sheer weirdness of apologetic claims that provincialism can be
defeated by the marketplace, that "cosmopolitan consumption
may be marked by driving a German car, wearing Italian shoes,
and dining in a French restaurant with other affluent whites"
(Poster, 17). Or does he sense something monstrous behind the
approving complacency with which Mark Poster claims that
middle-class families in Orange County

> are testing new family structures, some of which eliminate to
> a considerable degree earlier forms of domination in the fam-
> ily. . . . They want to remove restrictions of women's choices;
> the adults want to achieve emotional and sexual gratification;
> they want to develop in their children an ability for self-
> directed personal growth; they want to enjoy the sophisti-
> cated technologies available to them. (18)

Yet the absence of a determinate locale of Kroker's suburb,
being everywhere and nowhere, being a bower of diseased bliss
imported duty-free from the romance tradition, though appropriately gothic, dissolves what Edward Soja has called the "socio-
spatial dialectic," the productive interplay of the social order and
the space within which it unfolds (77–78). The very timeless-
ness of Kroker's monsters of enjoyment, beached in an endless
barbecue summer, invokes a banished but grumbling history,
slouching off in defeat. As such, Kroker is one of Foucault's "pi-
ous descendants of time" who oppose "the determined inhabitants of space" (22). As does his mentor Baudrillard, Kroker keys
his terror to a nostalgia for what the excremental present has unalterably replaced. Neither the apparently real space nor the ap-

parently real materials occupying it has any ontological ground in this suburb. The "real, imitation life" has sucked ontology dry, leaving only a husk, and the critic, beside.

Such remnants bring with them consolatory assurances of the critic's own realness and of the realness of whatever urban or rural locale the critic calls "home." But what signifies this real? What are the crosses, wafers, garlic bulbs, and holy water necessary to keep off identification, coalescence, with such places, such beings? Kroker, typically, has no answer here, but our second form of critical gothicizing strives, inadvertently, to provide one.

> [The city bristles with malice.] The carefully manicured lawns of Los Angeles's Westside sprout forests of ominous little signs warning: "Armed Response!" Even richer neighborhoods in the canyons and hillsides isolate themselves behind walls guarded by gun-toting private police and state-of-the-art electronic surveillance. (Davis 223)[5]

Thus begins Mike Davis's "Fortress L.A.," his properly terrifying account of L.A.'s version of what Michael Sorkin calls "parallel suburban cities growing on the fringes of old centers abandoned to the poor" (xiv). As firmly located in geographical space as Kroker's suburbs are removed from it, Davis's scenes for terror sport street addresses and names. We can fly to Los Angeles and take pictures of ourselves outside the walls. In Davis's account the guarded, gated community is bastion and beacon to a barbarian majority. Those suburbanites who cannot afford the armed guards and castellations dream that they could and make whatever gestures at enclaving they can. Thus the gated community becomes the key signifier and reinscribes—in refurbished, Disneyfied inversions—Otranto, Udolpho, and their ilk. The gated community is an architectural avatar of the threatened maiden of gothic fiction, but the threatened maiden has inherited Udolpho, has gentrified and secured its ramparts, and has hired Montoni's demobbed banditti to patrol its walls. For Davis the moment when the heroine, or her surrogates, turns upon the usurper has become an ossified road-to-Damascus moment for an entire population. Convinced of its virtue and its victimizability, this community is always at the point of appalling feats of self-defense.

For those inside, the barbarians are always at the gates—and they are a sort of solution. For those outside, like Davis and such other urbanologists as Sorkin, Edward Soja, and M. Christine Boyer, the barbarians are within the gates, capable of any enormity. Like the gothic succession of abbots and prioresses who will confine, entomb, and ritually murder to protect their cloistered spaces, the suburbanites are permitted by their constant state of siege and the knowledge of their cause's justice to abrogate any law and countervail any principle. These are not Kroker's pod folk; they are panicked, hystericized beings given over entirely not to mere growth but to the instinct for self-preservation, Hobbists who know no bodily sensation save fear. Such beings see threat everywhere, as in Davis's example of

> Hidden Hills, a Norman Rockwell painting behind high security walls, [which] has been bitterly divided over compliance with a Superior Court order to build forty-eight units of seniors' housing outside its gates. At meetings of the city's all-powerful homeowners' association (whose membership includes Frankie Avalon, Neil Diamond, and Bob Eubanks) opponents of compliance have argued that the old folks' apartments will attract gangs and dope. (246)

Davis, then, offers the reader something real to be scared of: the effects of a place in which the dream of security, from which no bourgeois North American can be entirely free, has (perhaps) been achieved, but at the cost of delivering those secured into the hands of a drive to self-preservation indistinguishable from the death drive (which is, of course, where the dream of security is rooted anyway—this is an instinctual homecoming of sorts). For the observer, though, there may be separation, but there is no security from the suburban guerrillas who have long since possessed the continent.

But this separation is won at a cost as well. What are the oppositional signs when protection is the enemy, when the crime-and-trash-free Disneyscape has escaped the theme park and, creeping like kudzu, covered the country? While Davis himself is careful not quite to succumb to the temptations implicit here, others, like Sorkin, Boyer, and some contributors to the collection *Sex, Death, and God in L.A.*, come perilously close to advocating homelessness, criminality, casual street violence, and what we might call, following Dean MacCannell, "primitivity" as the truest markers of the authentic.[6] Without people sleeping on the streets and gunshots in the distance, how would we know we weren't captive behind community gates? In order to separate the critic must embrace and take as real the very set of signs that have raised the security fences.

Which is not a danger, quite, in the third of our forms, a form the more insidious as it assumes an antigothic stance as part of its nest of defenses. (It would argue also that Davis's suburbanites are neither fearful nor fearsome [Jameson 118].) This is the quietest of our forms: arrives proclaiming utopian hope rather than fear and in fact spends much time explaining that there is nothing left by which we can be scared. In this stational formation the suburb emerges, in metonymic morsels, as revenant, residual—not so much a scene in itself as a specter haunting the postmodern condition, or perhaps as the guilty exposed secret around which postmodernity has wrapped itself. Consider an early manifestation of the suburb in Fredric Jameson's *Postmodernism, or the Cultural Logic of Late Capitalism*:

> As you go up the still old-fashioned stairs of the Gehry house, you reach an old-fashioned door, through which you enter an old-fashioned maid's room (although it might just as well be the bedroom of a teenager). The door is a time-travel device; when you close it, you are back in the old twentieth-century American suburb—the old concept of the room, which includes my privacy, my treasures, and my kitsch, chintzes, old teddy bears, old LP records. (118)

First there is/was a maid, then a phantasmatic teenager, then a personal possessive pronoun, redecorating. And this possession maintains itself, despite Gehry's having enclosed it within "the cube [of distended glass parallelograms] and the slab (of corrugated metal); these ostentatious markers, planted in the older building like some lethal strut transfixing the body of a car crash victim" (113).

If nothing else, the metaphoric energies of suburban survival are awesome, even when that energy finds its figurative vehicle in a violated corpse. I emphasize these passages because they show a marked tendency in Jameson's reconstructions: the suburban house, especially in its upper interior, becomes by metaphor or metonymy the human. The identity may be occluded, but it endures. This human, though, emerges as gothicized revenant, as the pinned corpse that might get up and shamble, a benign, beneficent, but futile zombie.

This is, of course, another variant on being afraid—not fearing that the undead walk but rather that they don't, that the energies of enlightenment (seen here as Horkheimer and Adorno's remorseless engines of disenchantment customized by Sloterdijk's cynical reason) have fully disinfected the landscape. A number of curiosities inhere in this structure of fear. Some of these must be passed over, but Jameson's recurrent figuration of the suburban doorframe as something like the tree encasing *The Tempest*'s Sycorax radically internalizes the gothic scene and does so in a literal, material way. Gehry's postmodern structures wrap the doorframe just as postsuburbanization encloses the bedroom community, as edge cities encase decaying older suburbs and white flight zones, as the gates of gated communities . . .

And the inhabitants dwell in fear of fear because terror—against which anesthetizing postmodernism sets itself—is one of "the great negative [and negating] emotions of the modernist moment" (117). Thus a kind of utopian gothic founds itself on the spirit ambered, or rather enameled, in the suburban doorframe. And the first word of the charm that breaks the spell and releases the ghost is "nostalgia":

mourning for a lost object which can scarcely even be remembered as such, a path back through other objects shows them radically modified and transformed as well. The doorframe—the metonym of cultural habitation and the social—now turns out to have been not merely cultural, and a representation, but a nostalgic representation of a more natural form of dwelling. It now "opens the door" to a host of economic and historical anxieties. (170)

That is, the doorframe as metonym for the suburban house as "more natural form of dwelling" produces politically employable anxieties. In Jameson's formulation "from mere nostalgic reflexes, these articles slowly take on the positive and active value of conscious resistance, as choices and symbolic acts that . . . assert themselves as something emergent rather than something residual" (171).

Which is to think utopianly indeed, if in an oddly, or appropriately, old-fashioned way. The moment here described has its analogue in much earlier gothic in those moments when the protagonist is addressed by the signs of her or his past. The purest version, perhaps, is that of Adeline in Radcliffe's *The Romance of the Forest* reading the journal of the captive—she does not yet know that the writer is her father. The captive is a displaced metonym for the bourgeois family life from which both captive and reader have been catastrophically torn. As Adeline reads, however, she firms her resolve to resist all futures except that continuous with the half-recalled, half-imagined past conjured by the manuscript. Adeline's nostalgia for what never really was, a nostalgia present but unformed before the moldering manuscript, becomes its signifier, forms the basis for her ongoing project of critical resistance. And this is what Jameson's doorframe should do. It ought to be the friendly ghost of a lost order on which the subject may found an edifice of critical thought.

What happens, or may happen, is different. The postmodern subject is arrested in the merely nostalgic first phase, the moment before the time of haunting. Gazing anxiously at the not-quite-lost object, the subject awaits spectral glimmerings that may not arrive. Jameson assures us that the gothic moment will arrive on contact with material conditions even if those conditions are mere local concerns: "real estate speculation and the disappearance of the construction of older single-family housing" (170). And these certainly are the anxieties besetting

Douglas Coupland's Generation X characters, though Coupland's figures are anxious only reflexively. And such anxieties may well precede the gating—doorframing writ large and supported with armed response unit—of Davis's communities. That either of these responses has a utopian dimension seems to me unproved.

But even these dystopic versions register insufficiently the reflexivity of Jameson's foundational gothic moment. In gazing at the doorframe, the subject encounters as revenant an earlier version of the subject. The anxiety-nostalgia network set up is constructed upon a sudden recognition of temporal rupture (Žižek, *Looking Awry* 137). The nostalgic gaze laments not time passing but the passing of the *locale* of the gaze; one will never find again the right prospect on the doorframe. Yet that this lost place was ever properly a locale is open to question; that it has been trotted out and marketed as oppositional makes it look perilously like a station. Jameson's suburban doorframe opens not onto the conditions of real estate in the time of savings and loan associations but onto an utterly disrupted temporality in the subject.

Which is something really to be scared of and is why Jameson and those makers of nostalgic works he discusses repress the suburb, except in its most attenuated metonyms. When, in redescribing *Something Wild*, Jameson wonders that there are no conformists, quite, on the landscape, he avoids registering that the track of the film moves from city to small town, a variation of the small town that centers the work of David Lynch. "There are no middle classes left to be found in the heartland," notes Jameson (292–293), having failed to recognize that both the middle classes and the heartland have moved to the suburbs and the suburbs are nowhere to be seen, in *Something Wild* or, excepting doorframes, in *Postmodernism*.

The suburb as all-but-vanished sign of the utopian specter haunting the postmodern condition is, then, the first derivative of a deeper anxiety (kitsch attribution and urban, or college town, or Internet bohemias might be considered second derivatives). This anxiety registers the foundational character of the suburban moment for the dominant classes of cultural producers and critics, recognizes that the vast majority of cherished cultural chattels are propped against the metonymic doorframe, and acknowledges the postmodern subject's alienation in having lost its connections with that point of presumed origin. What it lies against, covers, *stations*, is the possibility that the utopian hope discerned in nostalgia is itself founded upon a conditioned longing for visitation by that most meager of simulacral figures: the ghost who isn't there, and never was.

NOTES

1. Each of these terms marks the attempt of theorists of the postmodern condition to designate a limited, antihegemonic agency clinging still to individual human subjects. Michel de Certeau's "tactics" designate the appropriation of the tools of the powerful for other purposes (29–42). Jean Baudrillard's "fatality" suggests a deep refusal on the part of what he calls the "silent majorities" to take seriously the directives of power (7–24). Dick Hebdige's "impossible object" is a slipperier notion but suggests that a certain intensity of affective relation with any artifact can heave that artifact out of its mass-produced, dulling anonymity, can confer upon it aura, thus removing the affected subject from the inhuman circuit of consumption/production (47–76).

2. One might remark that the myth has perhaps more power still for those attempting to approximate the position of the exiled European despite the handicap of having come from the very suburbs being described. And this attempt can begin early. Finding copies of such popularizing books as David Riesman's *The Lonely Crowd* on the parental bedside table can do much to explain to the fifteen year old that she or he has been made miserable by the soulless suburbs rather than by being fifteen.

3. This particular trope maintains itself as one of the ways in which the alien presence in signed in the current television series *The X-Files*. Rogue aliens in the series may be distinguishable, but the "naturalized" aliens, those who have adapted to life on earth, are clones and have respectable bourgeois occupations. In the 1995 episode "Colony," Scully and Mulder discover a set of identical alien doctors who are being pursued and killed by an alien bounty hunter. In a further turn, one of these cloned aliens has played father—in the best 1950s television fashion—to Mulder's abductee sister. In the mid-1990s, perhaps *only* podded aliens are capable of "living" out still the dreams of Gans's Levit-

towners. My thanks to Terri Monture for recalling the title of the episode.

4. "Multinucleated metropolitan regions" is a term coined by M. Gottdeiner; "centerless cities" is suggested by Kenneth Jackson; "Edge Cities" is Joel Garreau's term; "Technoburbs" is the proposal of Robert Fishman. Rob Kling, Spencer Olin, and Mark Poster, while preferring Gottdeiner's term for its descriptive and analytical precision, noted that "it sounds more like something in a chemical laboratory than a place where people live and that they may actually come to love, or at least enjoy." For this reason they embrace the simpler, and temporally predictable, "postsuburban" as their marker.

5. Curiously, the first sentence here does not appear in the version of "Fortress" published in *City of Quartz*. It does show up in the version published in Sorkin (154). The addition appears to reflect the longing for authenticating violence that is so much an unannounced theme in Sorkin's collection.

6. "The term 'primitive' is increasingly only a response to a mythic necessity to keep the idea of the primitive alive in the modern world and consciousness. And it will stay alive because there are several empires built on the necessity of the 'primitive': included among these are anthropology's official versions of itself, an increasing segment of the tourist industry, the economic base of ex-primitives who continue to play the part of primitives-for-moderns, now documentary film-making, and soon music, art, drama, and literature" (MacCannell 34).

WORKS CITED

Baudrillard, Jean. *Fatal Strategies*. Trans. Philip Beitchman and W. G. J. Niesluchowski. New York: Semiotext(e)/Pluto, 1990.

Boyer, Christine M. "Cities for Sale: Merchandising History at South Street Seaport." *Variations on a Theme Park*. Ed. Michael Sorkin. New York: Hill and Wang, 1992, 181–204.

Clover, Carol J. *Men, Women, and Chainsaws: Gender in the Modern Horror Film*. Princeton, NJ: Princeton UP, 1992.

Craig, Lois. "Suburbs." *Design Quarterly* 132 (1986): 29–30.

Davis, Mike. *City of Quartz*. New York: Verso, 1990.

de Certeau, Michel. *The Practice of Everyday Life*. Trans. Steven Rendell. Berkeley: U of California P, 1984.

Dolar, Mladan. "Die Einführung in das Serail." *Wo es war* 2 (1987).

Feuer, Jane. *Seeing through the Eighties: Television and Reaganism*. Durham and London: Duke UP, 1995.

Fishman, Robert. *Bourgeois Utopias: The Rise and Fall of Suburbia*. New York: Basic, 1987.

Fiske, John. *Power Plays, Power Works*. London and New York: Verso, 1993.

Foucault, Michel. "Of Other Spaces." Trans. Jay Miskowiec. *Diacritics* 16 (1986): 22.

Gans, Herbert J. *The Levittowners: Ways of Life and Politics in a New Suburban Community*. New York: Pantheon, 1967.

Garreau, Joel. *Edge City: Life on the New Frontier*. New York: Doubleday, 1991.

George, Lynell. "City of Specters." *Sex, Death, and God in L.A.* Ed. David Reid. Berkeley: U of California P, 1992, 154–172.

Gottdeiner, M. *The Social Production of Urban Space*. Austin: U of Texas P, 1985.

Graña, Cesar. "Social Optimism and Literary Depression." *Fact and Symbol: Essays in the Sociology of Art and Literature*. New York: Oxford UP, 1971.

Hebdige, Dick. "The Impossible Object: Towards a Sociology of the Sublime." *New Formations* 1 (Spring 1987): 47–76.

Jackson, Kenneth. *Crabgrass Frontier: The Suburbanization of the United States*. New York: Oxford UP, 1985.

Jameson, Fredric. *Postmodernism, or the Cultural Logic of Late Capitalism*. Durham: Duke UP, 1991.

Kling, Rob, Spencer Olin, and Mark Poster, eds. *Postsuburban California: The Transformation of Orange County since World War II*. Berkeley: U of California P, 1995.

Kroker, Arthur, Marilouise Kroker, and David Cook. *Panic Encyclopedia: The Definitive Guide to the Postmodern Scene*. Montreal: New World Perspectives, 1989.

MacCannell, Dean. *Empty Meeting Grounds: The Tourist Papers*. London and New York: Routledge, 1992.

Michasiw, Kim Ian. "Haunting the Unremembered World: Shelley's Gothic Practice." *Gothic Fictions: Prohibition/Transgression*. Ed. Kenneth W. Graham. New York: AMS P, 1989, 199–225.

Poster, Mark. "The Emergence of Postsuburbia: An Introduction." *Postsuburban California*. Ed. Rob Kling, Spencer Olin, and Mark Poster. Berkeley: U of California P, 1995, 1–42.

Reid, David, ed. *Sex, Death, and God in L.A.* Berkeley: U of California P, 1992.

Soja, Edward M. *Postmodern Geographies: The Reassertion of Space in Critical Social Theory*. London and New York: Verso, 1989.

Sorkin, Michael, ed. *Variations on a Theme Park: The New American City and the End of Public Space*. New York: Hill and Wang, 1992.

Žižek, Slavoj. *Looking Awry: An Introduction to Jacques Lacan through Popular Culture*. Cambridge, MA: MIT P, 1991.

———. *The Sublime Object of Ideology*. London: Verso, 1989.

NOTES ON CONTRIBUTORS

ROBERT K. MARTIN

Robert K. Martin is professor of English and chair of the department at the Université de Montréal. He is the author of *The Homosexual Tradition in American Poetry* (1979) and *Hero, Captain, and Stranger: Male Friendship, Social Critique, and Literary Form in the Sea Novels of Herman Melville* (1986), as well as editor of *The Continuing Presence of Walt Whitman* (1992).

ERIC SAVOY

Eric Savoy is associate professor of English at the University of Calgary, where he teaches American literature and literary theory. He has published recently on James and queer theory, Hawthorne and psychoanalysis, and 1950s American cinema.

WILLIAM VEEDER

William Veeder is professor of English at the University of Chicago. His work on gothic includes essays and lectures on Bierce, Gilman, Hardy, James, LeFanu, Poe, and Stoker and books on Mary Shelley and Stevenson. He is currently completing an essay on "The Turn of the Screw" and a novel on Ambrose Bierce.

MAGGIE KILGOUR

Maggie Kilgour is associate professor of English at McGill University and the author of *From Communion to Cannibalism: An Anatomy of Metaphors of Incorporation* (1990) and *The Rise of the Gothic Novel* (1995). After too many years of living with cannibals and other ghouls, she is now writing on water.

DAVID R. JARRAWAY

David R. Jarraway is associate professor of English at the University of Ottawa, where he specializes in modern American literature and contemporary gay and lesbian writing. He is the author of *Wallace Stevens and the Question of Belief: "Metaphysician in the Dark"* (1993) and has published most recently in the *Minnesota Review*, *American Literature*, and *English Studies in Canada*.

STEVEN BRUHM

Steven Bruhm is assistant professor of English at Mount Saint Vincent University in Halifax. He is the author of *Gothic Bodies: The Politics of Pain in Romantic Fiction* (U of Pennsylvania P, 1994) and is currently finishing *Reflecting Narcissus: A Queer Aesthetic*, a book-length examination of the Narcissus myth in queer cultural production.

LESLEY GINSBERG

Lesley Ginsberg is a postdoctoral visiting scholar at the Women's Leadership Institute at Mills College. Her essay is part of a larger study entitled *The Romance of Dependency: Childhood and the Ideology of Love in American Literature, 1825–1870*. Her work has also appeared in *American Literature*.

GEORGE PIGGFORD

George Piggford is assistant professor of English at Tufts University. He is coeditor with Robert K. Martin of *Queer Forster* (Chicago, 1997). His essays have appeared in *Modern Drama* and *Mosaic*.

MARIANNE NOBLE

Marianne Noble received her Ph.D. from Columbia University and is an assistant professor at American University. She has published articles on *Uncle Tom's Cabin* and Emily Dickinson and is currently writing a book entitled *The Masochistic Pleasures of the Sentimental Voice*, which addresses the erotics of domination in Evangelical sentimentalism.

MARY CHAPMAN

Mary Chapman is associate professor of English at the University of Alberta in Edmonton, Canada. She has published articles on Cooper, Alcott, Silko, and Erdrich and is the editor of Broadview Press's paperback edition of Charles Brockden Brown's gothic novel *Ormond, or The Secret Witness*.

C. JODEY CASTRICANO

C. Jodey Castricano lives and writes in Vancouver, Canada. She has a Ph.D. in English from the University of British Columbia and has published poetry as well as criticism. Her dissertation, *In Derrida's Dream: A Poetic of a Well-Made Crypt*, draws upon her love of the gothic to discuss Derrida's writing practice in terms of specters, haunting, and mourning.

NICOLA NIXON

Nicola Nixon is assistant professor of English at Concordia University. She has published articles on Melville and James and on the popular genres of science fiction, detective fiction, and vampire films.

KIM IAN MICHASIW

Kim Ian Michasiw teaches eighteenth-century literature and psychoanalytic theory at York University. His edition of Charlotte Dacre's *Zofloya, or The Moor* (1806) has just been published. He is working on a book-length study of real-life aesthetics.

INDEX